4

Compact
ACTUAL iBT Reading & Listening Book 4

Publisher Chung Kyudo
Editors Cho Sangik, Hong Inpyo
Authors Darakwon TOEFL Research Team
Proofreader Michael A. Putlack
Designers Zo Hwayoun, Park Sunyoung

First published in Novermber 2011
By Darakwon, Inc.
Darakwon Bldg., 211, Munbal-ro, Paju-si, Gyeonggi-do 10881
Republic of Korea
Tel: 82-2-736-2031 (Ext. 250)
Fax: 82-2-732-2037

Copyright © 2011 Darakwon, Inc.

All rights reserved. No part of this publication may be reproduced, stored in a retrieval system, or transmitted in any form or by any means, electronic, mechanical, photocopying or otherwise, without the prior consent of the copyright owner. Refund after purchase is possible only according to the company regulations. Contact the above telephone number for any inquiries. Consumer damages caused by loss, damage, etc. can be compensated according to the consumer dispute resolution standards announced by the Korea Fair Trade Commission. An incorrectly collated book will be exchanged.

ISBN 978-89-277-0609-0 18740
      978-89-277-0581-9 18740 (set)

www.darakwon.co.kr

Components Main Book / Answer Book
11 10 9 8 7 6 5   23 24 25 26 27

Contents

- Introduction — 6
- Actual Test **01** — 8
- Actual Test **02** — 20
- Actual Test **03** — 32
- Actual Test **04** — 44
- Actual Test **05** — 56
- Actual Test **06** — 68
- Actual Test **07** — 80
- Actual Test **08** — 92
- Actual Test **09** — 104
- Actual Test **10** — 116

Introduction

One of the most important standardized tests students of the English language may ever take is the TOEFL® iBT. Because getting a high score on the test is so crucial, it is important to prepare for the test as much as possible prior to taking it.

That is the purpose of *Compact Actual iBT Reading & Listening* series. This book focuses on two of the four sections on the TOEFL® iBT: the Reading and Listening sections. These are arguably the two most difficult parts of the TOEFL® iBT. In both the Reading and the Listening sections, test takers will face passages and lectures that cover a wide variety of topics. These include subjects in the arts, social sciences, physical sciences, and life sciences. For that reason, a familiarity with many of these topics is crucial. So is having an extensive vocabulary that includes knowledge of specialized words in each of the fields. Fortunately, *Compact Actual iBT Reading & Listening* provides exactly what students need. The Reading passages and Listening lectures cover many of the very topics that often appear on the TOEFL® iBT. In addition, the Listening conversations do the same: They cover topics that frequently appear on the TOEFL® iBT, which can only serve to assist test takers when they sit for the actual test.

Compact Actual iBT Reading & Listening has been designed to be used both in the classroom and by test takers working on an individual basis. Each compact test consists of one Reading passage, one Listening conversation, and one Listening lecture. All three of them are the standard length of actual TOEFL® iBT passages, conversations, and lectures. In addition, they all have the same number of questions and the same types of questions that are found on the actual test. By using this book, test takers will be more prepared for the test when they actually take it.

This book, however, is merely a tool. Both students and teachers must make use of this tool in the best possible manner so that test takers may do as well as possible when they take the TOEFL® iBT.

About This Book

Compact Actual iBT Reading & Listening consists of ten units. Each unit consists of one compact test. A single compact test contains one Reading passage, one Listening conversation, and one Listening lecture. The passage, conversation, and lecture are followed by questions. These questions are of the same type and number that are found on the TOEFL® iBT.

In addition, the subjects of the passages in the Reading section are those that have all appeared on recent TOEFL® iBT tests. As many topics on the TOEFL® iBT Reading section tend to repeat, this can be a great benefit to test takers. By familiarizing themselves with the topics, subject matter, and vocabulary used in the passages in the Reading section of each compact test, test takers can be more confident when they take the Reading section of the TOEFL® iBT.

The same is true of the conversation and lectures in the Listening section. The Listening conversations contain situations that have appeared on recent TOEFL® iBT tests while the Listening lectures are all on topics that have occurred recently as well. By familiarizing themselves with the topics, subject matter, situations, and vocabulary used in the conversations and lectures, test takers can be more confident when they take the Listening section of the TOEFL® iBT.

Reading Section

The Reading section of each compact test consists of one full-length Reading passage followed by either thirteen or fourteen questions. Each passage covers a field that commonly occurs on the TOEFL® iBT. This includes fields such as history, archaeology, biology, and art.

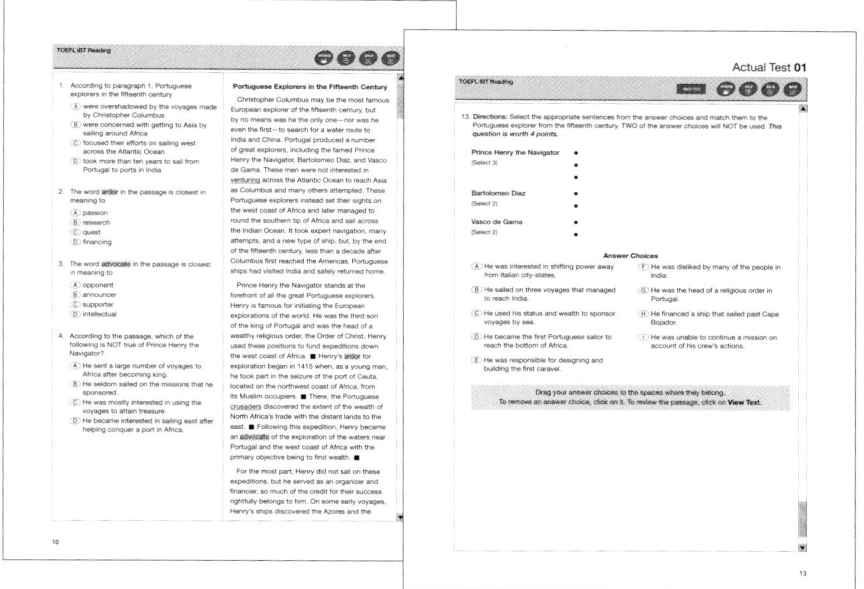

Listening Section

The Listening section of each compact test consists of one full-length Listening conversation followed by five questions and one full-length Listening lecture followed by six questions. Each conversation concerns either an office hours situation or a service situation whereas each lecture covers a topic that commonly occurs on the TOEFL® iBT. These topics are in the following four categories: arts, life sciences, physical sciences, and social sciences.

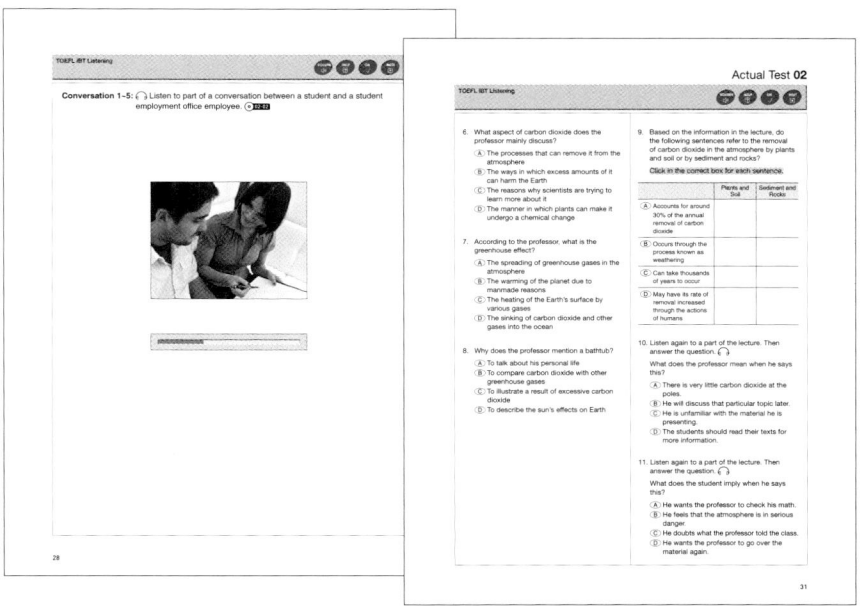

Actual Test 01

TOEFL iBT Reading

Reading
Section Directions

This section measures your ability to understand academic passages in English.

In this part, you will read 1 passage and answer reading comprehension questions about the passage. Most questions are worth one point, but the last question is worth more than one point. The directions indicate how many points you may receive.

Some passages include a word or phrase that is underlined in blue. Click on the word or phrase to see a definition or an explanation.

When you want to move on to the next question, click on **Next**. You may skip questions and go back to them later. If you want to return to previous questions, click on **Back**. You can click on **Review** at any time and the review screen will show you which questions you have answered and which you have not answered. From this review screen, you may go directly to any question you have already seen in the Reading section.

You may now begin the Reading section. You will read 1 reading passage. You will have **20 minutes** to read the passage and answer the questions.

Click on **Continue** to go on.

TOEFL iBT Reading

1. According to paragraph 1, Portuguese explorers in the fifteenth century
   - (A) were overshadowed by the voyages made by Christopher Columbus
   - (B) were concerned with getting to Asia by sailing around Africa
   - (C) focused their efforts on sailing west across the Atlantic Ocean
   - (D) took more than ten years to sail from Portugal to ports in India

2. The word ardor in the passage is closest in meaning to
   - (A) passion
   - (B) research
   - (C) quest
   - (D) financing

3. The word advocate in the passage is closest in meaning to
   - (A) opponent
   - (B) announcer
   - (C) supporter
   - (D) intellectual

4. According to the passage, which of the following is NOT true of Prince Henry the Navigator?
   - (A) He sent a large number of voyages to Africa after becoming king.
   - (B) He seldom sailed on the missions that he sponsored.
   - (C) He was mostly interested in using the voyages to attain treasure.
   - (D) He became interested in sailing east after helping conquer a port in Africa.

Portuguese Explorers in the Fifteenth Century

Christopher Columbus may be the most famous European explorer of the fifteenth century, but by no means was he the only one—nor was he even the first—to search for a water route to India and China. Portugal produced a number of great explorers, including the famed Prince Henry the Navigator, Bartolomeo Diaz, and Vasco de Gama. These men were not interested in venturing across the Atlantic Ocean to reach Asia as Columbus and many others attempted. These Portuguese explorers instead set their sights on the west coast of Africa and later managed to round the southern tip of Africa and sail across the Indian Ocean. It took expert navigation, many attempts, and a new type of ship, but, by the end of the fifteenth century, less than a decade after Columbus first reached the Americas, Portuguese ships had visited India and safely returned home.

Prince Henry the Navigator stands at the forefront of all the great Portuguese explorers. Henry is famous for initiating the European explorations of the world. He was the third son of the king of Portugal and was the head of a wealthy religious order, the Order of Christ. Henry used these positions to fund expeditions down the west coast of Africa. ■ Henry's ardor for exploration began in 1415 when, as a young man, he took part in the seizure of the port of Ceuta, located on the northwest coast of Africa, from its Muslim occupiers. ■ There, the Portuguese crusaders discovered the extent of the wealth of North Africa's trade with the distant lands to the east. ■ Following this expedition, Henry became an advocate of the exploration of the waters near Portugal and the west coast of Africa with the primary objective being to find wealth. ■

For the most part, Henry did not sail on these expeditions, but he served as an organizer and financier, so much of the credit for their success rightfully belongs to him. On some early voyages, Henry's ships discovered the Azores and the

5. In paragraph 2, the author of the passage implies that Prince Henry the Navigator

   Ⓐ would have been more influential than he was had he ever become king
   Ⓑ wanted to expand the amount of territory that Portugal possessed
   Ⓒ never sailed on a ship from Portugal after he visited the port of Ceuta
   Ⓓ was the greatest of the Portuguese explorers during the fifteenth century

6. The word treacherous in the passage is closest in meaning to

   Ⓐ hidden
   Ⓑ abundant
   Ⓒ sharp
   Ⓓ dangerous

7. The author's description of Cape Bojador mentions which of the following?

   Ⓐ It was located within a week's sailing distance of Portugal.
   Ⓑ It is situated in the same geographical region as the Canary Islands.
   Ⓒ Many Portuguese ships that sailed there sank on its coral reefs.
   Ⓓ It became the center of the African slave trade Portugal was involved in.

8. The word there in the passage refers to

   Ⓐ the shores of modern-day South Africa
   Ⓑ the eastern coast of Africa
   Ⓒ the Indian Ocean
   Ⓓ India

Madeira Islands, which the Portuguese claimed and subsequently colonized. In 1434, one of his expeditions sailed past Cape Bojador, just south of the Canary Islands, which was located further south than any European ship had sailed before. Cape Bojador was infamous among sailors for its treacherous reefs and strange currents, so getting past it was a major accomplishment. Soon afterward, the Portuguese reached the coasts of sub-Saharan Africa and found wealth in the form of gold and captured Africans, whom they sold as slaves. By the time Henry died in 1460, Portuguese ships were sailing almost as far south as present-day Sierra Leone.

Over the next several decades, the Portuguese continued to push further south. They established forts and trading posts in several places and used them as bases on their voyages. Finally, in 1488, Bartolomeo Diaz rounded the southern tip of Africa and saw the Indian Ocean; however, his crew refused to continue. After leaving some markers along the shores of modern-day South Africa, the expedition returned home. Ten years later, Vasco de Gama set out to reach India. He explored the eastern coast of Africa and found a navigator who guided his ships across the Indian Ocean. The expedition made landfall in southwestern India in May of 1498. De Gama made two more voyages to India, and he eventually died of an illness there in 1524. While de Gama was well respected in Portugal, among the Arabs and Indians in that region, he gained the reputation of a pirate who brutally seized whatever he wanted.

These long explorations past Africa and to India were made possible by a new type of ship, the caravel, which came into use in the mid-fifteenth century. Caravels had shallow drafts, which allowed them easily to sail in coastal waters, possessed triangular sails designed to let them sail into the wind by tacking, and had large cargo spaces. With caravels, smart navigation,

9. According to paragraph 4, why did Bartolomeo Diaz return to Portugal instead of sailing to India in 1488?

   Ⓐ He lacked a competent navigator who was familiar with the Indian Ocean.
   Ⓑ His crew refused to sail any further than the southern tip of Africa.
   Ⓒ He was unaware of which direction he should sail in order to reach India.
   Ⓓ He was under orders not to sail past the southern coast of Africa.

10. Why does the author mention the Arabs and Indians' opinion of Vasco de Gama?

    Ⓐ To prove that he was little more than a pirate
    Ⓑ To note his responsibility for the deaths of thousands
    Ⓒ To contrast it with that of the Portuguese
    Ⓓ To explain why he was not universally well regarded

11. The author's description of the caravel mentions all of the following EXCEPT:

    Ⓐ The ship was designed to let it sail into the wind.
    Ⓑ It was larger than most of the other ships of its time.
    Ⓒ It was capable of carrying large amounts of goods.
    Ⓓ The ship could sail in shallow water near the coast.

12. Look at the four squares [■] that indicate where the following sentence could be added to the passage.

    These riches inspired Henry to do all that he could to send Portuguese ships to India and elsewhere in Asia.

    Where would the sentence best fit?

    Click on a square [■] to add the sentence to the passage.

and ruthless men like de Gama, the Portuguese carved out a global empire. They began the first large-scale African slave trade, opened the door to the Indian spice trade by sea, and eventually discovered and colonized Brazil in South America. Significantly, the Portuguese also took much of Europe's trade with India away from the Italian city-states, which resulted in a power shift from regions in the Mediterranean Sea to those in Western Europe.

Glossary
venture: to begin one's travels somewhere
crusader: a soldier on a holy mission
ruthless: cruel; merciless

Actual Test 01

TOEFL iBT Reading

13. **Directions:** Select the appropriate sentences from the answer choices and match them to the Portuguese explorer from the fifteenth century. TWO of the answer choices will NOT be used. *This question is worth 4 points.*

Prince Henry the Navigator
(Select 3)
-
-
-

Bartolomeo Diaz
(Select 2)
-
-

Vasco de Gama
(Select 2)
-
-

Answer Choices

(A) He was interested in shifting power away from Italian city-states.

(B) He sailed on three voyages that managed to reach India.

(C) He used his status and wealth to sponsor voyages by sea.

(D) He became the first Portuguese sailor to reach the bottom of Africa.

(E) He was responsible for designing and building the first caravel.

(F) He was disliked by many of the people in India.

(G) He was the head of a religious order in Portugal.

(H) He financed a ship that sailed past Cape Bojador.

(I) He was unable to continue a mission on account of his crew's actions.

Drag your answer choices to the spaces where they belong.
To remove an answer choice, click on it. To review the passage, click on **View Text**.

TOEFL iBT Listening

Listening
Section Directions

This section measures your ability to understand conversations and lectures in English.

In this part, you will listen to 1 conversation and 1 lecture. You will hear the conversation or lecture only **one** time. After the conversation or lecture, you will answer some questions about it. The questions typically ask about the main idea and supporting details. Some questions ask about a speaker's purpose or attitude. Answer the questions based on what is stated or implied by the speakers.

You may take notes while you listen. You may use your notes to help you answer the questions. Your notes will **not** be scored.

If you need to change the volume while you listen, click on the **Volume** icon at the top of the screen.

In some questions, you will see this icon: 🎧 This means that you will hear, but not see, part of the question.

Some of the questions have special directions. These directions appear in a gray box on the screen.

Most questions are worth one point. If a question is worth more than one point, it will have special directions that indicate how many points you can receive.

You must answer each question. After you answer, click on **Next**. Then click on **OK** to confirm your answer and go on to the next question. After you click on **OK**, you cannot return to previous questions.

A clock at the top of the screen will show you how much time is remaining. The clock will not count down while you are listening. The clock will count down only while you are answering the questions.

Now you may begin the Listening section.

Conversation 1~5: Listen to part of a conversation between a student and a professor.

Actual Test 01

TOEFL iBT Listening

1. Why does the student visit the professor?
   - Ⓐ To discuss some issues she has with the class
   - Ⓑ To find out what her grade in the class is
   - Ⓒ To tell the professor that she is dropping the class
   - Ⓓ To ask about a recent homework assignment

2. What does the student say about the class?
   - Ⓐ It has convinced her to become a chemistry major.
   - Ⓑ It is the most difficult one that she is taking.
   - Ⓒ She believes that it will be an easy A for her.
   - Ⓓ She is having trouble keeping up with the material.

3. What is the professor's opinion of some students in her class?
   - Ⓐ She thinks that they do not work hard enough.
   - Ⓑ She believes they have promising careers ahead of them.
   - Ⓒ She thinks they are able to do all of the work.
   - Ⓓ She feels that they can excel in her class.

4. What will the student probably do next?
   - Ⓐ Ask to join a study group
   - Ⓑ Leave the professor's office
   - Ⓒ Have the professor explain the homework
   - Ⓓ Drop the professor's class

5. Listen again to a part of the conversation. Then answer the question.

   What is the purpose of the professor's response?
   - Ⓐ To acknowledge that she understands the student's concerns
   - Ⓑ To admit that her class can be somewhat difficult
   - Ⓒ To encourage the student to give her some more information
   - Ⓓ To thank the student for coming to speak with her

Lecture 6~11: Listen to part of a lecture in a mass media class.

Actual Test 01

TOEFL iBT Listening

6. What is the main topic of the lecture?
   Ⓐ The men who invented the first television
   Ⓑ The early years of television broadcasting
   Ⓒ The reasons why television became more popular than radio
   Ⓓ The history of television broadcasting during World War II

7. Why does the professor explain the role of the FCC during television broadcasting's early years?
   Ⓐ To note why broadcasting attempts then failed
   Ⓑ To describe the desire of broadcasters to earn money
   Ⓒ To mention why Germany developed clearer images faster than the U.S. did
   Ⓓ To complain about the lack of quality programming then

8. Why does the professor discuss Philo Farnsworth?
   Ⓐ To say that he was one of the early employees at the FCC
   Ⓑ To claim that he was the person who first thought of making a television
   Ⓒ To state that he was the first president of NBC's station in New York City
   Ⓓ To name him as the person who developed the first working television

9. What comparison does the professor make between radio and early television broadcasts?
   Ⓐ The individuals they both hired
   Ⓑ The money that each of them earned
   Ⓒ The type of content they each aired
   Ⓓ The times when they both aired shows

10. What does the professor imply about early TV broadcasts?
    Ⓐ They were lower in quality than modern programs.
    Ⓑ They were shown in color and in black and white.
    Ⓒ They were dominated mostly by variety shows.
    Ⓓ They cost a lot of money for companies to produce.

11. According to the professor, when was the Golden Age of TV?
    Ⓐ The years from 1884 to 1928
    Ⓑ The late 1920s and early 1930s
    Ⓒ The years during World War II
    Ⓓ The late 1940s and 1950s

Actual Test 02

Reading
Section Directions

This section measures your ability to understand academic passages in English.

In this part, you will read 1 passage and answer reading comprehension questions about the passage. Most questions are worth one point, but the last question is worth more than one point. The directions indicate how many points you may receive.

Some passages include a word or phrase that is underlined in blue. Click on the word or phrase to see a definition or an explanation.

When you want to move on to the next question, click on **Next**. You may skip questions and go back to them later. If you want to return to previous questions, click on **Back**. You can click on **Review** at any time and the review screen will show you which questions you have answered and which you have not answered. From this review screen, you may go directly to any question you have already seen in the Reading section.

You may now begin the Reading section. You will read 1 reading passage. You will have **20 minutes** to read the passage and answer the questions.

Click on **Continue** to go on.

Inflation

Inflation is a general rise in prices in an economy. Not all prices may rise at the same time, and the increase may be small, but, in general, when prices go up, economists call this inflation. Prices typically increase because there is a large supply of money in the economy. Each piece of printed paper money or minted coin has a value based upon how much money is in the economy. When there is less money available, each piece has a greater value and can therefore be used to purchase more goods and services. When this occurs, prices tend to drop, which results in deflation. Conversely, when there is too much money in an economy, the opposite occurs: People have more money to make purchases, and prices tend to rise, which results in inflation. Governments are responsible for increasing the money supply, which they may do for three main reasons: to pay debts, to please certain voters, and to stimulate the economy.

In every country, the government controls the money supply by printing paper money and minting coins. Governments depend on tax revenues to pay for their responsibilities and debts, yet when the amount of tax revenues raised fails to meet these obligations, a government may be tempted to print more money to pay off its debt. This results in an increase in the money supply, and inflation occurs. At certain times in history, this process has gotten out of control, so hyperinflation has occurred. For example, in Weimar Germany in 1923, the value of money was reduced so much that people had to pay millions of marks for a mere loaf of bread. Many nations, such as the United States, avoided similar problems by utilizing the gold standard. A nation that is on the gold standard backs its currency with gold, for which it can be exchanged at any time. This often has a stabilizing effect on an economy. Nevertheless, President Richard Nixon took the United States off the gold standard

1. According to paragraph 1, inflation may occur because
   A) people are unable to afford the products they want to buy
   B) the government prints more paper money than it mints coins
   C) people lack the money to buy goods and services in general
   D) the prices of most items that are being sold increase

2. The author discusses deflation in paragraph 1 in order to
   A) show how it differs from inflation
   B) prove that it is less harmful than inflation
   C) explain how often it happens in most economies
   D) describe its connection with the government

3. Which of the sentences below best expresses the essential information in the highlighted sentence in the passage? *Incorrect* answer choices change the meaning in important ways or leave out essential information.
   A) Governments raise money by taxing their citizens, but this is usually not enough to pay their debts, so they have to print money.
   B) Unless a government prints money in addition to collecting tax revenues, it will not be able to meet most of its financial obligations.
   C) Governments may have to increase the supply of money when they do not collect enough taxes to cover all of their debts.
   D) The obligations of a typical government demand that it collect taxes from its people so that it does not have to print too much money.

4. The word **backs** in the passage is closest in meaning to
   - (A) rewards
   - (B) prints
   - (C) supports
   - (D) combines

5. The author uses **Weimar Germany** as an example of
   - (A) the worst case of inflation the world has ever experienced
   - (B) a country that experienced hyperinflation
   - (C) the negative effects of collecting too many taxes
   - (D) a nation that should have used the gold standard

6. In paragraph 2, the author's description of the gold standard mentions all of the following EXCEPT:
   - (A) There are some nations that still make use of it today.
   - (B) The United States is one country that no longer employs it.
   - (C) It is often able to keep inflation out of an economy.
   - (D) It enables people to trade their money for gold at any time.

7. The word **contribute** in the passage is closest in meaning to
   - (A) promise
   - (B) donate
   - (C) loan
   - (D) withdraw

8. The word **them** in the passage refers to
   - (A) countless businesses
   - (B) governments
   - (C) lobbyists
   - (D) their debts

in 1971. Now, American money is simply backed by the confidence that people have in its value. As a result, prices have risen both steadily and dramatically since 1971.

The second primary reason that governments print more money is to please specific voters. These voters are borrowers—people who have taken out loans that they must repay with interest. If these borrowers are wage earners, then they are uninterested in seeing prices rise. However, if they are businesspeople who produce and sell products, then inflation can benefit them. The prices of their products increase, so they make more money selling the same products and therefore earn enough money to pay off their debts faster. Whether there is inflation or not, the amount of money they owe remains constant. Businesses can often greatly influence the government, particularly if they **contribute** large sums to politicians' reelection campaigns. Businesses also serve as the **backbone of an economy**, so most governments attempt to please them. Finally, countless businesses pay lobbyists to pressure governments to print more money and thus increase inflation to help **them** eliminate their debts.

The third and final major reason that governments print more money is to stimulate the economy. One resulting side effect of stimulus spending is inflation. When an economy is in a recession, the government may print more money and then spend it on goods and services in an effort to cause economic growth. The government might also lend money to businesses for them to spend on job creation, which can stimulate the economy and help drag the country out of a recession.

Inflation may seem to be economically beneficial in some ways, but the individuals that suffer from it the most are typical wage earners who must purchase goods and services. When prices rise but people's wages remain the same, their buying

TOEFL iBT Reading

9. According to paragraph 3, some voters desire inflation because

   A it gives them more access to politicians that they can influence
   B they are able to borrow money from banks at lower interest rates
   C it enables them to earn money much more quickly than before
   D the values of the loans they provide people tend to decrease

10. In stating that businesses serve as the backbone of an economy, the author means that businesses are

    A major employers
    B a source of funds
    C the causes of most recessions
    D economically important

11. The word it in the passage refers to

    A an economy
    B a recession
    C the government
    D more money

12. According to paragraph 5, which of the following is true of inflation?

    A It tends to cause a certain amount of harm to regular workers.
    B It can increase the value of people's investments.
    C It encourages people to save their money for the future.
    D It makes it possible for people to purchase more goods and services.

13. Which of the following can be inferred from paragraph 5 about inflation?

    A It can result in people losing their money despite having invested it.
    B It may force people to work many years past the traditional retirement age.
    C It can cause typical wage earners to feel resentful of the government.
    D It rarely exceeds an annual basis of five percent in most modern-day economies.

power decreases, so they cannot purchase even the same amount of goods and services that they previously had. Additionally, many people save money for the future or invest it in retirement plans. Yet, by the time they retire, because of inflation, the value of their money will be less than it was when they began saving it. Unfortunately, in most economies, inflation is a virtually constant presence since prices climb gradually year after year.

Glossary
stimulate: to arouse; to increase the activity of someone or something
hyperinflation: a type of extreme inflation in which prices rise very quickly over a short period of time
mark: the name of the currency that was once used in Germany

14. **Directions:** An introductory sentence for a brief summary of the passage is provided below. Complete the summary by selecting the THREE answer choices that express the most important ideas of the passage. Some sentences do not belong because they express ideas that are not presented in the passage or are minor ideas in the passage. *This question is worth 2 points.*

Inflation, which is the rising of prices in an economy, may occur for a number of different reasons.

-
-
-

Answer Choices

(A) Weimar Germany experienced a case of hyperinflation in the 1920s, so prices increased dramatically over a short period of time.

(B) People tend to dislike inflation since it causes their buying power to decrease while also lowering the values of their savings and investments.

(C) Governments may sometimes induce inflation in order to satisfy certain voting classes that want to make more money.

(D) Employing the gold standard is one way that a government can prevent most prices from rising too high too quickly.

(E) Inflation can be caused by a government spending money in an effort to stimulate the economy and to improve its performance.

(F) By increasing the supply of money in the economy, a government can cause inflation to take place.

Drag your answer choices to the spaces where they belong.
To remove an answer choice, click on it. To review the passage, click on **View Text**.

Listening
Section Directions

This section measures your ability to understand conversations and lectures in English.

In this part, you will listen to 1 conversation and 1 lecture. You will hear the conversation or lecture only **one** time. After the conversation or lecture, you will answer some questions about it. The questions typically ask about the main idea and supporting details. Some questions ask about a speaker's purpose or attitude. Answer the questions based on what is stated or implied by the speakers.

You may take notes while you listen. You may use your notes to help you answer the questions. Your notes will **not** be scored.

If you need to change the volume while you listen, click on the **Volume** icon at the top of the screen.

In some questions, you will see this icon: 🎧 This means that you will hear, but not see, part of the question.

Some of the questions have special directions. These directions appear in a gray box on the screen.

Most questions are worth one point. If a question is worth more than one point, it will have special directions that indicate how many points you can receive.

You must answer each question. After you answer, click on **Next**. Then click on **OK** to confirm your answer and go on to the next question. After you click on **OK**, you cannot return to previous questions.

A clock at the top of the screen will show you how much time is remaining. The clock will not count down while you are listening. The clock will count down only while you are answering the questions.

Now you may begin the Listening section.

Conversation 1~5: Listen to part of a conversation between a student and a student employment office employee.

TOEFL iBT Listening

1. Why does the student visit the student employment office?
   - (A) To apply for a job there
   - (B) To inquire about employment opportunities
   - (C) To ask the woman to help him find a job
   - (D) To find out the location of the engineering library

2. What kind of job does the student say that he is uninterested in?
   - (A) A landscaping job
   - (B) A job in the library
   - (C) A job at the school gym
   - (D) An engineering job

3. What is the woman's attitude toward the student?
   - (A) She is friendly and helpful.
   - (B) She is polite yet hurried.
   - (C) She is considerate but unsupportive.
   - (D) She is impatient and upset.

4. Listen again to a part of the conversation. Then answer the question.

   Why does the student say this?
   - (A) To describe his dream job
   - (B) To help the woman learn more about him
   - (C) To tell the woman his work requirements
   - (D) To attempt to make a joke

5. Listen again to a part of the conversation. Then answer the question.

   What does the student imply when he says this?
   - (A) He thinks that the woman is much smarter than he is.
   - (B) The woman should give him a letter of recommendation for a job.
   - (C) He believes the woman knows a lot about on-campus jobs.
   - (D) He wants the woman to choose his new working hours.

Lecture 6~11: Listen to part of a lecture in an environmental sciences class.

6. What aspect of carbon dioxide does the professor mainly discuss?

    Ⓐ The processes that can remove it from the atmosphere
    Ⓑ The ways in which excess amounts of it can harm the Earth
    Ⓒ The reasons why scientists are trying to learn more about it
    Ⓓ The manner in which plants can make it undergo a chemical change

7. According to the professor, what is the greenhouse effect?

    Ⓐ The spreading of greenhouse gases in the atmosphere
    Ⓑ The warming of the planet due to manmade reasons
    Ⓒ The heating of the Earth's surface by various gases
    Ⓓ The sinking of carbon dioxide and other gases into the ocean

8. Why does the professor mention a bathtub?

    Ⓐ To talk about his personal life
    Ⓑ To compare carbon dioxide with other greenhouse gases
    Ⓒ To illustrate a result of excessive carbon dioxide
    Ⓓ To describe the sun's effects on Earth

9. Based on the information in the lecture, do the following sentences refer to the removal of carbon dioxide in the atmosphere by plants and soil or by sediment and rocks?

    Click in the correct box for each sentence.

	Plants and Soil	Sediment and Rocks
Ⓐ Accounts for around 30% of the annual removal of carbon dioxide		
Ⓑ Occurs through the process known as weathering		
Ⓒ Can take thousands of years to occur		
Ⓓ May have its rate of removal increased through the actions of humans		

10. Listen again to a part of the lecture. Then answer the question.

    What does the professor mean when he says this?

    Ⓐ There is very little carbon dioxide at the poles.
    Ⓑ He will discuss that particular topic later.
    Ⓒ He is unfamiliar with the material he is presenting.
    Ⓓ The students should read their texts for more information.

11. Listen again to a part of the lecture. Then answer the question.

    What does the student imply when he says this?

    Ⓐ He wants the professor to check his math.
    Ⓑ He feels that the atmosphere is in serious danger.
    Ⓒ He doubts what the professor told the class.
    Ⓓ He wants the professor to go over the material again.

Actual Test
03

Reading
Section Directions

This section measures your ability to understand academic passages in English.

In this part, you will read 1 passage and answer reading comprehension questions about the passage. Most questions are worth one point, but the last question is worth more than one point. The directions indicate how many points you may receive.

Some passages include a word or phrase that is underlined in blue. Click on the word or phrase to see a definition or an explanation.

When you want to move on to the next question, click on **Next**. You may skip questions and go back to them later. If you want to return to previous questions, click on **Back**. You can click on **Review** at any time and the review screen will show you which questions you have answered and which you have not answered. From this review screen, you may go directly to any question you have already seen in the Reading section.

You may now begin the Reading section. You will read 1 reading passage. You will have **20 minutes** to read the passage and answer the questions.

Click on **Continue** to go on.

The Desalination of Sea Water

Water is necessary for all life on Earth, but, unfortunately for many, it is not evenly distributed. Many lands have an abundance of water, yet others have an insufficient supply. There is one place, however, where there is plenty of water: the oceans. However, the salt content of sea water makes it undrinkable and unsuitable for agriculture. Human ingenuity has solved this problem though by discovering methods to remove the salt from the water in order to make it usable. The most common methods—brute-force desalination and reverse osmosis desalination— are expensive, so engineers are searching for new methods. Three are being experimented with: forward osmosis, carbon nanotubes, and biomimetics. While all three are currently expensive, it is hoped that, once perfected, they will provide cheaper ways to desalinate sea water.

The original, and still most commonly used desalination method, is called brute-force desalination. In this method, a large amount of sea water is heated until it turns to steam. The salt is left behind, and the steam is then condensed to produce fresh water. At present, approximately 85% of all desalinated water is produced by this method. The second method used is reverse osmosis desalination. ■ Inside a desalination plant, high-pressure pumps force sea water through extremely thin membranes that capture the salt and transform sea water into fresh water. ■ Both methods require a lot of energy so are quite expensive. ■ In an oil-rich Persian Gulf nation such as Saudi Arabia, this may not be a problem, but in a poor, coastal African country, the inordinate cost may prevent the manufacturing of a desalination plant. ■

The three new methods of desalination are also expensive and need more improvement to make them affordable. All three methods pass the sea water through a membrane, just as does reverse

1. The word ingenuity in the passage is closest in meaning to
   Ⓐ conditioning
   Ⓑ manufacturing
   Ⓒ resourcefulness
   Ⓓ industrialization

2. According to paragraph 1, which of the following is true of water?
   Ⓐ There is an equivalent amount of fresh water and salt water on the planet.
   Ⓑ There are some places on Earth that have more water than other regions.
   Ⓒ Every organism on Earth must consume some amount of water on a daily basis.
   Ⓓ More people live closer to salt water than they do to fresh water.

3. The word inordinate in the passage is closest in meaning to
   Ⓐ redundant
   Ⓑ excessive
   Ⓒ intimidating
   Ⓓ long-term

4. In paragraph 2, the author uses Saudi Arabia as an example of
   Ⓐ a country that has no fresh water sources of its own
   Ⓑ a nation that can afford to use desalination methods
   Ⓒ a state that is found in the Persian Gulf region
   Ⓓ a place that has more fresh water than most African countries

5. The author's description of brute-force desalination mentions which of the following?

   Ⓐ It employs high-pressure pumps in order to separate the salt from the water.
   Ⓑ It transforms salt into its gaseous form to remove it from the ocean water.
   Ⓒ It is the most expensive of all of the desalination methods currently in use.
   Ⓓ It is by far the most regularly used method of creating fresh water from salt water.

6. According to paragraph 3, which of the following is NOT true of the forward osmosis method of desalination?

   Ⓐ It requires high-pressure pumps to push the water through a membrane.
   Ⓑ It is a relatively new method of desalination that people are using.
   Ⓒ Much of its effectiveness rests upon the draw solution that it employs.
   Ⓓ It utilizes less energy than do other methods of desalination.

7. The word cores in the passage is closest in meaning to

   Ⓐ centers
   Ⓑ bases
   Ⓒ innards
   Ⓓ foundations

8. According to paragraph 4, biomimetics is effective as a desalination method because

   Ⓐ the holes in the membrane do not permit salt particles to pass through it
   Ⓑ carbon nanotubes help it create an electric charge
   Ⓒ the salt ions are attracted to the aquaporins and become attached to them
   Ⓓ the aquaporins it utilizes remove the salt from the water

osmosis, but there are some major differences. In the forward osmosis method, sea water is drawn through the membrane into a salt solution—called a draw solution—that has a higher salt content and which contains salt that is different from sea salt. The draw solution attracts the sea water, causing it to flow through the membrane, which is between the draw solution and the sea water, and the seawater salt ions are left behind. Then, low heat is utilized to evaporate the salt from the new solution. This works because the salt used in the draw solution is easier to remove from water than seawater salt ions. The advantage of forward osmosis is that no high-pressure pumps are needed to force water through the membrane, which thereby reduces the energy requirements for desalination.

The carbon nanotubes method and biomimetics method have redesigned membranes at their cores. A nanotube is made of carbon and has an electric charge at one end. By placing multiple nanotubes in a membrane, their electric charges repel the positively charged salt ions and allow uncharged water molecules to pass through the membrane. In the biomimetics method, living cells called aquaporins are placed in a membrane. These are proteins that help water pass into and out of cells in living things. Again, an electric charge near the center of each aquaporin repels the salt ions and allows only the water to pass through.

It is hoped that these three new methods, once perfected, will one day be affordable and will provide fresh water to the nearly one billion people who live without easy access to fresh water. Currently, 300 million people worldwide rely on desalination plants for fresh water. Around 14,500 desalination plants in 150 countries produce approximately sixteen billion gallons of fresh water daily. Some countries, such as those in the Persian Gulf region, rely entirely on desalination for their freshwater supplies. However, producing

TOEFL iBT Reading

9. The word it in the passage refers to
   A desalination
   B double
   C fresh water
   D sea water

10. The author's description of desalination plants mentions all of the following EXCEPT:
    A the approximate number of plants that exist around the world
    B the amount of water that is purified on a daily basis
    C the costs that desalination plants incur as they purify salt water
    D the number of people who rely upon the plants for fresh water

11. In paragraph 5, the author of the passage implies that
    A countries in the Persian Gulf receive little annual rainfall
    B the majority of desalination plants are found near deserts
    C most of the desalination plants are owned by private industries
    D around half of the world's countries have desalination plants

12. Look at the four squares [■] that indicate where the following sentence could be added to the passage.

    As a result, many people living in poor countries are presently deprived of clean drinking water.

    Where would the sentence best fit?

    Click on a square [■] to add the sentence to the passage.

fresh water is expensive and is not a solution for every nation. The costs of producing water from desalination can be almost double the cost of importing fresh water to users, assuming that it is available. Although the prices for making fresh water from sea water have dropped in recent years, they are still prohibitive. In the future, the freshwater problem will continue to grow as the world's population increases. Perhaps the real solution is conservation and the requirement that people use fresh water only when it is absolutely necessary.

Glossary
condense: to change from a gaseous to a liquid state
transform: to adjust; to alter; to change
prohibitive: expensive

13. **Directions:** Select the appropriate sentences from the answer choices and match them to the desalination method to which they relate. TWO of the answer choices will NOT be used. *This question is worth 3 points.*

Reverse Osmosis Method
(Select 3)
-
-
-

Forward Osmosis Method
(Select 2)
-
-

Answer Choices

(A) It uses electric charges to repel the salt ions from the water.

(B) It relies upon heat to remove the salt from the water.

(C) It requires a tremendous amount of energy to create fresh water.

(D) It employs a draw solution that contains salt.

(E) It is the most commonly used form of desalination today.

(F) It makes use of high-pressure pumps.

(G) It is an extremely costly method of desalination.

Drag your answer choices to the spaces where they belong.
To remove an answer choice, click on it. To review the passage, click on **View Text**.

Listening
Section Directions

This section measures your ability to understand conversations and lectures in English.

In this part, you will listen to 1 conversation and 1 lecture. You will hear the conversation or lecture only **one** time. After the conversation or lecture, you will answer some questions about it. The questions typically ask about the main idea and supporting details. Some questions ask about a speaker's purpose or attitude. Answer the questions based on what is stated or implied by the speakers.

You may take notes while you listen. You may use your notes to help you answer the questions. Your notes will **not** be scored.

If you need to change the volume while you listen, click on the **Volume** icon at the top of the screen.

In some questions, you will see this icon: 🎧 This means that you will hear, but not see, part of the question.

Some of the questions have special directions. These directions appear in a gray box on the screen.

Most questions are worth one point. If a question is worth more than one point, it will have special directions that indicate how many points you can receive.

You must answer each question. After you answer, click on **Next**. Then click on **OK** to confirm your answer and go on to the next question. After you click on **OK**, you cannot return to previous questions.

A clock at the top of the screen will show you how much time is remaining. The clock will not count down while you are listening. The clock will count down only while you are answering the questions.

Now you may begin the Listening section.

TOEFL iBT Listening

Conversation 1~5: Listen to part of a conversation between a student and a professor.

1. What are the speakers mainly discussing?
   - Ⓐ The upcoming semester
   - Ⓑ The student's recent grades
   - Ⓒ The student's future plans
   - Ⓓ The student's need to apply for a job

2. Why does the professor ask the student about her intentions after she graduates?
   - Ⓐ The school requires him to do so.
   - Ⓑ He is concerned about her personal life.
   - Ⓒ The student implied that she needed some help.
   - Ⓓ He wants to help her find a job.

3. Why does the student mention pharmaceutical companies?
   - Ⓐ To compare them with the government as an employer
   - Ⓑ To inquire about the professor's past work there
   - Ⓒ To indicate where she is interested in finding employment
   - Ⓓ To ask the professor to find some people to contact at them

4. What can be inferred about the professor?
   - Ⓐ He wants the student to enroll in one of his classes.
   - Ⓑ He has experience working in the private sector.
   - Ⓒ The student is the only one that he currently advises.
   - Ⓓ He is considering retiring because of his advanced age.

5. Listen again to a part of the conversation. Then answer the question.

   What does the student mean when she says this?
   - Ⓐ She is confident in her ability to improve.
   - Ⓑ She agrees with what the professor said.
   - Ⓒ She knows she could have done better at school.
   - Ⓓ She would like the professor to repeat himself.

Lecture 6~11: Listen to part of a lecture in an art history class.

6. Which aspect of Art Deco does the professor mainly discuss?
   - Ⓐ Its founding
   - Ⓑ Its style of design
   - Ⓒ Its influences
   - Ⓓ Its relationship with cars

7. According to the professor, which movement or culture influenced Art Deco?

   Click on 2 answers.
   - Ⓐ Impressionism
   - Ⓑ Roman culture
   - Ⓒ Aztec culture
   - Ⓓ Cubism

8. How does the professor organize the information about Art Deco that she presents to the class?
   - Ⓐ By giving explanations and then showing slides to provide visual stimulus
   - Ⓑ By covering the history of Art Deco in chronological order
   - Ⓒ By naming some of the major artists of the period and then focusing on their works
   - Ⓓ By pointing out examples of the influence of other cultures on Art Deco works

9. What will the professor probably do next?
   - Ⓐ Show some slides to the class
   - Ⓑ Ask the students to read from their books
   - Ⓒ Take a short break
   - Ⓓ Go over the material for the upcoming exam

10. Listen again to a part of the lecture. Then answer the question.

    What does the professor imply when she says this?
    - Ⓐ Most Art Deco designs are too complicated for people to understand.
    - Ⓑ There are many people who dislike the styles that Art Deco uses.
    - Ⓒ It is difficult to determine the period when most Art Deco works were made.
    - Ⓓ Not everyone agrees on whether some works are in the Art Deco style or not.

11. Listen again to a part of the lecture. Then answer the question.

    What does the professor mean when she says this?
    - Ⓐ She is not sure about the answer to his question.
    - Ⓑ The answer to his question is obvious.
    - Ⓒ The student has asked a good question.
    - Ⓓ There are multiple answers to the question.

Actual Test 04

Reading
Section Directions

This section measures your ability to understand academic passages in English.

In this part, you will read 1 passage and answer reading comprehension questions about the passage. Most questions are worth one point, but the last question is worth more than one point. The directions indicate how many points you may receive.

Some passages include a word or phrase that is underlined in blue. Click on the word or phrase to see a definition or an explanation.

When you want to move on to the next question, click on **Next**. You may skip questions and go back to them later. If you want to return to previous questions, click on **Back**. You can click on **Review** at any time and the review screen will show you which questions you have answered and which you have not answered. From this review screen, you may go directly to any question you have already seen in the Reading section.

You may now begin the Reading section. You will read 1 reading passage. You will have **20 minutes** to read the passage and answer the questions.

Click on **Continue** to go on.

TOEFL iBT Reading

1. The word <u>intact</u> in the passage is closest in meaning to
   - Ⓐ unique
   - Ⓑ colorful
   - Ⓒ undamaged
   - Ⓓ legible

2. The word <u>disseminated</u> in the passage is closest in meaning to
   - Ⓐ distributed
   - Ⓑ interpreted
   - Ⓒ evaluated
   - Ⓓ considered

3. The author's description of the eruption of Mount Vesuvius mentions which of the following?
   - Ⓐ Ash that spewed from the volcano covered the entire surrounding area.
   - Ⓑ Fewer than 1,500 people were killed when the volcano erupted.
   - Ⓒ Mount Vesuvius erupted over a period of seventy-nine days.
   - Ⓓ The people living there knew for days that the volcano was going to erupt.

4. The word <u>them</u> in the passage refers to
   - Ⓐ strict religious morals
   - Ⓑ the Romans
   - Ⓒ the walls
   - Ⓓ 140 years

5. According to paragraph 2, which of the following is NOT true about the rediscovery of Pompeii and Herculaneum?
   - Ⓐ People's attitudes when one town was rediscovered resulted in the walls being reburied.
   - Ⓑ A construction team was responsible for one of the rediscoveries of the towns.
   - Ⓒ Pompeii was uncovered in the eighteenth century by people trying to find it.
   - Ⓓ The rediscovery of the towns in the 1500s was the result of people looking for them.

Rediscovering Pompeii and Herculaneum

In 79 A.D., Mount Vesuvius, a volcano in southern Italy, erupted and destroyed the towns of Pompeii and Herculaneum. Thousands of people there and in nearby areas died in the disaster, and the entire area around the volcano was covered in a deep layer of hot ash and rocks. For more than 1,500 years, Pompeii and Herculaneum remained buried and slowly disappeared from people's memories. Then, first in 1599, and later in the 1730s and 1740s, both towns were rediscovered. Amazingly, the hot ash had preserved both towns to such an extent that a great number of artifacts and even painted works of art had remained intact. This provided historians and artists with a unique view of life in the Roman Empire during the first century. The discovery of these artifacts and the towns themselves also had a dramatic impact on European art and architecture as scholars studied and disseminated the knowledge they learned at the two ancient sites.

The eruption of Vesuvius was a documented event, but the existence and location of Pompeii and Herculaneum were lost over time. A part of Pompeii was revealed when a canal was dug in the area in 1599, but only a few walls were unearthed, and the area was soon covered again. Some historians regard this as an ancient act of censorship since many of the walls dug up contained well-preserved murals and frescos that were of a sexual nature. In a climate of strict religious morals, it would have been considered offensive to have revealed the more open sexual mores of the Romans in centuries past. Once the walls were covered back up, it took nearly 140 years for them to be rediscovered a second time. First, in 1738, workers digging at a site for a new palace discovered the remains of Herculaneum. Then, in 1748, a team that was actively searching for Pompeii uncovered it.

From that time up to the present day, extensive archaeological work has been done on both

6. In paragraph 2, the author implies that the walls of Pompeii were covered back up in 1599 because
   - (A) people knew they could not preserve the uncovered walls
   - (B) there was a lack of interest in archaeology then
   - (C) the social conditions at that time did not permit it to be excavated
   - (D) there were no funds to pay for the excavation

7. According to paragraph 3, the Romans made the wall paintings in Pompeii because
   - (A) they were intended to display various aspects of Roman fertility rites
   - (B) the Romans wanted to display their attitudes toward sexuality
   - (C) they wanted to display contemporary Roman clothing and jewelry styles
   - (D) they were meant to show Roman styles for people who looked at them in future times

8. The word budding in the passage is closest in meaning to
   - (A) itinerant
   - (B) famous
   - (C) classical
   - (D) nascent

9. Why does the author mention Neoclassicism?
   - (A) To show that the works from this period resembled those in the two uncovered towns
   - (B) To stress that it began before Pompeii and Herculaneum were rediscovered
   - (C) To focus on the artwork that was produced by the artists during the movement
   - (D) To note its relationship with the artwork found in Pompeii and Herculaneum

places by numerous teams of experts. One reason for the sites' popularity is their virtual treasure trove of artifacts from first-century Rome. Numerous wall paintings and frescos, some of which showed images of Romans and their clothing and jewelry, have been uncovered. As for the erotic paintings, art historians now believe that they were concerned with fertility rituals and were not intended to be obscene. Additionally, large numbers of daily items used by the Romans were preserved as were several buildings in the towns. From this information, scholars have learned a great deal about Roman social life, art, and architecture in the period leading up to the eruption of Vesuvius in 79. In particular, the many preserved works of art have given scholars an opportunity to study the styles of the ancient masters, the materials and methods they used, and the way that the styles changed over time.

Since very few other paintings from Roman times—and virtually none from ancient Greece—survived, the rediscovery of Pompeii and Herculaneum provided a unique look at the ancient world. The images uncovered at Pompeii were copied and spread throughout Europe in the decades after they were rediscovered. Pompeii became a major stopping point for budding artists and architects who wanted to learn as much as they could from the ancient Romans. The rediscovery of Pompeii and Herculaneum had a major impact on Neoclassicism, which was a movement that began in the mid-eighteenth century and drew heavily on the art and architecture of ancient Rome and Greece.

Although life in Pompeii and Herculaneum was instantly wiped out almost 2,000 years ago, the rediscovered towns have given mankind a view of life at a specific time in the past. Other ancient cities, such as Athens and Rome, have retained sites that permit glimpses at their past glory and grandeur, but not in the way that Pompeii and Herculaneum do. Because life continued in Athens

10. According to paragraph 4, the rediscovery of the paintings in Pompeii and Herculaneum was important to the art world because

    Ⓐ it provided the impetus for the Renaissance to begin
    Ⓑ it let people get a real look at life in ancient times
    Ⓒ it made Italy once again the center of the art world
    Ⓓ it forced most artists to visit Italy to study the works firsthand

11. The phrase wiped out in the passage is closest in meaning to

    Ⓐ altered
    Ⓑ buried
    Ⓒ transferred
    Ⓓ killed

12. The word their in the passage refers to

    Ⓐ glory and grandeur
    Ⓑ Pompeii and Herculaneum
    Ⓒ Athens and Rome
    Ⓓ changes

13. Which of the sentences below best expresses the essential information in the highlighted sentence in the passage? *Incorrect* answer choices change the meaning in important ways or leave out essential information.

    Ⓐ Historians are pleased because the volcanic ash, which destroyed the towns and killed their people, preserved both places and made them virtual museums of the past.
    Ⓑ The towns and their people were killed by the volcanic ash, which left the towns intact, so experts have learned more about them than any other places in the ancient world.
    Ⓒ Once the towns were destroyed, the volcanic ash covered them and made it possible for later historians to study the towns and to learn about life during the Roman Empire.

and Rome, they have undergone changes. As a result, many of their ancient secrets are buried under layers of modern life. This is not so with Pompeii and Herculaneum. In an instant, the two towns were lost, and the lives of their people were taken away, but, simultaneously, the volcanic ash preserved so much that today historians know more about the people of these two places than they do about almost any other ancient site.

Glossary
mural: a wall painting
more: a custom; traditions
ritual: a rite; a ceremony

Ⓓ Because historians have been able to view the two towns virtually intact, they have learned more about these places than historians have about any other ancient city or town.

14. **Directions:** An introductory sentence for a brief summary of the passage is provided below. Complete the summary by selecting the THREE answer choices that express the most important ideas of the passage. Some sentences do not belong because they express ideas that are not presented in the passage or are minor ideas in the passage. *This question is worth 2 points.*

The recovery of the Roman towns of Pompeii and Herculaneum has provided historians with a unique glimpse into how people lived in the Roman Empire during the first century.

-
-
-

Answer Choices

Ⓐ Many of the murals and frescoes recovered from the walls of the two towns have shown people how the Romans dressed at the time of the volcano's eruption.

Ⓑ Because life ceased to exist in the two towns following their destruction, they have been preserved much better than other ancient cities such as Rome and Athens.

Ⓒ There were few eyewitnesses to the eruption who survived to tell about it, which is one reason why the memory of the two towns slowly faded away.

Ⓓ The eruption of the volcano Mount Vesuvius in 79 A.D. was responsible for burying the two towns in a thick layer of ash that killed all of their people.

Ⓔ Much of the artwork recovered from the two towns helped influence many artists and also affected the period called Neoclassicism.

Ⓕ Some workers uncovered parts of Pompeii as far back as 1599, but the walls were later covered back up, and the town was forgotten once again.

Drag your answer choices to the spaces where they belong.
To remove an answer choice, click on it. To review the passage, click on **View Text**.

Listening
Section Directions

This section measures your ability to understand conversations and lectures in English.

In this part, you will listen to 1 conversation and 1 lecture. You will hear the conversation or lecture only **one** time. After the conversation or lecture, you will answer some questions about it. The questions typically ask about the main idea and supporting details. Some questions ask about a speaker's purpose or attitude. Answer the questions based on what is stated or implied by the speakers.

You may take notes while you listen. You may use your notes to help you answer the questions. Your notes will **not** be scored.

If you need to change the volume while you listen, click on the **Volume** icon at the top of the screen.

In some questions, you will see this icon: 🎧 This means that you will hear, but not see, part of the question.

Some of the questions have special directions. These directions appear in a gray box on the screen.

Most questions are worth one point. If a question is worth more than one point, it will have special directions that indicate how many points you can receive.

You must answer each question. After you answer, click on **Next**. Then click on **OK** to confirm your answer and go on to the next question. After you click on **OK**, you cannot return to previous questions.

A clock at the top of the screen will show you how much time is remaining. The clock will not count down while you are listening. The clock will count down only while you are answering the questions.

Now you may begin the Listening section.

Conversation 1~5: Listen to part of a conversation between a student and a student housing office employee.

Actual Test 04

TOEFL iBT Listening

1. What are the speakers mainly discussing?
   - Ⓐ The dormitory room the student has
   - Ⓑ The way that students can select their roommates
   - Ⓒ The manner in which the school must compensate the student
   - Ⓓ The living conditions at the school

2. Why does the student visit the student housing office?
   - Ⓐ To ask to change his dormitory room
   - Ⓑ To apply for a single room in a dormitory
   - Ⓒ To complain about his housing situation
   - Ⓓ To demand that he get the room that he wants

3. According to the student, what is wrong with his dormitory room?

   Click on 2 answers.
   - Ⓐ It has too many students in it.
   - Ⓑ It is located in the basement.
   - Ⓒ It is too small for him.
   - Ⓓ It lacks enough furniture.

4. Listen again to a part of the conversation. Then answer the question.

   What is the purpose of the student's response?
   - Ⓐ To let the woman know that he is highly displeased
   - Ⓑ To indicate that he has some more issues to discuss
   - Ⓒ To request that the woman stop interrupting him
   - Ⓓ To encourage the woman to hurry and solve his problem

5. Listen again to a part of the conversation. Then answer the question.

   What can be inferred about the student when he says this?
   - Ⓐ He needs some time to think about the woman's offer.
   - Ⓑ He is independently wealthy.
   - Ⓒ He is pleased with the woman's suggestion.
   - Ⓓ He wants to move in to his new place immediately.

Lecture 6~11: Listen to part of a lecture in a marine biology class.

TOEFL iBT Listening

6. What aspect of South Georgia Island does the professor mainly discuss?
   - (A) Its biodiversity
   - (B) Its geographical location
   - (C) Its relationship with Antarctica
   - (D) The feeding grounds that surround it

7. Why does the professor explain the whaling industry around South Georgia Island from previous centuries?
   - (A) To state why fewer people currently live on the island than formerly did
   - (B) To note that South Georgia Island was first sighted by sailors on whaling ships
   - (C) To mention why some species are less abundant than they were in the past
   - (D) To describe how changes in the ecosystem have had a lasting effect there

8. According to the professor, why is open water important to animals?

   Click on 2 answers.
   - (A) It makes breeding easier.
   - (B) It permits them to feed.
   - (C) It enables them to breathe air.
   - (D) It protects them from predators.

9. Why does the professor discuss the disappearing ice in Antarctica?
   - (A) To provide a possible explanation for declining krill populations
   - (B) To show that the ice is only vanishing in certain areas of the continent
   - (C) To argue that ice melts and freezes on a regular cycle
   - (D) To suggest that some animals will not adapt to the changing environment

10. Based on the information in the lecture, do the following sentences refer to penguins or whales that live on or around South Georgia Island?

    Click in the correct box for each sentence.

	Penguins	Whales
(A) They can breathe easily thanks to the open ice around the island.		
(B) Some species are still trying to recover from being hunted in previous times.		
(C) Up to 300,000 of them live on a section of the island during the breeding season.		
(D) They can hunt for food because of the open ice around the island.		

11. Listen again to a part of the lecture. Then answer the question.

    Why does the professor say this?
    - (A) To get the students to think about the consequences of their actions
    - (B) To emphasize the importance of the information he just gave the students
    - (C) To focus the lecture on the topic of krill and its necessity to animal life
    - (D) To make the students aware that he has just provided some trivial information

Actual Test 05

TOEFL iBT Reading

Reading
Section Directions

This section measures your ability to understand academic passages in English.

In this part, you will read 1 passage and answer reading comprehension questions about the passage. Most questions are worth one point, but the last question is worth more than one point. The directions indicate how many points you may receive.

Some passages include a word or phrase that is underlined in blue. Click on the word or phrase to see a definition or an explanation.

When you want to move on to the next question, click on **Next**. You may skip questions and go back to them later. If you want to return to previous questions, click on **Back**. You can click on **Review** at any time and the review screen will show you which questions you have answered and which you have not answered. From this review screen, you may go directly to any question you have already seen in the Reading section.

You may now begin the Reading section. You will read 1 reading passage. You will have **20 minutes** to read the passage and answer the questions.

Click on **Continue** to go on.

1. The word **enhanced** in the passage is closest in meaning to
   - Ⓐ renovated
   - Ⓑ connected
   - Ⓒ improved
   - Ⓓ removed

2. Which of the following can be inferred from paragraph 1 about the electric guitar?
   - Ⓐ It requires constant maintenance to work properly.
   - Ⓑ It can produce sounds that are fairly loud.
   - Ⓒ It is the preferred instrument of most musicians.
   - Ⓓ It is much more expensive than an acoustic guitar.

3. Which of the sentences below best expresses the essential information in the highlighted sentence in the passage? *Incorrect* answer choices change the meaning in important ways or leave out essential information.
   - Ⓐ By using its external systems, an electric guitar can produce a variety of different sounds.
   - Ⓑ There are a number of ways that the electric guitar has been made better over time.
   - Ⓒ Electric guitars have implements such as pedals and other devices that acoustic guitars lack.
   - Ⓓ On account of the improvements made to them, electric guitars have outstanding sound quality.

4. According to paragraph 2, which of the following is true of electric guitars?
   - Ⓐ Without electricity, their sound cannot be increased in volume.
   - Ⓑ Their designs have remained constant since they were first invented.
   - Ⓒ Some of them operate without the use of an electric cord.
   - Ⓓ Their bodies are similar to those that acoustic guitars have.

The Electric Guitar

The electric guitar is one of the most common instruments in rock and roll as well as other genres of music. This instrument is based on the acoustic guitar but operates with electricity, and its sound is projected through speakers after being enhanced with an amplification system. This enables an electric guitar to provide a wider range of sounds at a higher volume than an acoustic guitar. Over the past few decades, the electric guitar has been altered to improve its performance and to make it more versatile, yet its basic features have changed little since its development in the United States in the 1930s and 1940s.

Most electric guitars resemble normal acoustic guitars except for a few distinct differences. First, they usually have solid bodies rather than hollow ones like acoustic guitars have. As a result of this lack of a hollow body, an electric guitar requires sound pickups and an electric cord to connect the guitar to an amplifier and speaker system. The sound pickups are necessary to provide volume while the pickups change the vibration of the guitar strings into electronic signals that are sent to the amplifier, whereupon it is amplified and then projected through the speakers. Thanks to research and experience, electric guitars have seen great improvements in sound quality, amplification, and their ability to produce sound effects through devices built into the guitar or external systems such as effects pedals on the floor.

Historically, the electric guitar is a purely American invention. George Beauchamp is credited with inventing the first commercially produced electric guitar in 1931. His guitar was nicknamed "the frying pan" since its shape was similar to that of the cooking implement. Beauchamp was a musician who played Hawaiian music, which was very popular at that time. Almost every Hawaiian musical band then used an

5. The word **plucked** in the passage is closest in meaning to
   (A) strummed
   (B) tuned
   (C) attached
   (D) alternated

6. The author's description of George Beauchamp mentions which of the following?
   (A) He based the design of his electric guitar on that of a frying pan.
   (B) He invented the electric guitar because he was inept at playing the acoustic guitar.
   (C) He devised a way to make a guitar that used electricity to amplify sound.
   (D) He became a famous musician after performing in many places in Hawaii.

7. The word **gravitated** in the passage is closest in meaning to
   (A) run
   (B) walked
   (C) moved
   (D) jogged

8. The word **it** in the passage refers to
   (A) a long piece of wood
   (B) an amp and speaker system
   (C) the look of a guitar
   (D) the log guitar

9. Why does the author mention **Adolph Rickenbacker**?
   (A) To claim that he was associated with Les Paul
   (B) To blame him for George Beauchamp's lack of funding
   (C) To explain who received the first patent on the electric guitar
   (D) To give the name of George Beauchamp's business partner

acoustic steel lap guitar, which was like a regular guitar except for the fact that it rested on the guitarist's lap or on a stool. The guitarist plucked the strings with his right hand while using a guitar pick, and his left hand used a metal tube that slid over the strings on the neck to produce changes in the pitch. From this concept, Beauchamp hit on the idea of enhancing the steel lap guitar with magnetic sound pickups that would carry the vibrations of the strings to an amplifier, which could improve the sound before it passed through a loudspeaker.

In 1932, Beauchamp and manufacturer Adolph Rickenbacker founded a company to produce the frying pan guitar. Unfortunately, they were unable to secure a patent for Beauchamp's invention until 1937. In the interval, other inventors and companies were hard at work making their own versions of the electric guitar. Then, in 1940, Les Paul created one of the most famous electric guitars. A versatile acoustic guitar player and country music singer, Paul had gravitated toward the louder sound of the electric guitar in the 1930s. Unhappy with what was commercially available, Paul developed his own version, which he called "the log." Basically, it was a long piece of wood with guitar strings and pickups that were all connected to an amp and speaker system. Eventually, Paul developed a solid body for the log, which gave it the look of a guitar. Upon being manufactured, the log guitar became one of the first solid-body electric guitars. Paul eventually sold his guitar invention to the Gibson Guitar Corporation. The log guitar was called the Les Paul Gibson and is still considered one of the classic electric guitars of all time.

When the electric guitar was invented, it was primarily used for Hawaiian music and, later, for jazz, blues, and rockabilly music. Then, by the 1950s, it became the mainstay of rock and roll music. The origins of rock and roll music lay in the influences of country, blues, and rockabilly

10. According to paragraph 4, Les Paul invented his own electric guitar because

    A. he was interested in becoming wealthy from making guitars
    B. he disliked all of the ones that were available for him to purchase
    C. he wanted to come up with a unique sound for a new genre of music
    D. he worked with George Beauchamp yet did not like his guitar's design

11. The word mainstay in the passage is closest in meaning to

    A. revolutionary
    B. instrument
    C. foundation
    D. organizer

12. The author uses country, blues, and rockabilly music as examples of

    A. music that helped influence the creation of rock and roll
    B. the most popular styles of music when the electric guitar was invented
    C. the music that was the most affected by the electric guitar
    D. musical genres that had no need for electric guitars

music. Although rock and roll does not exist solely because of the electric guitar, it is hard to imagine it without the electric guitar. The guitars of Les Paul and another American inventor, Leo Fender, became the standard rock and roll guitars of the time. Since the 1950s, most electric guitar manufacturers have developed their products for the rock and roll genre and its many offshoots, such as heavy metal.

Glossary
versatile: flexible; adaptable
hollow: having a hole in one's center
secure: to attain; to get

13. **Directions:** Select the appropriate sentences from the answer choices and match them to the type of guitar to which they relate. TWO of the answer choices will NOT be used. *This question is worth 3 points.*

Electric Guitar
(Select 3)
-
-
-

Acoustic Guitar
(Select 2)
-
-

Answer Choices

(A) It makes use of an amplifier system.

(B) It is custom-made according to the musician's tastes.

(C) It can make a large number of different sounds.

(D) It does not need to be connected to a speaker system.

(E) It has a hollow body.

(F) It was first developed by George Beauchamp.

(G) It has the acoustic quality of a frying pan.

Drag your answer choices to the spaces where they belong.
To remove an answer choice, click on it. To review the passage, click on **View Text**.

Listening
Section Directions

This section measures your ability to understand conversations and lectures in English.

In this part, you will listen to 1 conversation and 1 lecture. You will hear the conversation or lecture only **one** time. After the conversation or lecture, you will answer some questions about it. The questions typically ask about the main idea and supporting details. Some questions ask about a speaker's purpose or attitude. Answer the questions based on what is stated or implied by the speakers.

You may take notes while you listen. You may use your notes to help you answer the questions. Your notes will **not** be scored.

If you need to change the volume while you listen, click on the **Volume** icon at the top of the screen.

In some questions, you will see this icon: 🎧 This means that you will hear, but not see, part of the question.

Some of the questions have special directions. These directions appear in a gray box on the screen.

Most questions are worth one point. If a question is worth more than one point, it will have special directions that indicate how many points you can receive.

You must answer each question. After you answer, click on **Next**. Then click on **OK** to confirm your answer and go on to the next question. After you click on **OK**, you cannot return to previous questions.

A clock at the top of the screen will show you how much time is remaining. The clock will not count down while you are listening. The clock will count down only while you are answering the questions.

Now you may begin the Listening section.

Conversation 1~5: Listen to part of a conversation between a student and a professor.

Actual Test 05

TOEFL iBT Listening

1. What are the speakers mainly discussing?
   - Ⓐ Some work that they will do in class soon
   - Ⓑ The mistakes the student made on his paper
   - Ⓒ An assignment the student needs to submit
   - Ⓓ The topic of the student's research paper

2. Why does the professor explain what a research paper is?
   - Ⓐ To convince the student that he is capable of doing the work
   - Ⓑ To encourage the student to work harder in class
   - Ⓒ To answer the question that the student just asked him
   - Ⓓ To let the student know how he improperly did his work

3. What is the professor's opinion of the student?
   - Ⓐ He feels that the student tries a little too hard.
   - Ⓑ He thinks the student should participate more in discussions.
   - Ⓒ He is impressed with the student's seriousness.
   - Ⓓ He thinks the student has a lot of potential.

4. What can be inferred about the professor?
   - Ⓐ He cares about how his students perform in his class.
   - Ⓑ He tries to return his students' assignments quickly.
   - Ⓒ He gives his students the opportunity to participate in class.
   - Ⓓ He grades his students' work very harshly.

5. Listen again to a part of the conversation. Then answer the question.

   Why does the student say this?
   - Ⓐ To confess to having intentionally written his paper improperly
   - Ⓑ To acknowledge that he knows the teacher is referring to him
   - Ⓒ To ask the teacher exactly what he made a mistake on
   - Ⓓ To get the teacher to provide him with some specific details

Lecture 6~11: Listen to part of a lecture in a history class.

History

Actual Test 05

TOEFL iBT Listening

6. Why does the professor explain the circumstances surrounding Henry VIII's first marriage?
   - (A) To show how irregular the marriage was
   - (B) To note why Henry split from the Catholic Church
   - (C) To state how many of Henry's children became adults
   - (D) To criticize Henry's subsequent actions

7. According to the professor, what did the pope do after Henry VIII married Anne Boleyn?
   - (A) He arranged a split between the Catholic Church and England.
   - (B) He excommunicated Henry.
   - (C) He ordered Henry to visit Rome.
   - (D) He made Henry ask for forgiveness.

8. Who was Thomas Cranmer?
   - (A) King Henry VIII's brother
   - (B) The pope
   - (C) An archbishop
   - (D) The English ambassador to Rome

9. How is the discussion organized?
   - (A) By describing the events in the order in which they occurred
   - (B) By providing biographies of the most important people of the era
   - (C) By encouraging the students to give their own interpretations of events
   - (D) By using the book to clarify some of the most important details

10. Listen again to a part of the lecture. Then answer the question.

    What does the professor imply when he says this?
    - (A) The students need to bring their books to class.
    - (B) He wants the students to open their books.
    - (C) The students' homework is to read the next chapter.
    - (D) He will not provide any details on that matter.

11. Listen again to a part of the lecture. Then answer the question.

    What does the professor imply when he says this?
    - (A) He wants the student to give him a quick answer.
    - (B) The student needs to pay more attention in class.
    - (C) He has not forgotten about the student's previous question.
    - (D) He always answers his students' questions during his lectures.

Actual Test 06

TOEFL iBT Reading

Reading
Section Directions

This section measures your ability to understand academic passages in English.

In this part, you will read 1 passage and answer reading comprehension questions about the passage. Most questions are worth one point, but the last question is worth more than one point. The directions indicate how many points you may receive.

Some passages include a word or phrase that is underlined in blue. Click on the word or phrase to see a definition or an explanation.

When you want to move on to the next question, click on **Next**. You may skip questions and go back to them later. If you want to return to previous questions, click on **Back**. You can click on **Review** at any time and the review screen will show you which questions you have answered and which you have not answered. From this review screen, you may go directly to any question you have already seen in the Reading section.

You may now begin the Reading section. You will read 1 reading passage. You will have **20 minutes** to read the passage and answer the questions.

Click on **Continue** to go on.

1. The word trappings in the passage is closest in meaning to
   A knowledge
   B accouterments
   C indications
   D awareness

2. The word assimilated in the passage is closest in meaning to
   A transferred
   B removed
   C absorbed
   D informed

3. According to paragraph 2, which of the following is true of where the Hadza live?
   A Part of their homeland borders the Indian Ocean to the east.
   B There are several rival tribes that live in the same area as them.
   C Their territory has mountains on one side and water on the other.
   D There are few rivers and streams that flow through the area.

4. Why does the author mention the Hadza's avoidance of warfare in paragraph 2?
   A To account for the fact that they have not become extinct as a people
   B To prove that there are some people to whom violence does not come naturally
   C To express puzzlement about why there are so few remaining Hadza
   D To explain one benefit of the manner in which they solve disputes

The Hadza

When humans first evolved, they were hunter-gatherers that survived thanks to the animals and plants they found. Then, approximately 10,000 years ago, humans developed agriculture and animal husbandry. From this start sprang the civilizations that exist almost everywhere on Earth today. However, in some corners of the planet, small groups of people still live without the trappings of modern civilization. One such group is the Hadza people of Tanzania. They have no agriculture, no permanent dwellings, and no possessions except for what they carry on their backs. They eat only what they hunt and gather as they live a virtually Stone Age existence.

The Hadza live in the northern area of Tanzania in eastern Africa on a harsh, dry, broad plain located between the Mbulu Highlands and the shores of salty Lake Eyasi. Many of the Hadza people have been assimilated by the modern world; however, around 1,000 of them still follow their traditional ways. They live in small groups that usually consist of no more than thirty people, most of whom are related. However, the groups are fluid since people come and go as they please, may move to other groups, and frequently eat and sleep wherever they happen to find themselves. If there is a dispute, then one or both of the parties involved merely separate and change groups. In this way, the Hadza have largely escaped from warfare and internal strife. Their sparse population density has also permitted the Hadza to avoid large-scale outbreaks of infectious diseases.

Like most other societies, a Hadza family consists of a father, mother, and their children. The Hadza have no concept of marriage, but if a man and a woman are attracted to one another, it is soon established that they are a couple. They may remain together for life and mutually raise their children, or they may split apart and find other mates. ■ Women seem to play a prominent role in these breakups as they often search for a

5. Which of the sentences below best expresses the essential information in the highlighted sentence in the passage? *Incorrect* answer choices change the meaning in important ways or leave out essential information.

   Ⓐ Most African men are unable to comprehend how Hadza women refuse to accept being inferior to them, so they divorce their Hadza wives and send them back to their homes.
   Ⓑ Only a few marriages of Hadza women and Tanzanian men have been successful and have not ended in divorce due to the men's ill treatment of the women.
   Ⓒ Unless African men begin to change their attitudes toward women, it is likely that few Hadza women will be willing to marry them.
   Ⓓ The majority of Hadza women who intermarry with men in other tribes come back home because of how they are treated as inferiors for being women.

6. The author's description of Hadza families mentions all of the following EXCEPT:

   Ⓐ Families do not always stay together but may in fact part.
   Ⓑ The Hadza have an elaborate marriage ceremony for couples.
   Ⓒ A family unit consists of the parents and their children.
   Ⓓ Women are often the reason that Hadza family units break up.

7. According to paragraph 4, the Hadza know little of the outside world because

   Ⓐ they are unable to afford to travel to other places
   Ⓑ most of them have no interest in learning about other cultures
   Ⓒ they rarely permit outsiders to spend any time with them
   Ⓓ they receive no formal schooling during their lives

man who is a better hunter and, therefore, a better provider. ■ Generally, Hadza men hunt while the women gather food, which mostly consists of fruits and edible plants. ■ Yet the Hadza have no dominant leaders, no authorities, and no beliefs that men should be in positions of power over women. ■ Some Hadza women marry outside their group—usually to other Tanzanians—but the majority return after a few years since they are unable to stand the way they are treated by males from other African tribes, who consider themselves dominant over women.

The Hadza know little of the outside world. As a result, most only speak their own <u>dialect</u> and a little Swahili, and few are educated enough to speak some non-African languages. This makes it difficult for anthropologists to study them since it is difficult to find interpreters and to persuade the Hadza to accept any outsiders to live among them. Arranging such a meeting is also difficult since the Hadza, most of whom do not know their own ages, do not think of time in the way that the rest of the world does. Yet the Hadza are not totally immune to modern influences since they wear modern clothes, use metal tools such as axes and knives, and cook their food in metal pots. Otherwise, they utilize nothing else from technologically advanced civilizations. For instance, the Hadza have no means of transportation other than their own legs, no machines to do their work, no electricity, and no permanent shelters. They move when they need to, hunt and gather food when they are hungry, and spend most of the rest of their time engaged in leisure activities.

Anthropologists are fascinated by the Hadza; they are a link to mankind's earliest days since their lifestyles are so similar to those of early humans. The <u>harshness</u> of the Hadza's territory accounts for why they have been left in relative peace for tens of thousands of years. The soil is poor for farming, there is little fresh water,

8. In paragraph 4, the author implies that the Hadza

   (A) are slowly learning foreign languages
   (B) have adapted to using cars
   (C) make no use of calendars
   (D) are unaware of the outside world

9. According to paragraph 4, which of the following is true of the Hadza?

   (A) They do not consider any single place to be their home.
   (B) They have learned how to raise a few crops.
   (C) They make all of the clothes that they wear.
   (D) They dedicate the majority of their time to working.

10. The word harshness in the passage is closest in meaning to

    (A) acidity
    (B) expansiveness
    (C) redundancy
    (D) ruggedness

11. According to paragraph 5, anthropologists study the Hadza because

    (A) their genetic makeup is similar to that of humans from the Stone Age
    (B) they are people residing in modern times but live like humans from the distant past
    (C) they are the remnants of some of the first tribes to emerge in Africa
    (D) it is likely that they will be extinct as a people within the next few decades

12. Which of the following can be inferred from paragraph 5 about the Hadza?

    (A) Their population is becoming too great for the land to support everyone.
    (B) More of them are abandoning their nomadic lives for modern civilization.
    (C) They must adopt modern farming methods in order to survive.
    (D) They currently have less land to roam on than they did in the past.

and there is a six-month dry season. However, the increasing population of Tanzania has led to human encroachment on Hadza land, so the Hadza now live in an area about one quarter the size they did sixty years ago. Perhaps one day, the Hadza lifestyle will also disappear.

Glossary
animal husbandry: the art of taming wild animals and domesticating them
dialect: a variety of a language
encroachment: infringement; advance

13. Look at the four squares [■] that indicate where the following sentence could be added to the passage.

    Because of this, most men in the tribes work hard to show their potential value to women.

    Where would the sentence best fit?

    Click on a square [■] to add the sentence to the passage.

14. **Directions:** An introductory sentence for a brief summary of the passage is provided below. Complete the summary by selecting the THREE answer choices that express the most important ideas of the passage. Some sentences do not belong because they express ideas that are not presented in the passage or are minor ideas in the passage. *This question is worth 2 points.*

    The Hadza are a group of people in Africa who reject most aspects of modern civilization and live like humans did during the Stone Age.

    -
    -
    -

    Answer Choices

    (A) Some Hadza women marry men in other tribes, but most of these marriages wind up as failures.

    (B) The people that comprise the Hadza tribe live in a part of the land that is found in eastern Tanzania in Africa.

    (C) The Hadza are a nomadic people who wander around their territory in search of animals to hunt and vegetation to gather.

    (D) Hadza culture lacks the concepts of both marriage and time as its members have very unstructured lives.

    (E) The Hadza have some metal tools and modern clothes, but that is virtually all they use from present-day society.

    (F) The harshness of the land that the Hadza live on makes it difficult for them to survive in any amount of comfort.

    Drag your answer choices to the spaces where they belong.
    To remove an answer choice, click on it. To review the passage, click on **View Text**.

Listening
Section Directions

This section measures your ability to understand conversations and lectures in English.

In this part, you will listen to 1 conversation and 1 lecture. You will hear the conversation or lecture only **one** time. After the conversation or lecture, you will answer some questions about it. The questions typically ask about the main idea and supporting details. Some questions ask about a speaker's purpose or attitude. Answer the questions based on what is stated or implied by the speakers.

You may take notes while you listen. You may use your notes to help you answer the questions. Your notes will **not** be scored.

If you need to change the volume while you listen, click on the **Volume** icon at the top of the screen.

In some questions, you will see this icon: 🎧 This means that you will hear, but not see, part of the question.

Some of the questions have special directions. These directions appear in a gray box on the screen.

Most questions are worth one point. If a question is worth more than one point, it will have special directions that indicate how many points you can receive.

You must answer each question. After you answer, click on **Next**. Then click on **OK** to confirm your answer and go on to the next question. After you click on **OK**, you cannot return to previous questions.

A clock at the top of the screen will show you how much time is remaining. The clock will not count down while you are listening. The clock will count down only while you are answering the questions.

Now you may begin the Listening section.

Conversation 1~5: 🎧 Listen to part of a conversation between a student and a librarian.

Actual Test 06

TOEFL iBT Listening

1. Why does the student visit the librarian?
   - Ⓐ To check out some books
   - Ⓑ To pay a fine
   - Ⓒ To ask about a missing book
   - Ⓓ To renew some of her books

2. Why does the student owe the library money?
   - Ⓐ To pay for some copies she made
   - Ⓑ To pay for a book that she damaged
   - Ⓒ To pay for an overdue book
   - Ⓓ To pay a rental fee

3. Why does the student ask the librarian how many books she can borrow at a time?
   - Ⓐ To find out the number of books that the librarian has checked out
   - Ⓑ To satisfy her curiosity about the number
   - Ⓒ To confirm that she has some other books checked out
   - Ⓓ To make sure that she is not going to exceed the limit

4. What can be inferred about the librarian?
   - Ⓐ He attends the school as a part-time student.
   - Ⓑ He is considering changing jobs soon.
   - Ⓒ He is helpful to the library's patrons.
   - Ⓓ He knows little about the library's computer system.

5. Listen again to a part of the conversation. Then answer the question.

   What does the student mean when she says this?
   - Ⓐ She thinks the librarian is joking.
   - Ⓑ She wants the librarian to leave.
   - Ⓒ She believes the amount is too much.
   - Ⓓ She has to go to her class soon.

Lecture 6~11: Listen to part of a lecture in a biology class.

Actual Test 06

TOEFL iBT Listening

6. What aspect of wolves does the professor mainly discuss?
   - (A) Their reappearance in the United States
   - (B) Their physical characteristics
   - (C) The regulations concerning hunting them
   - (D) The habits that individual packs exhibit

7. Why does the professor explain the absence of wolves from Yellowstone National Park?
   - (A) To say why many people were in favor of their reintroduction there
   - (B) To mention why so many elk and deer were living in the park
   - (C) To show how much of a negative effect it had on the park
   - (D) To account for the appearance of other predators in the park

8. According to the professor, which group of people opposed the reintroduction of wolves to Yellowstone National Park?
   - (A) Tourists
   - (B) Locals
   - (C) Farmers
   - (D) Naturalists

9. Based on the information in the lecture, do the following sentences refer to the time before or after wolves were reintroduced to Yellowstone National Park?

   Click in the correct box for each sentence.

	Before	After
(A) Many fish disappeared from the streams.		
(B) There were fewer coyotes in the park.		
(C) Tourists spent more money visiting the park.		
(D) Some trees never reached maturity since they were eaten by elk.		

10. Listen again to a part of the lecture. Then answer the question.

    What can be inferred about the student when he says this?
    - (A) He is interested in independently studying the wolves living in the park.
    - (B) He believes that the wolves have had some negative effects on the park.
    - (C) He would like the professor to provide more information about the wolves.
    - (D) He does not understand how people can be against wolves being in the park.

11. Listen again to a part of the lecture. Then answer the question.

    Why does the professor say this?
    - (A) To make an attempt at humor
    - (B) To give her opinion on hunting wolves
    - (C) To state that she is against killing wolves
    - (D) To lament the needless deaths of the wolves

Actual Test
07

Reading
Section Directions

This section measures your ability to understand academic passages in English.

In this part, you will read 1 passage and answer reading comprehension questions about the passage. Most questions are worth one point, but the last question is worth more than one point. The directions indicate how many points you may receive.

Some passages include a word or phrase that is underlined in blue. Click on the word or phrase to see a definition or an explanation.

When you want to move on to the next question, click on **Next**. You may skip questions and go back to them later. If you want to return to previous questions, click on **Back**. You can click on **Review** at any time and the review screen will show you which questions you have answered and which you have not answered. From this review screen, you may go directly to any question you have already seen in the Reading section.

You may now begin the Reading section. You will read 1 reading passage. You will have **20 minutes** to read the passage and answer the questions.

Click on **Continue** to go on.

The Wallace Line

Charles Darwin spent twenty years researching evolution without publishing his findings. But a letter he received in 1858 from another naturalist, Alfred Russell Wallace, prompted Darwin quickly to publish his own theories in the seminal work *The Origin of Species*. The contents of the letter included Wallace's own theories on evolution, which were quite similar to Darwin's. While Darwin became famous, Wallace's name is barely known outside scientific circles. He has, however, achieved a modicum of fame in modern times for being the father of biogeography as well as one of history's greatest specimen collectors. In addition, Wallace is best known for the Wallace Line, his theory that a line of deep water separated the fauna of Southeast Asia, New Guinea, and Australia into different types and which served as the basis for his ideas on evolution.

Alfred Russell Wallace was British, like Darwin, and a naturalist, but the similarities between the two end there. Wallace was younger than Darwin, did not come from wealth, and received no formal education after the age of fourteen. He was self-taught and worked as a land surveyor while pursuing his hobby of botany in Britain. Then, in the spirit of adventure, Wallace and a friend visited the Amazon rainforest in 1848 and spent four years there. ■ His expenses were paid by his shipping home of insect, animal, and plant specimens to British museums. ■ It was in this manner that Wallace funded practically all of his research over his entire career. ■ The bulk of his extensive research and specimen collecting was done in Southeast Asia, mostly in the Malay Peninsula and on the islands of modern-day Indonesia, where he spent eight years starting in 1854. ■

This endless collecting of specimens is what gave Wallace the ideas on evolution that he described to Darwin in his famous letter. Wallace noticed that, within individual species, there was

---

1. The word modicum in the passage is closest in meaning to
   - Ⓐ bit
   - Ⓑ question
   - Ⓒ supply
   - Ⓓ region

2. In paragraph 1, the author of the passage implies that Charles Darwin and Alfred Russell Wallace
   - Ⓐ came up with their theories on evolution independent of one another
   - Ⓑ argued over who would get the credit for the theory of evolution
   - Ⓒ were bitter rivals because of the lack of fame that Wallace received
   - Ⓓ criticized one another for perceived mistakes in their ideas on evolution

3. According to paragraph 2, which of the following is true of Alfred Russell Wallace's early life?
   - Ⓐ He was a childhood friend of Charles Darwin despite their difference in age.
   - Ⓑ He received little schooling and mostly taught himself everything that he knew.
   - Ⓒ He spent several years living in various parts of Southeast Asia during his youth.
   - Ⓓ He began collecting animal specimens in Britain to pay for his trips around the world.

4. Why does the author mention Alfred Russell Wallace's trip to the Amazon rainforest?
   - Ⓐ To state that he had gone there to work as a surveyor
   - Ⓑ To explain how he got the funding for his trip to Indonesia
   - Ⓒ To show where he got his start collecting specimens
   - Ⓓ To talk about the friend who accompanied him on his trip

5. The word **It** in the passage refers to
   - Ⓐ A line of deep water
   - Ⓑ The eastern part of the Indonesian archipelago
   - Ⓒ The Celebes Sea
   - Ⓓ The narrow strait

6. The word **dubbed** in the passage is closest in meaning to
   - Ⓐ pictured
   - Ⓑ reappointed
   - Ⓒ drew
   - Ⓓ named

7. According to paragraph 3, the deepwater line is important because
   - Ⓐ it covers a significant amount of land and water in Southeast Asia
   - Ⓑ Alfred Russell Wallace was the first to notice its existence
   - Ⓒ it makes a line that certain species of animals do not cross
   - Ⓓ it provided Alfred Russell Wallace with the fame that had previously eluded him

8. The author discusses the land and water through which the Wallace Line runs in paragraph 3 in order to
   - Ⓐ show that not all of the water the line goes through is deep
   - Ⓑ emphasize the importance of geography to Alfred Russell Wallace
   - Ⓒ go into detail on where exactly the line is
   - Ⓓ prove that the line actually does exist

9. The word **nonexistent** in the passage is closest in meaning to
   - Ⓐ missing
   - Ⓑ endangered
   - Ⓒ exterminated
   - Ⓓ extinct

a wide variety among the specimens that he was collecting. He had also noticed that geography played an important part in animal distribution. Wallace came to realize that a line of deep water divided the species of animals in the eastern part of the Indonesian archipelago, New Guinea, and Australia from those in the western part of Indonesia and the Malay Peninsula. It started in the Celebes Sea, ran between Borneo to the west and Celebes to the east, and then passed through the narrow strait in which Bali was to the west and Lombock Island was to the east. Eventually, naturalists dubbed this the Wallace Line.

Wallace discovered 177 species of birds, such as woodpeckers, hornbills, and pheasants, which were found predominately on the western side of the line. In addition, there were 215 species of mammals, such as rhinos, orangutans, tigers, and gibbons, on the western side of the line and which were not found in the east. Wallace found species east of the line that were almost unknown west of the line. Among them were marsupials such as the kangaroo and the koala and many birds, including the bird of paradise, the cockatoo, and the cassowary. Altogether, he identified 241 bird species and 79 mammal species east of the line that were practically nonexistent west of the line. Most animals on both sides of the line were relatively unknown outside the local area.

The Wallace Line is an example of what is now called biogeography, of which Wallace is considered the father. Wallace clearly deduced that some force was at work placing these animals in one location and not another and that the deepwater line between the two sides prevented the passage of species from one side to the other. Within each area, the variety of specimens he found belonging to the same species led him to conclude that each one had come into existence from a similar common species that had existed before them. In other words, they had evolved. Wallace did not, however, utilize the term. Darwin

10. According to paragraph 4, which of the following is true of the animals that lived west of the Wallace Line when Alfred Russell Wallace first identified it?

    (A) Almost 250 birds that were not found east of the line lived there.
    (B) There were marsupials such as kangaroos and koalas living there.
    (C) It included more than 200 mammals that did not live east of the line.
    (D) Rhinos and tigers lived west of the line but could also be found east of it.

11. Which of the sentences below best expresses the essential information in the highlighted sentence in the passage? *Incorrect* answer choices change the meaning in important ways or leave out essential information.

    (A) Wallace crossed the line repeatedly in an effort to determine why some animals only lived east of the line while others resided west of it.
    (B) The deepwater line effectively kept animals from crossing it, so there were smaller populations of animals living on either side of the line.
    (C) A force that Wallace did not understand was causing the animals to be divided onto one side of the line so that they would never meet.
    (D) Wallace came to understand that something had put the animals on one side of the line and then had prevented them from crossing it.

12. The word begrudged in the passage is closest in meaning to

    (A) denounced
    (B) complimented
    (C) resented
    (D) assaulted

recognized that Wallace's ideas were similar to his own and gave a presentation in July 1858 on his theories while also giving equal credit to Wallace. But it was Darwin who published first and is credited with coming up with the theory of evolution. To their lasting credit, both of the men remained friends, Wallace never begrudged Darwin's fame, and Darwin never denied the role Wallace had played in the theory of evolution.

Glossary
seminal: influential; groundbreaking
bulk: a majority of something
predominantly: mostly

13. Look at the four squares [■] that indicate where the following sentence could be added to the passage.

   While there, Wallace found an activity that he both enjoyed and profited from.

   Where would the sentence best fit?

   Click on a square [■] to add the sentence to the passage.

14. **Directions:** An introductory sentence for a brief summary of the passage is provided below. Complete the summary by selecting the THREE answer choices that express the most important ideas of the passage. Some sentences do not belong because they express ideas that are not presented in the passage or are minor ideas in the passage. *This question is worth 2 points.*

   Alfred Russell Wallace conducted groundbreaking work on the theory of evolution while he was in Southeast Asia, yet he never achieved the fame that Charles Darwin did.

   -
   -
   -

   Answer Choices

   (A) Most people know Wallace for the Wallace Line, which was a line in Southeast Asia that certain species of animals never crossed.

   (B) Charles Darwin and Alfred Russell Wallace were friends even though there were many differences between the two men.

   (C) Darwin hurried to publish his findings on evolution when he realized that Wallace was working on the same topic, so Darwin became famous worldwide.

   (D) Wallace was able to finance most of the expeditions that he went on by becoming a prodigious collector of plant and animal specimens around the world.

   (E) The deepwater line that separated numerous bird and mammal species from one another came to be called the Wallace Line.

   (F) Wallace never regretted that Darwin was the first to publish his theories on evolution since he was not interested in becoming a celebrity.

   Drag your answer choices to the spaces where they belong.
   To remove an answer choice, click on it. To review the passage, click on **View Text**.

TOEFL iBT Listening

Listening
Section Directions

This section measures your ability to understand conversations and lectures in English.

In this part, you will listen to 1 conversation and 1 lecture. You will hear the conversation or lecture only **one** time. After the conversation or lecture, you will answer some questions about it. The questions typically ask about the main idea and supporting details. Some questions ask about a speaker's purpose or attitude. Answer the questions based on what is stated or implied by the speakers.

You may take notes while you listen. You may use your notes to help you answer the questions. Your notes will **not** be scored.

If you need to change the volume while you listen, click on the **Volume** icon at the top of the screen.

In some questions, you will see this icon: 🎧 This means that you will hear, but not see, part of the question.

Some of the questions have special directions. These directions appear in a gray box on the screen.

Most questions are worth one point. If a question is worth more than one point, it will have special directions that indicate how many points you can receive.

You must answer each question. After you answer, click on **Next**. Then click on **OK** to confirm your answer and go on to the next question. After you click on **OK**, you cannot return to previous questions.

A clock at the top of the screen will show you how much time is remaining. The clock will not count down while you are listening. The clock will count down only while you are answering the questions.

Now you may begin the Listening section.

TOEFL iBT Listening

Conversation 1~5: Listen to part of a conversation between a student and a professor.

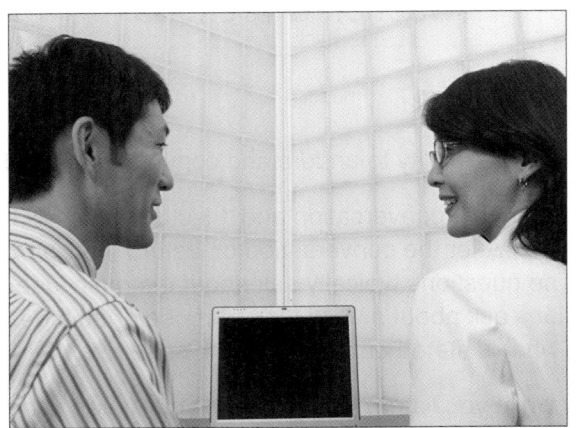

1. Why did the professor ask to see the student?
   - Ⓐ To go over his schedule for the next semester
   - Ⓑ To talk about some of the student's classes
   - Ⓒ To discuss the student's plans for after graduation
   - Ⓓ To find out which course requirements the student has fulfilled

2. What can be inferred about the student?
   - Ⓐ He prefers literature to history.
   - Ⓑ He likes speaking up during class.
   - Ⓒ He is planning to get a double major.
   - Ⓓ He is majoring in economics.

3. Why does the student mention his father?
   - Ⓐ To explain why he is planning to take a certain class
   - Ⓑ To say that his father is forcing him to change majors
   - Ⓒ To state that he wants to do the same work as his father
   - Ⓓ To claim that his father has a good sense of humor

4. What can be inferred about Professor Drake?
   - Ⓐ His office is located near Professor Thompson's.
   - Ⓑ He was the professor in a class the student took previously.
   - Ⓒ He teaches a course in marine biology.
   - Ⓓ He is willing to become the student's advisor.

5. What will the student probably do next?
   - Ⓐ Inquire about changing majors
   - Ⓑ Register for his new classes
   - Ⓒ Depart the professor's office
   - Ⓓ Get some information on a history class

Lecture 6~11: Listen to part of a lecture in an anthropology class.

Anthropology

Actual Test 07

TOEFL iBT Listening

6. What is the lecture mainly about?
   - (A) The reasons why humans have migrated over the centuries
   - (B) The battle for dominance between Cro-Magnons and Neanderthals
   - (C) Changes in humans that led to new races being created
   - (D) The spread of humans across the entire planet

7. According to the professor, where did the Cro-Magnons first go after they left their place of origin?
   - (A) The Middle East
   - (B) All throughout Africa
   - (C) Siberia and East Asia
   - (D) The Pacific Islands

8. Why does the professor mention Neanderthals?
   - (A) To compare their migrations with those of Cro-Magnons
   - (B) To describe some of their more obvious physical characteristics
   - (C) To suggest that humans once crossbred with them
   - (D) To say why Cro-Magnons were slow in moving to Europe

9. What is the professor's opinion of the individuals who sailed to various Pacific islands?
   - (A) He believes they could have sailed further.
   - (B) He thinks they progressed slowly.
   - (C) He is impressed by their skills.
   - (D) He offers no opinion on them.

10. What will the professor probably do next?
    - (A) Go over a new chapter
    - (B) Dismiss the class
    - (C) Begin a class discussion
    - (D) Collect the students' homework

11. Listen again to a part of the lecture. Then answer the question.

    What can be inferred from the professor's response to the student?
    - (A) The student needs to conduct some more research into the matter.
    - (B) It is possible that Cro-Magnons and Neanderthals crossbred in the past.
    - (C) He is going to search for archaeological evidence concerning Neanderthals.
    - (D) There is no evidence confirming Neanderthals are related to Cro-Magnons.

Actual Test 08

TOEFL iBT Reading

Reading
Section Directions

This section measures your ability to understand academic passages in English.

In this part, you will read 1 passage and answer reading comprehension questions about the passage. Most questions are worth one point, but the last question is worth more than one point. The directions indicate how many points you may receive.

Some passages include a word or phrase that is underlined in blue. Click on the word or phrase to see a definition or an explanation.

When you want to move on to the next question, click on **Next**. You may skip questions and go back to them later. If you want to return to previous questions, click on **Back**. You can click on **Review** at any time and the review screen will show you which questions you have answered and which you have not answered. From this review screen, you may go directly to any question you have already seen in the Reading section.

You may now begin the Reading section. You will read 1 reading passage. You will have **20 minutes** to read the passage and answer the questions.

Click on **Continue** to go on.

TOEFL iBT Reading

1. According to paragraph 1, the ancient Egyptians practiced animal mummification because
   - Ⓐ working with animals helped embalmers improve their human mummification methods
   - Ⓑ they wanted the mummified animals to be with humans in their tombs
   - Ⓒ many people believed that the animals would protect them in the afterlife
   - Ⓓ people often gave the mummies to the priests in the temples as a form of payment

2. The word heyday in the passage is closest in meaning to
   - Ⓐ advent
   - Ⓑ renaissance
   - Ⓒ onset
   - Ⓓ prime

3. The word it in the passage refers to
   - Ⓐ natron
   - Ⓑ moisture
   - Ⓒ fat
   - Ⓓ the animal's body

4. The author discusses natron in paragraph 2 in order to
   - Ⓐ note how the Egyptians dried the bodies of dead animals
   - Ⓑ describe its usefulness when the Egyptians removed animals' organs
   - Ⓒ state why the Egyptians wrapped dead bodies in linen
   - Ⓓ explain where the Egyptians were able to acquire it

Animal Mummification in Ancient Egypt

It is widely known that the ancient Egyptians mummified their dead due to their belief that the person would be preserved for the afterlife. What is less well-known is that the ancient Egyptians also mummified animals. Archaeologists have uncovered hundreds of thousands of mummified animals all throughout Egypt. Included among the preserved animals are cats, crocodiles, bulls, snakes, birds, fish, baboons, dogs, gazelles, lions, and even elephants. The main purpose of mummifying animals was for them to serve as companions for dead humans in the afterlife. Mummified animals were also offered to Egyptian gods on special holidays and were used as sacrifices to ask the gods for good weather and good harvests. Thanks to their extensive research, archaeologists have discovered the methods the Egyptians used for mummifying the animals.

During the heyday of archaeological expeditions to Egypt in the late nineteenth and early twentieth centuries, animal mummies were discovered but were considered to be of secondary importance to mummified human remains and the artifacts found alongside them. More extensive work has been done on mummified animals in recent years by experts called zooarchaeologists. They have uncovered the secrets of animal mummification. Typically, the animal's internal organs were manually removed or extracted through the addition of a turpentine and cedar-oil compound that liquefied the organs. Then, the embalmers placed small linen sacks of natron—a type of salt mined in Egypt since ancient times—inside the body to help absorb any moisture and fat as the animal dried. Once the animal's body had dried, the embalmers wrapped it in linen, upon which they usually wrote religious symbols. Some mummified animals were also placed inside wooden or stone sarcophagi.

Mummified animals were not exclusive to pharaohs and members of the upper class as

Actual Test 08

TOEFL iBT Reading

5. According to paragraph 2, which of the following is true of the process of animal mummification?
   - Ⓐ Natron was stuffed into the bodies to liquefy certain internal organs.
   - Ⓑ The embalmers wrapped the organs in cloths made of linen.
   - Ⓒ The organs of the dead animals had to be removed first.
   - Ⓓ It took a number of days for an embalmer to mummify a single animal.

6. According to paragraph 3, the animals that the Egyptians most commonly mummified
   - Ⓐ were considered to be effective guardians in the afterlife
   - Ⓑ were usually pets that people had owned during their lives
   - Ⓒ were ones that most people considered to be exotic animals
   - Ⓓ were captured by hunters who then sold them to embalmers

7. Which of the following can be inferred about exotic animals?
   - Ⓐ They were almost always highly dangerous.
   - Ⓑ They were very few in number.
   - Ⓒ They were expensive in ancient Egypt.
   - Ⓓ They came from lands other than Egypt.

8. The word them in the passage refers to
   - Ⓐ some animals
   - Ⓑ Apis bulls
   - Ⓒ crocodiles
   - Ⓓ gods

9. The word wailed in the passage is closest in meaning to
   - Ⓐ sobbed
   - Ⓑ yelled
   - Ⓒ celebrated
   - Ⓓ screamed

they have been discovered in the tombs of both the very rich and the very poor. Typically, the mummified animals were the beloved pets of the deceased. When a person died, his or her pet was frequently killed and mummified to serve as the individual's companion in the afterlife. For pharaohs and the extremely wealthy, these pets tended to be exotic animals, but tombs of common people have typically been found to have more normal pets such as dogs. When a pharaoh died, thousands of animals were regularly slaughtered and mummified as a part of the burial rites. In addition to whole animals, pieces of preserved meat were wrapped and placed in the tomb to serve as food sources for the person in the afterlife.

Some animals, such as Apis bulls and crocodiles, were believed to represent gods and were thus mummified to appease them. Often, an Apis bull was cared for all its life and was treated as if it were a god. Upon its death, it was set on a special stone to dry so that it could be mummified. Then, a large parade was held in its honor as priests, nobles, and commoners wailed at the loss of the bull. The tombs where these bulls were interred held many valuables too tempting for looters to pass up, so zooarchaeologists have yet to find an intact mummified Apis bull. The Egyptians also revered and mummified crocodiles since they believed crocodiles could predict the Nile River floods. The crocodiles living there instinctively laid their eggs above the waterline of the flooded Nile River, thus giving warning to the Egyptians of how high or low the coming flood would be.

Animal mummification was a big business in ancient Egypt. During festivals or in times of sorrow, the Egyptians offered mummified animals to their gods in the hope of pleasing them. Businesses were established to sell these mummified votives to pilgrims who had traveled far to temples to make sacrifices to the gods.

10. The word interred in the passage is closest in meaning to
    - (A) sacrificed
    - (B) buried
    - (C) burned
    - (D) hid

11. Which of the following can be inferred from paragraph 4 about animals?
    - (A) They played a major role in Egyptian religious rites.
    - (B) They were treated better than most humans were.
    - (C) The Egyptians rarely ate them but revered them instead.
    - (D) They could be found in virtually every household in Egypt.

12. The word votives in the passage is closest in meaning to
    - (A) presents
    - (B) offerings
    - (C) donations
    - (D) dolls

13. According to paragraph 5, which of the following is NOT true of the business of animal mummification?
    - (A) The majority of the mummified animal salesmen were based near temples.
    - (B) People who sold mummified animals often charged according to the animals' sizes.
    - (C) Mummified animals were sold to people who had gone on pilgrimages.
    - (D) Some of the people who were involved in the business were not particularly honest.

These mummified animals ranged from small insects and shrews to larger ones such as cats and birds. Typically, the price depended upon the size of the mummy. Zooarchaeologists have discovered that some of these animal mummy salesmen were not particularly honest. Some linen-wrapped mummies in ancient temples have been found to have contained nothing more than some bones or a few feathers of an animal while some merely held mud and stones. Nevertheless, most were legitimate mummified animals. As a result, the Egyptians left behind tens of thousands of examples that zooarchaeologists have been able to examine to help them learn more about ancient Egypt.

Glossary

afterlife: the spiritual world
embalmer: a person who prepares a dead body for burial
sarcophagus: a tomb; a coffin; a casket

14. **Directions:** An introductory sentence for a brief summary of the passage is provided below. Complete the summary by selecting the THREE answer choices that express the most important ideas of the passage. Some sentences do not belong because they express ideas that are not presented in the passage or are minor ideas in the passage. *This question is worth 2 points.*

In ancient Egypt, people practiced animal mummification for a number of different reasons.

-
-
-

Answer Choices

(A) By using natron, a type of salt found in Egypt, embalmers were able to dry the bodies of dead animals as they prepared them for mummification.

(B) Some mummified animal salesmen tricked their customers by selling them mummies that did not contain complete animals.

(C) Upon many people's deaths, their pets were killed and then made into mummies so that they could accompany the individuals in the afterlife.

(D) Some exotic animals, such as Apis bulls and crocodiles, were revered as gods and were then mummified and buried in temples upon their deaths.

(E) The Egyptians often sacrificed mummified animals to the gods when they wanted to pray for something that they considered important.

(F) Archaeologists have discovered huge numbers of mummified animals, so they have learned much about the process of animal mummification from them.

Drag your answer choices to the spaces where they belong.
To remove an answer choice, click on it. To review the passage, click on **View Text**.

Listening
Section Directions

This section measures your ability to understand conversations and lectures in English.

In this part, you will listen to 1 conversation and 1 lecture. You will hear the conversation or lecture only **one** time. After the conversation or lecture, you will answer some questions about it. The questions typically ask about the main idea and supporting details. Some questions ask about a speaker's purpose or attitude. Answer the questions based on what is stated or implied by the speakers.

You may take notes while you listen. You may use your notes to help you answer the questions. Your notes will **not** be scored.

If you need to change the volume while you listen, click on the **Volume** icon at the top of the screen.

In some questions, you will see this icon: 🎧 This means that you will hear, but not see, part of the question.

Some of the questions have special directions. These directions appear in a gray box on the screen.

Most questions are worth one point. If a question is worth more than one point, it will have special directions that indicate how many points you can receive.

You must answer each question. After you answer, click on **Next**. Then click on **OK** to confirm your answer and go on to the next question. After you click on **OK**, you cannot return to previous questions.

A clock at the top of the screen will show you how much time is remaining. The clock will not count down while you are listening. The clock will count down only while you are answering the questions.

Now you may begin the Listening section.

Conversation 1~5: Listen to part of a conversation between a student and a student housing office employee. 08-02

Actual Test 08

TOEFL iBT Listening

1. Why does the student visit the housing office?
   - Ⓐ To fill out a form about her housing preference
   - Ⓑ To complain about her housing situation
   - Ⓒ To file an official complaint
   - Ⓓ To attend a meeting with Mr. Mullen

2. What does the student say about her roommate?
   - Ⓐ She is a very conscientious student.
   - Ⓑ She is friendly and outgoing.
   - Ⓒ She seems to neglect her studies.
   - Ⓓ She has become a close friend.

3. What is the man's attitude toward the student?
   - Ⓐ He is concerned about her situation.
   - Ⓑ He believes that she is exaggerating.
   - Ⓒ He considers her to be too dramatic.
   - Ⓓ He is dismissive of her concerns.

4. What will the student probably do next?
   - Ⓐ Return to her dormitory room
   - Ⓑ Have a long talk with her roommate
   - Ⓒ Make arrangements to find a new roommate
   - Ⓓ Schedule a mediation period for her and her roommate

5. Listen again to a part of the conversation. Then answer the question.

   What is the purpose of the man's response?
   - Ⓐ To take her idea into consideration
   - Ⓑ To dispute the argument she is making
   - Ⓒ To rescind the offer he just made her
   - Ⓓ To reject the student's suggestion

Lecture 6~11: 🎧 Listen to part of a lecture in a geology class. 08-03

Actual Test 08

TOEFL iBT Listening

6. What is the main topic of the lecture?
   - Ⓐ How to apply pressure to rocks
   - Ⓑ The different types of stresses applied to rocks
   - Ⓒ The deformation of rocks
   - Ⓓ Rock strata

7. What is confining pressure?
   - Ⓐ Pressure that pulls on a rock
   - Ⓑ A force that causes a rock to stretch
   - Ⓒ The squeezing together of a rock
   - Ⓓ Equal pressure on all sides of a rock

8. What can be inferred about the student?
   - Ⓐ She does not understand the professor's explanation on rock deformation.
   - Ⓑ She wants the professor to show some slides to illustrate his lecture.
   - Ⓒ She feels that the professor needs to go back over the material from the beginning.
   - Ⓓ She is surprised by some of the information that the professor has covered.

9. Based on the information in the lecture, which types of rock deformation do the following sentences refer to?

   Click in the correct box for each sentence.

	Elastic Deformation	Ductile Deformation	Brittle Deformation
Ⓐ May fold the rock permanently but not break it			
Ⓑ Is a temporary change in the rock			
Ⓒ Results in the breaking of the rock			
Ⓓ Could cause the rock to appear to be flowing			

10. What will the professor probably do next?
    - Ⓐ Lecture some more on confining pressure
    - Ⓑ Discuss the compositions of rocks
    - Ⓒ Provide a demonstration of elastic deformation
    - Ⓓ Show a video on rock deformation

11. Listen again to a part of the lecture. Then answer the question.

    Why does the professor say this?
    - Ⓐ To indicate the importance of the material
    - Ⓑ To remind the students about their midterm exam
    - Ⓒ To say that he will pass out their exams soon
    - Ⓓ To answer a question that a student just asked

Actual Test
09

TOEFL iBT Reading

Reading
Section Directions

This section measures your ability to understand academic passages in English.

In this part, you will read 1 passage and answer reading comprehension questions about the passage. Most questions are worth one point, but the last question is worth more than one point. The directions indicate how many points you may receive.

Some passages include a word or phrase that is underlined in blue. Click on the word or phrase to see a definition or an explanation.

When you want to move on to the next question, click on **Next**. You may skip questions and go back to them later. If you want to return to previous questions, click on **Back**. You can click on **Review** at any time and the review screen will show you which questions you have answered and which you have not answered. From this review screen, you may go directly to any question you have already seen in the Reading section.

You may now begin the Reading section. You will read 1 reading passage. You will have **20 minutes** to read the passage and answer the questions.

Click on **Continue** to go on.

TOEFL iBT Reading

1. Which of the sentences below best expresses the essential information in the highlighted sentence in the passage? *Incorrect* answer choices change the meaning in important ways or leave out essential information.

   (A) A reduced amount of activity and achievement is one result of a person being a perfectionist who suffers from a psychological problem.
   (B) People who suffer from perfectionism often fear being wrong so much that they take no chances and thus lower their ability to succeed in life.
   (C) People who want to be perfect often fail to do so because they make a number of crucial mistakes while they are striving for perfection.
   (D) Perfectionists have a psychological condition that causes them to fear mistakes so much that they attain a higher level of achievement than most people.

2. The word paralyzed in the passage is closest in meaning to

   (A) frozen
   (B) shamed
   (C) forced
   (D) obligated

3. The word they in the passage refers to

   (A) parents
   (B) their children
   (C) others
   (D) their own desires and needs

4. The word reinforce in the passage is closest in meaning to

   (A) reject
   (B) emphasize
   (C) imply
   (D) initiate

Perfectionism

The desire to be perfect at something or, in many cases, everything, is known as perfectionism. Perfectionism is recognized as a psychological condition in which individuals may be so focused on being perfect and worrying about making mistakes that they are afraid to take risks and, as a result, reduce their levels of adaptability or creativity and their achievements. Psychologists believe that perfectionism develops in childhood. It is often the parents who are to blame since they create situations in which their children equate perfect schoolwork or performance in a sport or other endeavor with parental approval and love. Some indicators of a perfectionist are a person being overly concerned with mistakes, having high personal standards, being worried about parental expectations and criticism, doubting his or her own actions to the point where the perfectionist is paralyzed into inaction, and being overly focused on order.

Perfectionism typically begins at an early age. Parents stress the need for their children to be better than others, and they proceed to project their own desires and needs onto the lives of their children. Children learn that they can please their parents by being perfect at something. This may include achieving high grades, winning contests, and excelling at sports. If the parents reinforce this belief by rewarding success and criticizing or punishing failure, then they are setting up their children to become perfectionists. ■ Gradually, their children may become overly concerned with making mistakes as well as avoiding failure. ■ They eventually come to believe that people will think less of them if they make any errors. ■ Feelings of uncertainty often follow these children into adulthood. ■

Why parents do this to their children is related to two different sources of psychological control. In the first, the parents themselves are perfectionists, and they pass this attitude on to their children.

5. According to paragraph 2, which of the following is true of perfectionists?

    Ⓐ If they do not become perfectionists as children, they will never be successful.
    Ⓑ There are many times when they compete against their parents in certain endeavors.
    Ⓒ They are often forced into their condition through the actions of their parents.
    Ⓓ Their condition has been genetically inherited from their parents.

6. The word them in the passage refers to

    Ⓐ the parents
    Ⓑ fathers
    Ⓒ their own successes
    Ⓓ their sons

7. Which of the following can be inferred from paragraph 3 about the parents of perfectionists?

    Ⓐ They often push their children away from them so that they can attain perfection.
    Ⓑ They dislike seeing their children excel in fields that they themselves are good at.
    Ⓒ They may make their children perfectionists to compensate for their own failures in life.
    Ⓓ They are interested in controlling every aspect of their children's lives.

8. According to paragraph 3, some children become perfectionists because

    Ⓐ they are seeking some form of approval from their parents
    Ⓑ they have been ordered not to disappoint their parents
    Ⓒ their parents spend a great deal of time instructing them
    Ⓓ their parents refuse to allow them to spend any time on their own

The parents may or may not be successful in life, but they convey to their children that they will accept nothing less than perfection. The situation may be more severe if the parents are successful. Fathers in particular tend to project their own successes onto their sons. Some fathers expect them to achieve what they did in academia, sports, or business so much that their sons may be pushed into life choices they do not want but make solely because of their fathers. The second psychological aspect involved is the fear of separation. Parents with separation anxiety may only approve of their children's actions as long as they stay close and dependent on the parents. If the children attempt to become independent in any way—even at an early age—the parents will belittle and criticize them. The children then realize that parental approval, and maybe even love, can only be achieved by remaining close to their parents and by being perfect in their parents' eyes.

The outcomes of these fears can be quite negative. Some perfectionists never finish any tasks because they are afraid that their work is not perfect enough and requires further action to be complete. Others never even start anything because they dread failure. Additionally, having order in their lives allows perfectionists to control any uncertain elements that could upset their need for perfection. This leads some perfectionists to become control freaks who cannot stand any changes in their lives. Another negative aspect is that perfectionists tend to hide their mistakes. They fear the potential backlash of a mistake so much that they may blame others for their failures. Because of this trait, perfectionists rarely receive the feedback they require to overcome their mistakes and to achieve their goals. Ironically, by striving to be perfect, perfectionists frequently block the things that could make them successful.

The need to be perfect gets tied up in the children's—and later the adults'—views of their

9. The word dread in the passage is closest in meaning to
   - (A) anticipate
   - (B) consider
   - (C) fear
   - (D) reject

10. Why does the author mention control freaks?
    - (A) To criticize the behavior of some parents toward their children
    - (B) To show what the inability to accept failure may change a person into
    - (C) To explain why some perfectionists blame others for their own mistakes
    - (D) To discuss one negative aspect of a person being a perfectionist

11. The word lofty in the passage is closest in meaning to
    - (A) unreasonable
    - (B) imaginary
    - (C) apparent
    - (D) elevated

12. According to paragraph 5, some children may commit suicide because
    - (A) they can no longer accept making constant mistakes
    - (B) they feel a certain amount of pressure from their parents
    - (C) they are unable to handle the number of daily decisions they must make
    - (D) they feel that they have nothing left to accomplish in life

13. Look at the four squares [■] that indicate where the following sentence could be added to the passage.

    Some perfectionists have overcome these feelings, but it often takes a great effort and a long period of time to do so.

    Where would the sentence best fit?

    Click on a square [■] to add the sentence to the passage.

own sense of self. Perfectionists begin to believe that they are only as good as the feats that they accomplish. When coupled with being paralyzed into inactivity out of a fear of making mistakes, this can lead to extreme anxiety and depression. Such pressure has led to suicides among teens and young adults who believe that they have not lived up to their parents' lofty expectations. They can no longer stand the stress of trying to be perfect and thus end their lives.

Glossary
endeavor: an activity; an attempt at something
convey: to communicate; to pass on to someone else
belittle: to make fun of; to disparage; to put down

14. Directions: An introductory sentence for a brief summary of the passage is provided below. Complete the summary by selecting the THREE answer choices that express the most important ideas of the passage. Some sentences do not belong because they express ideas that are not presented in the passage or are minor ideas in the passage. *This question is worth 2 points.*

Many children become perfectionists because of their parents' actions, and, as a result, there are often a number of negative consequences.

-
-
-

Answer Choices

(A) Perfectionists may blame others for their own mistakes and even stop trying to accomplish anything because of their condition.

(B) A recent study has shown that teens who are perfectionists commit suicide at a greater rate than do teens who lead normal lives.

(C) Psychologists are actively studying the condition of perfectionism and consider it to be an actual problem, particularly for young children.

(D) Many parents transform their children into perfectionists by being unwilling to accept even the slightest bit of failure by their children.

(E) Many parents feel that their lives have been less than successful, so they hope that their children can outperform them in some manner.

(F) When children feel a need to receive parental approval in all aspects of their lives, they may become perfectionists.

Drag your answer choices to the spaces where they belong.
To remove an answer choice, click on it. To review the passage, click on **View Text**.

Listening
Section Directions

This section measures your ability to understand conversations and lectures in English.

In this part, you will listen to 1 conversation and 1 lecture. You will hear the conversation or lecture only **one** time. After the conversation or lecture, you will answer some questions about it. The questions typically ask about the main idea and supporting details. Some questions ask about a speaker's purpose or attitude. Answer the questions based on what is stated or implied by the speakers.

You may take notes while you listen. You may use your notes to help you answer the questions. Your notes will **not** be scored.

If you need to change the volume while you listen, click on the **Volume** icon at the top of the screen.

In some questions, you will see this icon: 🎧 This means that you will hear, but not see, part of the question.

Some of the questions have special directions. These directions appear in a gray box on the screen.

Most questions are worth one point. If a question is worth more than one point, it will have special directions that indicate how many points you can receive.

You must answer each question. After you answer, click on **Next**. Then click on **OK** to confirm your answer and go on to the next question. After you click on **OK**, you cannot return to previous questions.

A clock at the top of the screen will show you how much time is remaining. The clock will not count down while you are listening. The clock will count down only while you are answering the questions.

Now you may begin the Listening section.

Conversation 1~5: Listen to part of a conversation between a student and a professor.

Actual Test 09

TOEFL iBT Listening

1. What are the speakers mainly discussing?
   - Ⓐ The classes the student will take next semester
   - Ⓑ The student's new major
   - Ⓒ The student's decision to major in physics
   - Ⓓ The student's academic achievements

2. According to the professor, how are the student's grades in physics?
   - Ⓐ They are merely average.
   - Ⓑ They are slowing improving.
   - Ⓒ They are close to failing.
   - Ⓓ They are getting progressively worse.

3. Why does the professor mention psychology?
   - Ⓐ To name some psychology books the student should read
   - Ⓑ To suggest that the student might want to study that subject
   - Ⓒ To compliment the student on the A+ he got on a psychology test
   - Ⓓ To pass on some information a psychology professor gave him

4. Listen again to a part of the conversation. Then answer the question.

   What does the professor imply when he says this?
   - Ⓐ Some students are trying to eavesdrop on them.
   - Ⓑ He believes the student may become upset soon.
   - Ⓒ He wants no one else to hear their conversation.
   - Ⓓ The student has just gotten into some trouble.

5. Listen again to a part of the conversation. Then answer the question.

   What does the professor imply when he says this?
   - Ⓐ He remembers when the student had some problems.
   - Ⓑ The student needs to improve his behavior.
   - Ⓒ An important day is coming up soon.
   - Ⓓ The student is a law-abiding individual.

Lecture 6~11: Listen to part of a lecture in a history class.

6. What is the lecture mainly about?
   - Ⓐ The differences between Christian and Muslim Arabs
   - Ⓑ The reasons why Christian Arabs have left the Middle East
   - Ⓒ The influence of Israel on Christian-Muslims relations
   - Ⓓ The views of Westerners concerning Christian Arabs

7. What is the Levant?
   - Ⓐ All of the countries in the Middle East
   - Ⓑ The countries in Africa that border the Mediterranean Sea
   - Ⓒ The countries in the Middle East with Arab populations
   - Ⓓ The countries in the weastern part of the Mediterranean Sea

8. Why does the professor provide the modern-day Christian populations of several countries in the Levant?
   - Ⓐ To prove that they have sizable Christian populations
   - Ⓑ To explain why there are more Muslims than Christians there
   - Ⓒ To contrast them with the number of Christians during the Byzantine period
   - Ⓓ To show how much they have decreased over the decades

9. Why does the professor mention Israel?
   - Ⓐ To discuss its relationship with Christian Arabs
   - Ⓑ To say that it distrusts Christian Arabs more than Muslim Arabs
   - Ⓒ To explain why so few Muslim Arabs live there
   - Ⓓ To describe its connection with the Christian West

10. What comparison does the professor make between Christian Westerners and Israelis?
    - Ⓐ They have integrated Christian Arabs with the rest of their populations.
    - Ⓑ Neither of them has a large Muslim population.
    - Ⓒ They both associate all Arabs with terrorism.
    - Ⓓ Neither of them attempts to understand the feelings of Arabs.

11. What can be inferred about the professor?
    - Ⓐ He believes that Israel has caused the most harm to Christian Arabs.
    - Ⓑ He is against the departure of Christian Arabs from the Levant.
    - Ⓒ He would like to see more Christian Arabs living in Egypt.
    - Ⓓ He is a descendant of a family of Christian Arabs.

Actual Test
10

TOEFL iBT Reading

Reading
Section Directions

This section measures your ability to understand academic passages in English.

In this part, you will read 1 passage and answer reading comprehension questions about the passage. Most questions are worth one point, but the last question is worth more than one point. The directions indicate how many points you may receive.

Some passages include a word or phrase that is underlined in blue. Click on the word or phrase to see a definition or an explanation.

When you want to move on to the next question, click on **Next**. You may skip questions and go back to them later. If you want to return to previous questions, click on **Back**. You can click on **Review** at any time and the review screen will show you which questions you have answered and which you have not answered. From this review screen, you may go directly to any question you have already seen in the Reading section.

You may now begin the Reading section. You will read 1 reading passage. You will have **20 minutes** to read the passage and answer the questions.

Click on **Continue** to go on.

Oil Spills

Oil is the lifeblood of the world's industries and transportation systems and is commonly transported around the world by pipelines and tankers. Although most oil cargoes safely reach their destinations, accidents sometimes occur during which some oil gets spilled. When this happens on the ocean because of an oil tanker spill, a major environmental disaster can happen; the oil can kill fish and seabirds, foul coastal regions, and destroy local fishing industries. Oil companies and governments must scramble to stop the spill from spreading and attempt to cleanse the environment as quickly as possible. Over time, numerous ways to contain and clean up oil spills have been discovered and invented. These include mechanical, chemical, biological, and physical means.

The initial effort to contain an oil spill frequently involves mechanical means. Booms, which are barriers that float on the water and are placed there by small boats, are utilized to contain the spill and to prevent it from spreading any further. Once the booms localize the spill, then other methods can be used to cleanse the affected region. One method involves burning the oil; however, this has drawbacks, the most significant of which is the air pollution created by the smoke emitted during this process. Other methods involve using skimmers to remove the oil from the water. There are three main types of skimmers: weirs, oleophilic, and suction skimmers. Weir skimmers act like dams in that they permit oil floating on the surface to flow over a barrier and then trap it in a contained area while collecting as little water as possible. The oil-water mixture is subsequently removed by pumps for later storage or disposal. Meanwhile, oleophilic skimmers utilize oil-attracting materials in the forms of chains of mops or belts that absorb the oil, which is later squeezed from these devices. Finally, suction skimmers resemble vacuum cleaners by

1. The word foul in the passage is closest in meaning to
    Ⓐ dampen
    Ⓑ invade
    Ⓒ suffocate
    Ⓓ taint

2. According to paragraph 1, which of the following is NOT true of the results of an oil spill in the ocean?
    Ⓐ A large number of means are utilized in order to prevent the spill from spreading.
    Ⓑ The people whose lives are disrupted by the spill receive financial compensation.
    Ⓒ Much of the aquatic life that dwells in the area of the spill may be injured or killed.
    Ⓓ Organizations attempt to clean the spill in as timely a manner as is possible.

3. The word there in the passage refers to
    Ⓐ the initial effort
    Ⓑ the water
    Ⓒ one method
    Ⓓ the oil

4. In stating that the booms localize the spill, the author means that the booms
    Ⓐ stop the oil from spreading
    Ⓑ break down the oil
    Ⓒ siphon off the oil
    Ⓓ make the oil less harmful

5. The author's description of the skimmers used to clean oil spills mentions which of the following?
    Ⓐ Suction skimmers are able to extract more oil than the other types of skimmers can.
    Ⓑ Oleophilic skimmers use a method to clean oil that operates much like a dam does.
    Ⓒ The skimmers used depend upon a number of circumstances surrounding the oil spill.
    Ⓓ All three types of skimmers are unable to thoroughly remove the oil from the water.

6. Which of the sentences below best expresses the essential information in the highlighted sentence in the passage? *Incorrect* answer choices change the meaning in important ways or leave out essential information.

   Ⓐ Because the dispersants contain dangerous ingredients, oil companies must get permission from the government to use them to clean up oil spills.
   Ⓑ Governments and oil companies are concerned about the damage to the environment that the use of dispersants can result in.
   Ⓒ In some instances, dispersants have been known to cause even more damage to the environment than the oil slick itself has.
   Ⓓ While the dispersants are harmful to the environment, they are less damaging than the oil, so companies make the choice to utilize dispersants.

7. According to paragraph 3, dispersants work on oil spills because

   Ⓐ they break down the oil so that it degrades somewhat quickly
   Ⓑ they can be used in great quantities despite containing dangerous chemicals
   Ⓒ it is simple to change the oil molecules through chemical reactions
   Ⓓ companies have spent considerable time and money perfecting them

8. The word these in the passage refers to

   Ⓐ biodegrading bacteria
   Ⓑ the areas
   Ⓒ the oil spills
   Ⓓ tests

sucking up oil on the surface. All three skimmers have advantages and disadvantages, and their usage depends on the location of the spill and the weather conditions, among other factors.

Chemical means for oil spill cleanups involve using dispersants, which airplanes or boats spray onto the region covered by the spill. The chemicals in the dispersants bond with the oil molecules, and then they separate the oil from the water molecules. As a result, there are millions of tiny oil droplets rather than one giant mass of oil floating on the water. The advantage of this method is that these individual droplets are able to biodegrade more easily and swiftly than an enormous oil slick. The drawback to using dispersants is that they are chemicals that can damage the environment. The industries that produce dispersants and the oil companies that use them both recognize that their ingredients are dangerous, yet they reason that since the oil is more harmful than the chemicals, the dispersants are the lesser of two evils.

The biological method typically utilized to remove oil spills is called bioremediation. The purpose of bioremediation is to accelerate the biodegrading of the oil. Two main methods—fertilization and seeding—are used. With fertilization, nutrients such as nitrogen and phosphorus are added to the water. This hastens the growth of certain microorganisms that can break down oil. Seeding involves adding biodegrading bacteria that are not native to the areas where the oil spills have occurred. By adding these, the oil degrades at a much faster rate. Tests have shown that under certain conditions, bioremediation methods can increase the rate of oil deterioration by more than 200 times.

If these methods fail, the oil spill is too large, or the oil companies and governments fail to work swiftly enough, the slick may reach the coastline. At that point, physical means are used to remove

9. Why does the author mention nitrogen and phosphorous?

   Ⓐ To note their usefulness to the fertilization method of oil removal
   Ⓑ To declare that they are two of the primary elements founds in oil
   Ⓒ To show how they can be used to help seed the water surrounding an oil spill
   Ⓓ To provide a detailed explanation on how they are used in bioremediation

10. According to paragraph 4, which of the following is true of seeding?

    Ⓐ It is safer for the environment than using skimmers.
    Ⓑ It requires the introducing of a nonnative species to the environment.
    Ⓒ It is a more preferred method than fertilization.
    Ⓓ It requires adding both nitrogen and phosphorous to the water.

11. The word marred in the passage is closest in meaning to

    Ⓐ inert
    Ⓑ scarred
    Ⓒ active
    Ⓓ unbalanced

12. The word vestiges in the passage is closest in meaning to

    Ⓐ traces
    Ⓑ leaks
    Ⓒ problems
    Ⓓ pollutants

13. In paragraph 5, the author of the passage implies that

    Ⓐ most oil spills will biodegrade in a matter of months
    Ⓑ oil slicks in the ocean do not always make landfall
    Ⓒ cleaning oil that reaches the shore is expensive
    Ⓓ it is common for oil removal methods to fail

the oil. Workers equipped with buckets, shovels, and hoses clean the damaged areas. The oil is physically scooped up off the sand and rocks or blasted off with high-pressure water hoses. A large stretch of coastline can be marred for months or even years by an oil spill. Even with thousands of volunteers working in concert, oil spills are not easy to clean up, nor can every spot of oil be removed. However, over time, the last vestiges of the oil spill will eventually disappear.

Glossary

dispersant: a chemical substance that is able to break up various particles when it comes into contact with them

biodegrade: to decay or break down naturally

oil slick: a large pool or puddle of oil, which is often found on the water

14. **Directions:** An introductory sentence for a brief summary of the passage is provided below. Complete the summary by selecting the THREE answer choices that express the most important ideas of the passage. Some sentences do not belong because they express ideas that are not presented in the passage or are minor ideas in the passage. *This question is worth 2 points.*

Oil companies and governments have developed many methods to deal with oil spills when they occur.

-
-
-

Answer Choices

(A) There are several types of skimmers that, depending on a variety of conditions, can be used to collect oil from the ocean's surface.

(B) Bioremediation involves adding certain substances to the oil in an attempt to get it to break down at a faster-than-normal rate.

(C) Many times, oil slicks cannot be prevented from reaching the shore, whereupon they contaminate vast areas of land by the ocean.

(D) Oil booms may be dropped in the water in an attempt to prevent an oil slick from spreading too much.

(E) The causes of many oil spills are tankers running aground and then springing leaks, which make them release oil into the ocean.

(F) An oil spill that is not rapidly contained can spread and kill many fish, birds, and other creatures that live in or around the water.

Drag your answer choices to the spaces where they belong.
To remove an answer choice, click on it. To review the passage, click on **View Text**.

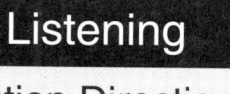

This section measures your ability to understand conversations and lectures in English.

In this part, you will listen to 1 conversation and 1 lecture. You will hear the conversation or lecture only **one** time. After the conversation or lecture, you will answer some questions about it. The questions typically ask about the main idea and supporting details. Some questions ask about a speaker's purpose or attitude. Answer the questions based on what is stated or implied by the speakers.

You may take notes while you listen. You may use your notes to help you answer the questions. Your notes will **not** be scored.

If you need to change the volume while you listen, click on the **Volume** icon at the top of the screen.

In some questions, you will see this icon: 🎧 This means that you will hear, but not see, part of the question.

Some of the questions have special directions. These directions appear in a gray box on the screen.

Most questions are worth one point. If a question is worth more than one point, it will have special directions that indicate how many points you can receive.

You must answer each question. After you answer, click on **Next**. Then click on **OK** to confirm your answer and go on to the next question. After you click on **OK**, you cannot return to previous questions.

A clock at the top of the screen will show you how much time is remaining. The clock will not count down while you are listening. The clock will count down only while you are answering the questions.

Now you may begin the Listening section.

TOEFL iBT Listening

Conversation 1~5: Listen to part of a conversation between a student and a Registrar's Office employee. 10-02

Actual Test 10

TOEFL iBT Listening

1. Why does the student visit the Registrar's Office?
   - Ⓐ To change one of his grades
   - Ⓑ To ask for some copies of his transcript
   - Ⓒ To fix a error on his transcript
   - Ⓓ To submit a note from his professor

2. According to the student, what might he do after he graduates?
   - Ⓐ Find a job related to his major
   - Ⓑ Conduct some independent research on medieval history
   - Ⓒ Attend graduate school in a few years
   - Ⓓ Return to school in order to become a teacher

3. What can be inferred about the woman?
   - Ⓐ She takes her job duties seriously.
   - Ⓑ She has little interest in helping the student.
   - Ⓒ She has been working there for a short time.
   - Ⓓ She does not enjoy her job.

4. Listen again to a part of the conversation. Then answer the question.

   What does the woman mean when she says this?
   - Ⓐ Something just fell on the ground.
   - Ⓑ She lost the student's transcript.
   - Ⓒ There was a mistake made.
   - Ⓓ Her computer malfunctioned.

5. Listen again to a part of the conversation. Then answer the question.

   What is the purpose of the student's response?
   - Ⓐ To accept the woman's compliment
   - Ⓑ To brag about his abilities
   - Ⓒ To talk about how good his grades are
   - Ⓓ To point out some of his abilities

Lecture 6~11: Listen to part of a lecture in a meteorology class.

6. What is the main topic of the lecture?
   - Ⓐ The composition and structure of the atmosphere
   - Ⓑ The effects of the atmosphere on the Earth
   - Ⓒ The ozone layer and how it protects humanity
   - Ⓓ The movement of air throughout the atmosphere

7. Why does the professor explain the division of the atmosphere?
   - Ⓐ To show how the troposphere affects the weather
   - Ⓑ To describe the particles that are found in each layer
   - Ⓒ To show how weather forms in each layer
   - Ⓓ To go into detail on its four layers

8. According to the professor, which of the following are aerosols?

   Click on 2 answers.
   - Ⓐ Argon
   - Ⓑ Carbon dioxide
   - Ⓒ Smoke particles
   - Ⓓ Ice crystals

9. What does the professor imply about the ozone layer?
   - Ⓐ It is unlikely to vanish.
   - Ⓑ It has been damaged recently.
   - Ⓒ Humans have made it very thin.
   - Ⓓ It can be repaired by humans.

10. Listen again to a part of the lecture. Then answer the question.
    What does the professor imply when he says this?
    - Ⓐ The students have to know the information that he is about to give.
    - Ⓑ The class has already studied the composition of the atmosphere.
    - Ⓒ The contents of the atmosphere are not of particular importance.
    - Ⓓ Scientists are not totally sure which elements make up the atmosphere.

11. Listen again to a part of the lecture. Then answer the question.
    What does the professor mean when he says this?
    - Ⓐ Many people get exposed to ultraviolet rays.
    - Ⓑ Ultraviolet rays are constantly hitting the planet.
    - Ⓒ Earth may soon be exposed to ultraviolet rays.
    - Ⓓ Ultraviolet rays are able to kill life forms.

Compact
Actual iBT
10 mini TOEFL® Tests

Reading & Listening

Answer Book

4

DARAKWON

Compact Actual iBT 4
Reading & Listening

Answer Book

Actual Test 01

Reading Section p.9

Answers

1. (B) [Factual Question]
2. (A) [Vocabulary Question]
3. (C) [Vocabulary Question]
4. (A) [Negative Factual Question]
5. (D) [Inference Question]
6. (D) [Vocabulary Question]
7. (B) [Factual Question]
8. (D) [Reference Question]
9. (B) [Factual Question]
10. (C) [Rhetorical Purpose Question]
11. (B) [Negative Factual Question]
12. 3rd [Insert Text Question]
13.

	Portuguese Explorer From the Fifteenth Century
Prince Henry the Navigator	(C), (G), (H)
Bartolomeo Diaz	(D), (I)
Vasco de Gama	(B), (F)

[Fill in a Table Question]

Translation

15세기 포르투갈의 탐험가들

크리스토퍼 콜럼버스가 15세기의 가장 유명한 유럽의 탐험가이기는 하지만, 인도와 중국으로 가는 항로를 찾으려 했던 유일한 탐험가는 아니었으며, 심지어 최초의 탐험가도 아니었다. 포르투갈에는 헨리 항해왕과 바르톨로 뮤 디아스, 그리고 바스코 다 가마에 이르기까지 수 많은 위대한 탐험가들이 있었다. 이들은 콜롬버스와 다른 탐험가들처럼 위험을 무릅쓰고 대서양을 가로질러 아시아에 도달하는 데에는 관심이 없었다. 그 대신, 이 포르투갈의 탐험가들은 아프리카의 서해안에 관심을 가지고 있었으며, 그 후 아프리카의 최남단을 경유하여 인도양을 가로질러 항해하는데 성공했다. 이를 위해서 전문적인 항해술과, 여러 번의 시도, 그리고 새로운 형태의 선박이 필요했지만, 콜럼버스가 처음으로 아메리카 대륙에 도착한 지 10년도 되지 않은 시기인 15세기가 끝나갈 무렵, 포르투갈의 선박들이 인도를 방문한 다음 안전하게 본국으로 돌아왔다.

헨리 항해왕은 포르투갈의 모든 위대한 탐험가들 중에서도 선구자와 같은 인물이다. 헨리는 유럽의 세계 탐험을 이끌어낸 인물로서 잘 알려져 있다. 그는 포르투갈 왕의 세 번째 왕자였으며 부유한 종교 교단이었던, 크리스트교 교단의 수장이었다. 헨리는 자신의 지위를 이용하여 아프리카 서해안을 탐험하기 위한 기금을 마련했다. 그가 젊은 시절이었던 1415년, 이슬람교도들이 점령하고 있었던 아프리카 북서부 해안의 세우타 항을 점령했을 때부터, 헨리의 탐험에 대한 열정이 시작되었다. 이곳에서, 포르투갈의 십자군들이 북아프리카의 엄청난 부를 이용하여 동쪽 멀리 떨어진 지역과 교역을 할 수 있다는 사실을 알게 되었다. (이러한 부는 헨리로 하여금 모든 수단을 동원하여 포르투갈 선박들을 인도 및 기타 아시아 지역에 보내도록 만들었다.) 이러한 탐험에 뒤이어, 헨리는 부의 획득을 주목적으로 하는, 포르투갈 근해와 아프리카의 서해안의 탐험에 대한 옹호자가 되었다.

대부분의 경우, 헨리는 직접 이러한 탐험을 하지는 않았지만, 이를 조직하고 재정지원을 했다. 그래서 탐험대의 성공은 당연히 헨리의 공적이 되었다. 초기의 몇몇 항해에서, 헨리의 선박들은 아조레스 제도와 마데이라 군도를 발견했는데, 그 후 포르투갈은 이 지역에 대한 권리를 주장하며 식민지화했다. 1434년, 그의 탐험대는 카나리아 제도 남쪽에 위치한 보자도르 곶을 지나서 항해했는데, 이곳은 예전에 유럽의 선박들이 항해했던 지역들 보다 더 남쪽에 위치하고 있었다. 보자도르 곶은 위험한 암초와 이상한 해류로 인하여 항해사들 사이에서 악명이 높았기 때문에, 이 지역을 지나간 것은 중요한 성과였다. 얼마 지나지 않아서, 포르투갈은 사하라사막 이남의 해안에 도달했으며, 이곳에서 금을 발견했을 뿐만 아니라, 아프리카인들을 포획하여 노예로 팔아버리기도 했다. 1460년 헨리가 사망했을 때, 포르투갈의 선박은 오늘날의 시에라리온의 남쪽 지역까지 항해했다.

그 후로 수십 년 동안, 포르투갈인들은 더 남쪽으로 탐험을 계속했다. 그들은 요새를 세웠고 수많은 장소에 무역항을 건설했으며, 이곳을 그들의 항해기지로 사용했다. 마침내, 1488년, 마르톨로 뮤 디아스가 아프리카 최남단을 지나서 인도양을 발견했다; 하지만, 그의 선원들은 더 나아가기를 거절했다. 오늘날의 남아프리카 공화국의 해안에 몇몇 위치 표식을 남긴 뒤, 탐험대는 본국으로 돌아왔다. 10년 뒤, 바스코 다 가마가 인도에 도착하기 위한 항해를 시작했다. 그는 아프리카의 동해안을 탐험했고 인도양을 가로질러 그의 선박을 안내할 수 있는 항해사를 찾아냈다. 그의 탐험대는 1498년 5월에 인도의 남서부에 상륙했다. 다 가마는 인도로 두 번 더 항해를 했는데, 결국 1524년, 병에 걸려 사망했다. 다 가마는 포르투갈에서 인정을 받았지만, 아랍인들과 인도인들 사이에서는, 자신이 원하는 것은 무엇이든 잔인하게 약탈했던 해적으로서의 평판을 얻었다.

아프리카를 경유하여 인도까지 이르는 기나긴 탐험의 여정은 15세기 중반에 사용된 새로운 종류의 선박인 카라벨(작은 범선) 덕분에 가능했다. 카라벨은 물에 얕게 잠기기 때문에, 이 배는 해안을 따라서 항해를 하는 것이 용이하고, 바람의 방향에 따라 조절할 수 있는 삼각형 돛을 달고 있으며, 수많은 짐을 실을 수 있었다. 카라벨과 발달된 항해술, 그리고 다 가마와 같은 무자비한 탐험가들이 있었기 때문에, 포르투갈은 세계적인 제국을 만들 수 있었다. 그들은 대규모의 아프리카 노예무역을 시작했고, 인도 향신료에 대한 해상무역을 시작했으며, 브라질과 남아메리카를 발견하여 식민지화했다. 또한 중요한 점은, 포르투갈인들이 인도와의 무역에서 이탈리아의 도시국가들보다 우위에 있게 되었다는 점인데, 이로 인하여 유럽의 권력이 지중해 지역에서 서유럽으로 이동하게 되었다.

Listening Section
p.15

Answers

1. Ⓐ [Gist-Purpose Question]
2. Ⓓ [Detail Question]
3. Ⓐ [Understanding Attitude Question]
4. Ⓑ [Making Inferences Question]
5. Ⓒ [Understanding Function Question]
6. Ⓑ [Gist-Content Question]
7. Ⓐ [Gist-Purpose Question]
8. Ⓓ [Understanding Organization Question]
9. Ⓒ [Connecting Content Question]
10. Ⓐ [Making Inferences Question]
11. Ⓓ [Detail Question]

Script

| 01-02 |

W1 Student: Professor Jenkins, would it be all right if I had a chat with you for a few minutes?

W2 Professor: Well, uh, I . . . You see . . . I've got a meeting to attend in a couple of minutes . . .

W1: Oh, please. I really need to talk to you, ma'am. I'm a student in your basic chemistry class, and I'm having all sorts of problems. I really, really need to talk about them with you. This shouldn't take too long.

W2: Well, when you put it that way . . . I'd be glad to help you out. Why don't you come on in and have a seat . . . ? Um, sorry, but it's kind of a big class. Your name is . . . ?

W1: Sara. I'm Sara Sellers. I'm a freshman.

W2: Thanks. It's nice to meet you, Sara. Now, you mentioned that you're having some problems in my class.

W1: Uh-huh.

W2: 5 Well, why don't you, um, expand upon them for me so that I can figure out how to help you?

W1: Sure. I just, uh, don't get this class.

W2: Um . . . that doesn't really tell me too much you know.

W1: Oh, right. Well, uh, I'm a little confused. You see, I was really good at chemistry in high school. I got an A in it, and it was my favorite class as well.

W2: But you're having problems with this class, right?

W1: Exactly. I mean, um, I just can't seem to keep up with all of the information we're covering in class. I had given some thought to becoming a chemistry major, but I'm not sure about that anymore.

W2: Well, the first thing to remember, Sara, is that we're only in the first two weeks of the semester.

W1: Uh, right . . . Wait. What does that have to do with anything?

W2: You're a freshman, right?

W1: Yes, that's correct.

W2: Well, college takes some getting used to. For instance, this is probably the first time that you've lived away from home. Am I correct about that?

W1: Yes.

W2: And, I must say that the level of instruction at this school is probably much higher than that which you got in high school. After all, we're a pretty good school, and my class—even though it's an introductory-level class—is not for slackers. I teach at a pretty good pace, so the kids who sign up for my course thinking they're going to get an easy A fortunately tend to drop out quickly. So, what I am basically trying to say is that . . . well, there's going to be an adjustment period that you are going to have to go through.

W1: Okay. That makes sense. So, um, what do I do about it?

W2: Well, you're probably going to have to study a lot harder than you did when you were in high school. But, most of all, just give yourself some time to get used to being in college. It's a whole different world from high school.

W1: Okay, thanks, Professor. I feel much better now.

W2: That's good. So stay with the class, and don't give up on majoring in chemistry. And if you have any problems, you come back here and talk to me immediately.

W1: Yes, ma'am. I will. Thanks.

Translation

W1 Student: *Jenkins* 교수님, 잠시 저와 이야기 나눌 시간이 되시나요?

W2 Professor: 음, 어, 제가… 음… 제가 잠시 후에 회의에 참석해야 하는데…

W1: 아, 부탁 드려요. 저 교수님하고 꼭 말씀 나눠야 하거든요. 저는 기초 화학 수업을 듣는 학생인데요, 문제가 좀 있어서요. 그래서 교수님과 그 문제에 대해서 말씀을 나눠야 해요. 오래 걸리지 않을 겁니다.

W2: 음, 그렇게 까지 얘기를 하니… 기꺼이 도와드리죠. 이쪽으로 와서 좀 앉지 그래요…? 음, 미안하지만, 학생 수가 많은 수업이라서, 학생 이름이 뭐죠…?

W1: *Sara*예요. 저는 *Sara Sellers*입니다. 1학년이고요.

W2: 고마워요. 만나서 반가워요, *Sara*. 그러면, 학생이 제 수업시간과 관련해서 어떤 문제가 있다고 했었는데요.

W1: 네.

W2: 음, 제가 어떤 도움을 드릴 수 있는지 더 자세히 설명해 주시겠어요?

W1: 네. 저는, 그러니까, 수업을 따라가지 못하겠어요.

W2: 음… 좀 더 자세히 설명해 주세요.

W1: 네, 알겠어요. 음, 저도 조금 혼란스러워요. 그러니까, 저는 고등학교 때 화학을 참 잘했었거든요. A학점을 받았고, 제가 좋아하는 과목이기도 했고요.

W2: 하지만 이 수업을 따라가는데 문제가 있다 그거군요, 맞죠?

W1: 맞아요. 제 말은, 음, 우리가 수업 시간에 다루고 있는 내용을 제가 다 이해하지 못하는 것 같아요. 저는 화학을 전공할 생각을 가지고 있었는데요. 이제는 망설여 지는군요.

W2: 음, Sara, 한 가지 기억해야 할 것은, 이제 겨우 새 학기가 시작한지 2주 밖에 지나지 않았어요.

W1: 음, 그래요… 잠시만요. 그 사실이 무슨 관계가 있죠?

W2: 당신은 신입생이예요, 그렇죠?

W1: 네, 그래요.

W2: 음, 대학에 익숙해지려면 시간이 좀 걸려요. 예를 들면, 학생은 아마 집을 떠나서 생활하는 것이 처음일 거예요. 그렇죠?

W1: 네.

W2: 그리고, 우리 학교의 교육 수준은 학생이 고등학교 때 배웠던 수준보다 훨씬 높을 거예요. 뭐니뭐니해도, 우리 학교는 상당히 좋은 학교이며, 제 수업이 비록 입문 과정의 수업이라고 해도 게으른 사람들은 수업을 따라갈 수가 없어요. 저는 상당히 빠른 속도로 가르치고 있기 때문에, 제 수업을 신청한 학생들 중에서 쉽게 A학점을 받고자 하는 학생들은 다행스럽게도 빨리 수강을 철회한답니다. 그래서, 제가 하고자 하는 이야기는… 음, 학생에게는 어느 정도 적응 기간이 필요한 것 같네요.

W1: 네, 무슨 말씀인지 알겠습니다. 그래서, 음, 저는 어떻게 해야 할까요?

W2: 음, 학생이 고등학교 때 공부하던 것에 비해서 훨씬 더 열심히 공부해야만 할 것입니다. 무엇보다도, 대학 생활에 적응할 시간을 좀 가져보세요. 고등학교와 완전히 다른 세상이니까요.

W1: 네, 감사합니다. 교수님. 기분이 한결 나아졌어요.

W2: 잘됐군요. 그러면 수업은 계속 듣고, 화학 전공도 포기하지 마세요. 다른 문제가 생기면, 즉시 나에게로 와서 이야기 나누도록 해요.

W1: 네, 교수님. 그럴게요. 감사합니다.

Script

| 01-03 |

M Professor: I'm fairly positive that everyone knows Alexander Graham Bell invented the telephone, Thomas Edison invented the light bulb, and the Wright Brothers invented the airplane, but does anyone know who invented the television . . . ? No . . . ? No one at all . . . ? Well, I must admit that I'm not the least bit surprised because, uh, in truth, there was no single inventor of the television. Instead, it was created thanks to the contributions of several inventors, each of whom came from different nations. Inventors in Germany, Hungary, Russia, England, and the United States all played individual roles in TV's creation. Between the years, um, 1884 and 1928, these men gradually developed the various pieces of technology that, when combined, became television.

So, what was early television like? It was, of course, nothing like what we watch nowadays. To begin with, the quality of the first broadcasts was extremely poor. There were some limited broadcasts of moving images in the U.S. during the late 1920s and early 1930s, but these early attempts at television failed. The Federal Communications Commission, which is usually called the FCC, was a major reason for this. The FCC regarded TV as an experimental device that had no consistency or standards. Therefore, the FCC didn't grant TV broadcasters commercial licenses like it did for radio stations. So, uh, basically, TV broadcasters couldn't make any money. As a result, there was no financial incentive for them to perfect the technology. Fortunately, some individual inventors took up the slack and worked hard to perfect television. Then, in 1934, an American inventor, Philo Farnsworth, developed the first all-electronic TV broadcasting and receiving system. This was the basis for the television.

W Student: Professor McBride, does that mean Farnsworth was the real inventor of television?

M: Well . . . Not exactly. Farnsworth was just one of those several inventors that I mentioned a minute ago. He did play a big role in television's development, but we cannot solely credit him with inventing it since his work was based on the contributions of many others. Giving him sole credit would just be, uh . . . i-i-it just wouldn't be right. That being said, thanks to Farnsworth's system, broadcasting of a . . . um, a higher quality than ever before became possible. Now, the first real high-quality broadcast—by that I mean one with clear images—was the Summer Olympic Games in Berlin, Germany, in 1936. However, it was broadcast in only a few places in Germany. Three years later, in 1939, the opening of the New York World's Fair was broadcast live in the New York area. Soon, New York City had a broadcasting system that could transmit TV signals to distances of around sixteen kilometers. Yet only a few thousand people in the area had TV sets then since most were expensive and unaffordable. However, with New York having millions of people living within this sixteen-kilometer radius, the potential for earning money from advertising was great. So, in 1941, the American FCC finally set some standards for TV broadcasting and granted commercial licenses for TV broadcasting to NBC and CBS, which both operated out of New York.

The big TV companies in America all got their starts in radio. So early television broadcasting took its lead from that broadcast medium. Like radio, television aired a mixture of news, dramas, comedy, and sports. Also like radio, television earned money through advertising. Companies recognized TV's potential and were willing to spend a great deal of money to make their products become known far and wide. It seemed that the key elements were in place for TV to take off, uh, well, everywhere. But World War II changed this. It started in Europe in 1939, and the U.S. entered the war in late 1941. At that time, virtually all progress on television came to a halt. Because factories needed to make guns, tanks, airplanes, and other war materials, the production of commercial products, including TV sets, stopped until the war's end. In addition, companies mostly suspended television broadcasting and concentrated on radio for war reporting.

After the war, TV found its niche. This was aided by improved technology, the mass production of TV sets, which reduced their prices, and the spread of broadcasting stations, which enabled more people to view broadcasts. The late 1940s and the 1950s are now regularly referred to as the Golden Age of TV. Most of the shows were still news, sports, dramas, and comedies, yet movies were sometimes broadcast. Educational and children's programming became common, too. Early TV broadcasting was in black and white, not color, and didn't broadcast twenty-four hours a day like today. Most stations went off the air at midnight and started airing shows again at six AM. Many big stars from the movies and theater took roles on TV shows, which helped popularize it. Okay, now, let's take a look at some of the earliest TV shows that were broadcast. I think you'll find some of them rather enjoyable.

Translation

M Professor: 알렉산더 그레이엄 벨이 전화기를 발명했고, 전구는 에디슨이, 비행기는 라이트 형제가 발명했다는 사실은 모든 사람들이 알고 있겠지만, 텔레비전은 누가 발명했을까요…? 아무도 모르시나요…? 정말 아무도 몰라요…? 음, 조금도 놀랄 만한 일은 아닌 것이, 음, 사실은, 텔레비전은 혼자서 발명한 것이 아니기 때문이죠. 대신, 여러 명의 발명가들에 의해 텔레비전이 탄생했는데, 이 발명가들은 서로 다른 나라의 사람들이었습니다. 독일, 헝가리, 러시아, 영국, 그리고 미국의 발명가들이 모두 TV의 발명에 있어서 저마다의 역할을 해냈지요. 음, 1884년부터 1928년 사이에, 이들은 다양한 기술들을 발달시켰는데, 이 기술들이 합쳐져서 텔레비전이 탄생했던 것입니다.

그러면, 초기의 텔레비전은 어땠을까요? 그것은, 물론, 오늘날 우리가 시청하는 텔레비전과는 전혀 달랐죠. 우선, 최초의 방송 품질은 정말 형편없었어요. 미국에서 1920년대와 1930년대에 영상을 전송하는 방송이 다소 존재하기는 했지만, 텔레비전 방송 시도는 실패했어요. FCC라 불리는 연방통신위원회가 이러한 실패의 주요한 원인이었지요. FFC는 TV를 일관성이나 기준이 없는 실험적인 장치로 인식했어요. 그렇기 때문에, FFC는 TV 방송사에 라디오 방송국에 부여했던 것과 같은 사업 허가서를 부여하지 않았던 것이죠. 그래서, 음, 기본적으로, TV 방송사들은 이익을 남길 수가 없었어요. 그 결과, 그들에게는 기술을 완성시킬 만한 재정적인 동기가 없었던 것입니다. 다행히도, 몇몇 개인적인 발명가들이 분위기를 다잡고 텔레비전을 완성시키기 위해서 열심히 연구를 했죠. 그리고 나서, 1934년에, 미국의 과학자 필로 판스워즈가, 전전자식 TV 방송 송수신 시스템을 개발해 냈죠. 이것이 텔레비전의 기초가 되었습니다.

W Student: *McBride* 교수님, 그렇다면 판스워즈가 텔레비전을 실제로 발명한 사람이라는 말씀인가요?

M: 음… 그렇지는 않아요. 판스워즈는 조금 전에 언급했던 여러 발명가들 중 한명일 뿐이죠. 그가 텔레비전의 발명에 있어서 중요한 역할을 했던 것은 분명하지만, 그의 연구는 여러 명의 다른 발명가들의 연구에 바탕을 두었기 때문에 그 혼자서 텔레비전을 발명했다고 보기는 힘듭니다. 혼자서 텔레비전을 발명했다고 인정해버린다면, 음… 그-그-그것은 잘못된 것이라고 생각해요. 판스워즈의 시스템 덕분에, 방송이… 음, 방송의 품질이 예전보다 향상될 수 있었다고 말할 수는 있겠군요. 음, 제가 의미하는 최초의 진정한 깨끗한 영상의 고품질 방송은 1936년, 독일의 베를린 하계 올림픽 방송입니다. 하지만, 이는 독일의 몇몇 지역에만 방영되었어요. 삼 년이 흐른 뒤, 1939년에, 뉴욕 세계 박람회 개막식이 뉴욕에서 생방송으로 방영되었습니다. 곧이어, 뉴욕시에는 16킬로미터 정도의 거리까지 TV 신호를 전송할 수 있는 방송 시스템이 구축되었죠. 하지만 이 지역의 천여 명의 사람들만 TV를 보유하고 있었는데, 이는 TV가 너무 비싸서 대부분의 사람들은 이를 구입할 여력이 없었기 때문이었습니다. 하지만, 뉴욕에는 60킬로미터의 범위 이내에 수백만 명의 사람들이 살고 있었기 때문에, 잠재적인 광고 수입이 엄청났죠. 그래서, 1941년, 미국의 FCC는 마침내 TV 방송의 기준을 마련했고, TV 방송 사업 허가서를 NBC와 CBS에 부여했는데, 이 두 방송사는 뉴욕시 밖에서 운영되었습니다.

미국의 거대 TV 회사들은 모두 라디오 방송을 하던 회사들이었어요. 그래서 초기 텔레비전 방송은 라디오 방송을 본보기로 삼고 있었죠. 라디오와 마찬가지로, 텔레비전에서는 뉴스, 드라마, 코미디, 그리고 스포츠 경기를 모두 다 방송했어요. 텔레비전 역시 광고를 통해서 수입을 올렸다는 사실 또한 라디오의 경우와 같았죠. 기업에서는 TV의 잠재성을 인식하고 제품을 널리 알리기 위해 기꺼이 엄청난 돈을 쏟아 부었어요. TV가 성장할 수 있었던 중요한 요인들은, 어, 음, 어디에서나 있었던 것 같습니다. 그러나 제2차 세계 대전에 의해서 이러한 상황이 바뀌었죠. 전쟁은 1939년에 유럽에서 시작되었고, 1941년 후반에는 미국이 참전하게 되었죠. 그 때, 사실상 텔레비전의 발전은 중지되었습니다. 공장에서는 총, 탱크, 비행기, 그리고 다른 전쟁 물자를 생산해야 했기 때문에, 전쟁이 끝날 때까지 TV를 포함한 상업 제품의 생산은 중단될 수밖에 없었죠. 게다가, 방송사들은 텔레비전 방송을 중단하고 라디오를 통해서 집중적으로 전쟁 소식을 전했습니다.

전쟁이 끝나고, TV는 틈새시장을 발견했습니다. 이는 TV의 대량 생산이라는 진보된 기술 덕분에 가능했는데, 이를 통해서 TV 가격이 하락했고, 방송국이 늘어나면서, 더 많은 사람들이 방송을 시청할 수 있게 되었던 것입니다. 1940년대 후반과 1950년대는 TV의 황금기라고 일컬어 지고 있습니다. 대부분의 프로그램은 여전히 뉴스, 스포츠, 드라마, 그리고 코미디였지만, 때때로 영화가 방송되기도 했죠. 교육 프로그램과 어린이 프로그램도 흔히 방송되었고요. 초기의 TV 방송은 컬러가 아니라 흑백이었고, 오늘날과 같은 종일 방송도 아니었어요. 대부분의 방송국들은 자정에 방송을 끝내고 오전 6시에 다시 방송을 시작했죠. 영화와 연극의 여러 유명인사들이 TV 프로그램에서 역할을 맡음으로써 프로그램의 인기에 기여하기도 했습니다. 좋아요, 이제, 최초로 방송되었던 TV 프로그램들에 대해 알아보도록 하죠. 여러분들이 매우 재미있어 할만한 내용들이 있을 것입니다.

Actual Test 02

Reading Section   p.21

Answers

1. D [Factual Question]
2. A [Rhetorical Purpose Question]
3. C [Sentence Simplification Question]
4. C [Vocabulary Question]
5. B [Rhetorical Purpose Question]
6. A [Negative Factual Question]
7. B [Vocabulary Question]
8. A [Reference Question]
9. C [Factual Question]
10. D [Vocabulary Question]
11. D [Reference Question]
12. A [Factual Question]
13. A [Inference Question]
14. C, E, F [Prose Summary]

Translation

인플레이션

경제에서 인플레이션은 일반적인 가격 상승을 의미한다. 모든 가격이 동시에 상승하지는 않을 수도 있으며 소폭이긴 하지만, 일반적으로 가격이 상승한다면, 경제학자들은 이를 인플레이션이라고 한다. 경제 내에 통화 공급이 많으면 일반적으로 가격이 상승한다. 인쇄된 지폐나 주조된 동전은 경제 내의 통화 공급에 따라서 그 가치가 결정된다. 통화 공급량이 적으면, 화폐의 가치가 상승해서 더 많은 상품과 용역을 구입할 수 있다. 이러한 상황이 발생했을 때에도, 가격이 하락한다면, 이를 디플레이션이라고 한다. 반면에, 경제 내에 통화 공급이 초과상태인 경우, 반대의 상황이 발생할 수 있다: 사람들이 소비할 수 있는 돈이 충분하여 가격이 상승하게 되면, 인플레이션이 발생한다. 통화 공급의 증가에 대한 책임은 정부에게 있는데, 정부가 그렇게 하는 이유는 다음 세 가지 이유 때문이다: 부채 상환, 투표자들의 환심을 사기 위한 목적, 그리고 경제 활성화가 그것이다.

모든 국가에서, 정부는 화폐의 발행을 통하여 통화 공급을 조절한다. 정부는 지불 능력과 부채 상환을 위해 세수에 의존하는데, 세수의 증가가 지출액에 미치지 못하게 되면, 정부는 부채를 상환하기 위해서 더 많은 화폐를 발행할 수밖에 없다. 그 결과 통화 공급이 증가하고, 인플레이션이 발생한다. 역사적으로 어떤 시기에는, 이러한 진행 과정이 통제 불가능한 상황이 되어서, 초인플레이션이 발생하기도 했다. 예를 들면, 1923년 바이마르 공화국에서, 화폐의 가치가 너무 많이 하락해서 사람들은 한 덩어리의 빵을 사는데 수백만 마르크를 지불해야 했다. 미국과 같은 여러 국가들은 이와 같은 문제를 해결하기 위하여 금본위제도를 활용했다. 금본위제도를 채택한 국가는 금을 바탕으로 통화를 발행하는데, 이러한 경우에는 언제든지 금과 화폐를 교환할 수 있다. 금본위제도는 종종 경제에 안정적인 영향을 미쳤다. 그럼에도 불구하고, 미국의 리처드 닉슨 대통령은 1971년에 금본위제도를 철회했다. 이제, 미국의 화폐는 단지 그 가치에 대한 판단에 따라서 발행된다. 그 결과, 1971년 이후로 화폐 가치는 꾸준히, 어떤 때에는 급격하게 상승해왔다.

정부가 화폐를 발행하는 두 번째 중요한 원인은 특정한 유권자들의 환심을 사기 위해서이다. 유권자들은 대출자로서 - 즉, 이자를 상환해야 하는 대출금을 빌린 사람들이다. 대출자들이 임금을 받는 노동자일 경우, 이들은 가격 상승에 별로 관심이 없다. 하지만, 대출자들이 제품을 생산하고 판매하는 사업가일 경우, 인플레이션은 그들에게 이익이 될 수 있다. 제품의 가격이 상승하면, 동일한 제품을 판매하여 더 많은 돈을 벌 수 있으며, 부채를 더 빨리 상환할 수 있게 된다. 인플레이션이 일어나건 일어나지 않건, 그들이 대출한 금액은 변하지 않는다. 기업은 종종 정부에게 중대한 영향을 미치는데, 특히 그들이 정치인의 재선 운동에 많은 액수의 돈을 기부할 때는 더욱 그렇다. 기업은 또한 경제의 중추적인 역할을 하므로, 대부분의 정부는 이들의 환심을 사려한다. 마지막으로, 수많은 기업들은 정부가 더 많은 화폐를 발행하도록 압력을 행사하기 위해 로비스트를 고용하는데, 이를 통해 인플레이션을 일으켜 자신들의 부채 상환에 도움을 받으려 한다.

정부가 더 많은 화폐를 발행하는 세 번째이자 마지막 주요 원인은 경제의 활성화를 위해서이다. 경제 활성화를 위한 지출의 부작용이 바로 인플레이션이다. 경제가 침체기에 들어섰을 때, 정부는 더 많은 화폐를 발행하여 상품과 용역에 대한 소비를 촉진시킴으로써 경제 성장을 유도한다. 정부는 기업에 자금을 대여하여 일자리 창출에 사용하도록 하는데, 이를 통해서 경제를 활성화 시키고, 국가 경제를 침체기에서 벗어나게 하려 노력한다.

인플레이션은 어떤 면에서 경제적으로 이익이 되기도 하지만, 대부분의 사람들은 상품과 용역을 구매하는 일반적인 임금 노동자들이므로, 개인들은 인플레이션으로 고통을 겪는다. 가격은 상승하지만 급여는 계속 같은 수준에 머물러 있기 때문에 구매력이 감소하게 되고, 예전에 구매했던 것과 같은 양의 제품과 용역을 구매할 수 없게 된다. 게다가, 많은 사람들이 미래를 위해서 저축을 하거나 은퇴 이후에 대비하여 투자를 한다. 하지만, 그들이 은퇴를 하게 되면, 인플레이션 때문에 저축을 시작했을 때에 비해서 화폐 가치가 떨어진다. 불행하게도, 대부분의 경제에서 사실상 인플레이션은 항시 존재하고 있다.

Listening Section   p.27

Answers

1. B [Gist-Purpose Question]
2. A [Detail Question]
3. A [Understanding Attitude Question]

4. Ⓓ [Understanding Function Question]
5. Ⓒ [Making Inferences Question]
6. Ⓐ [Gist-Purpose Question]
7. Ⓒ [Detail Question]
8. Ⓒ [Understanding Organization Question]
9.

	Plants and Soil	Sediment and Rocks
Ⓐ	X	
Ⓑ		X
Ⓒ		X
Ⓓ	X	

[Connecting Content Question]

10. Ⓑ [Understanding Attitude Question]
11. Ⓒ [Understanding Function Question]

Script

| 02-02 |

M Student: Good morning. Is this the, uh, the student employment office?

W Student Employment Office Employee: It sure is, young man. How may I be of service to you today? Let me guess . . . You're here to find a job.

M: Yeah, totally. How did you ever . . . Oh, right. Stupid question. Never mind.

W: Freshman, right?

M: Is it that obvious?

W: Well, let me say that I've been here for quite a few years. ⁴At least you can laugh about it though. I've seen some students that just walk off in a huff when I say something like that. So, anyway, what kind of job are you looking for?

M: One that pays a lot for as little work as possible.

W: Hmm . . . Unfortunately, I don't think you're going to find anything like that on this campus, but we do have many other jobs available. It's a good thing you came right now. There are always lots of jobs available during the first week of the semester, but the good ones get snapped up almost immediately.

M: Yeah, I figured I ought to get here as quickly as possible. I have to pay my own way here since I couldn't earn a scholarship yet. And tuition sure is expensive. So I really need a job.

W: ⁵I know what you mean. My son and daughter are both students here, and it's not cheap. Anyway, we've got a book that has some job listings in it. Why don't you look through that and see what you're interested in?

M: Okay, but do you mind if I pick your brain for a minute?

W: Not at all.

M: What kind of job would you recommend that I get?

W: That depends. Why don't you tell me a little about yourself first?

M: Sure. I'm a student in the school of engineering. I've got to take two lab classes in addition to a full course load. I live on campus though, so working on the weekends is fine. I'm not really the outdoors type either, so I'm not interested in doing landscaping or anything like that.

W: That's a good start. Okay . . . Hmm . . . How about the engineering library? It's fairly small and quiet, so you wouldn't get bothered by too many patrons.

M: Is that important?

W: Well, it means that you'd have an opportunity to study while you're working if nobody's asking you questions or you're not checking out books or that kind of thing. So, in a way, you'd be getting paid to study.

M: Hey, I like the sound of that. So, uh, are there any jobs available at the library?

W: There sure are. John Hanlin—he's the director of the library—called me a few minutes ago and told me there are several shifts available. Apparently, some of the students he had lined up to work there are studying abroad this semester.

M: That sounds promising.

W: So, uh, shall I call him up and tell him there's someone here interested in the job?

M: That would be great. Uh, that's Lufkin Library you're talking about, right?

W: That's correct. It's in Anderson Hall, which is probably where you're going to have a lot of your classes over the next four years.

M: Awesome. Thank you so much. If you don't mind, would you let Mr. Hanlin know that I'm going to be there in a few minutes? I'd really appreciate that.

Translation

M Student: 안녕하세요. 음, 여기가 학생고용사무처 맞나요?

W Student Employment Office Employee: 네, 학생, 여기가 맞아요. 무엇을 도와드릴까요? 제 생각에는… 일자리를 찾아온 것 같은데요.

M: 네, 맞아요. 어떻게 그걸… 아, 그래요. 어리석은 질문이군요. 신경 쓰지 마세요.

W: 신입생이군요, 그렇죠?

M: 그렇게 티가 나요?

W: 음, 제가 여기에서 근무한지 꽤 오래 됐거든요. 학생은 지금 웃고 있지만요. 제가 이렇게 말하면 씩씩거리며 나가버리는 학생들도 몇몇 본적이 있어요. 자, 그건 그렇고, 어떤 일자리를 찾고 있나요?

M: 가능한 업무량은 적으면서 급여는 높은 일자리요.

W: 흠… 안됐지만, 교내에서는 그런 일자리를 찾기 어렵고, 다른 일자리는 많이 있긴 해요. 지금 오길 잘 했네요. 학기가 시작한 후 1주일 동안은 항상 일자리가 많지만, 좋은 일자리들은 금방

사라지거든요.

M: 네, 가능한 빨리 와봐야겠다는 생각을 했거든요. 아직은 장학금을 받을 수 없기 때문에 제 힘으로 이곳의 학비를 벌어야 해서요. 그리고 학비가 좀 비싸야 말이죠. 그래서 전 꼭 일자리가 필요해요.

W: 무슨 말인지 잘 알겠어요. 내 아들하고 딸도 이 학교에 다니고 있는데, 학비가 저렴하지는 않더라고요. 그건 그렇고, 일자리 목록이 적혀있는 책이 여기 있어요. 읽어보시고 관심 있는 일자리를 찾아보는 것이 어떨까요?

M: 좋아요, 하지만 선생님의 지혜를 잠시만 빌릴 수 있을까요?

W: 물론이죠.

M: 제가 어떤 일을 하는 것이 좋을지 추천해 주실 수 있으세요?

W: 상황에 따라 다르죠. 우선 학생에 대한 이야기를 좀 해줄 수 있나요?

M: 물론이죠. 저는 공과 대학 학생이에요. 수업은 전체 과정을 모두 듣고 있고, 그 밖에 실험 실습이 두 시간 있어요. 저는 교내에서 생활하고 있기 때문에, 주말 근무도 상관없어요. 야외에서 일하는 것은 싫어하기 때문에, 조경이나 그와 비슷한 일자리에는 관심이 없고요.

W: 시작이 좋네요. 좋아요… 흠… 공대 도서관 일은 어떤가요? 상당히 작고 조용하며, 너무 많은 사람들이 찾아와 성가시게 굴지도 않을 거예요.

M: 그게 중요한 일인가요?

W: 음, 누군가 학생에게 질문을 한다거나, 학생이 책들을 점검하거나, 그와 같은 종류의 일을 하지 않는다면, 근무 시간에 공부할 기회가 생기는 것이죠. 그래서, 어떤 면에서는, 공부하면서 돈을 벌 수 있는 것이죠.

M: 와, 정말 좋겠는데요. 그러면, 음, 도서관에 일자리가 남아있나요?

W: 네, 있어요. 도서관장님이신 *John Hanlin*이라는 분이 몇 분 전에 저한테 전화하셔서 교대 근무할 사람이 필요하다고 말씀하셨어요. 제가 듣기로는, 그곳에서 일하던 학생들이 이번 학기에 해외에서 공부를 한다는 것 같아요.

M: 정말 솔깃하네요.

W: 그러면, 음, 제가 그 분께 전화해서 일자리에 관심이 있는 학생이 있다고 말씀을 드릴까요?

M: 아주 잘됐네요. 음, 말씀하신 도서관이 *Lufkin* 도서관 맞죠?

W: 맞아요. *Anderson Hall* 내에 있는데, 앞으로 4년 동안 많은 수업을 듣게 될 건물이죠.

M: 잘됐네요. 정말 감사합니다. *Hanlin* 선생님께 제가 몇 분 내로 도착할 것이라고 말씀드려 주시겠어요? 정말 감사합니다.

Script

| 02-03 |

M1 Professor: Okay, break's over. Everyone settle down so that we can continue talking about carbon dioxide . . . Ready . . . ? Good. Some scientists speculate that one reason global temperatures seem to be rising is the presence of carbon dioxide emissions in the atmosphere. Somewhere around nine billion metric tons of carbon dioxide are estimated to be released into the atmosphere each year. Most of this—oh, about four-fifths or so—comes from the burning of fossil fuels. The remainder comes from burning vegetation—that can be caused by forest fires—from erupting volcanoes, and, um, from many other reasons. This carbon dioxide—and other greenhouse gases—absorbs heat that comes off the Earth's surface. Then, the carbon dioxide radiates the heat back to the surface, which thereby increases the temperatures on the planet. This is the greenhouse effect.

Carbon dioxide is entering the atmosphere faster than it gets removed by natural means. I just said that about nine billion metric tons is emitted into the atmosphere each year, right? Well, only around five billion metric tons get removed. Even if every human on the planet were to stop burning fossil fuels immediately, it would still take an incredibly long time to remove the excess carbon dioxide. Why is this . . . ? Well, the reason is that the natural processes for removing it are very slow.

M2 Student: What are some of those natural processes, sir?

M1: Good question, Matt. Well, let's see . . . First, plants use it. Plants, uh, breathe carbon dioxide I guess you could say. Also, it can get absorbed by the soil and the ocean. Sometimes, sediment and rocks absorb it and transform into carbonate. There are many ways really.

Let's break it down further, shall we . . . ? About 30% of those nine billion metric tons is absorbed by plants and soil. They absorb carbon dioxide faster than the other methods, but they have limited capabilities. Of course, we can help increase the process by planting more trees and making cities green. But there is so much carbon dioxide now that doing those things isn't a complete solution. ¹⁰Also, the oceans absorb around, oh, around 25% or so of the carbon dioxide, but they do this relatively slowly. One problem is that, in order for the ocean to remove carbon dioxide from circulation, it needs to sink deep beneath the surface. But, for various reasons that I won't get into yet, carbon dioxide only does this at the two poles.

That leaves us with sediment and rocks. They absorb carbon dioxide through the process of weathering, which is a form of erosion. What weathering does is . . . uh, it changes the carbon dioxide to carbonate sediment and rocks, thereby removing it from the atmosphere. Unfortunately, this process takes, er, thousands of years. As a result, only about 1% of those nine billion tons gets removed in this manner.

The rest of the carbon dioxide remains in the atmosphere. And many people believe that it's partially responsible for the increase in temperatures some places are reporting. Here's an example . . . Think of the atmosphere as, um, a big bathtub. Now, imagine you're filling the bathtub with water. What happens if you add more water than drains out? Eventually, the tub will fill and then overflow, right? Well, we're adding more carbon dioxide than we're removing. Essentially, we're adding four billion metric tons of carbon dioxide each year. Currently, there are about 385 parts of carbon dioxide for every million parts of atmosphere. If this number rises above 450 parts per million, some experts believe that the effects on the environment may not be reversible for thousands—or maybe even hundreds of thousands—of years. Yes, Matt?

M2: [11]I'm sorry to interrupt, sir, but you just said that there are currently 385 parts of carbon dioxide per million parts of atmosphere, right?

M1: Correct.

M2: As a percentage, isn't that an incredibly minute number? I mean, how can something that's present in such a small, uh, quantity have such an enormous effect on the entire atmosphere? I'm rather confused about that.

M1: That's a good observation, Matt. The thing is . . . We're not totally sure if carbon dioxide is the culprit for any warming that's going on. We do know that the amount of carbon dioxide in the atmosphere is increasing rapidly. At the same time, the Earth appears to be warming. So, lately, many scientists have been trying to make a connection between the two. Plus, when the Earth used to be warmer—much warmer than today—we believe that atmospheric carbon dioxide levels were higher. But, really, more work in the field of climate research needs to be done before we can be positive about anything.

Still, just in case carbon dioxide is the reason that the Earth is warming, there are a good number of individuals working on finding ways to, uh, to remove excess amounts of it from the atmosphere. Burning fewer fossil fuels would help, but there would still be much carbon dioxide for us to get rid of. So, um, let me talk about some methods that scientists are working on that would remove carbon dioxide from the atmosphere.

Translation

M1 Professor: 좋아요. 쉬는 시간이 끝났군요. 모두 조용히 하시고 이산화탄소 이야기를 계속 해봅시다… 준비됐죠…? 좋아요. 몇몇 과학자들은 지구의 기온이 상승하는 이유가 대기 중으로 배출되는 이산화탄소 때문이라고 생각하고 있습니다. 해마다 약 900만 미터 톤의 이산화탄소가 대기 중으로 배출되는 것으로 추정되고 있습니다. 이 가운데 대부분이 – 오, 대략 5분의 4정도가 – 화석연료의 연소에 의해서 생성되죠. 나머지는 화산 폭발로 인한 산불에 의해서 발생할 수 있는 식물의 연소를 통해서도 발생하며, 그리고, 음, 여러 가지 다른 원인들에 의해서도 발생합니다. 이러한 이산화탄소와 다른 온실가스들은 지표면에서 방출되는 열을 흡수합니다. 그리고 나면, 이산화탄소는 지표면으로 열을 다시 방출하는데, 이렇게 되면 지구의 온도가 상승하게 되죠. 이를 온실효과라고 합니다.

이산화탄소는 자연적으로 소멸되는 속도보다 대기에 진입하는 속도가 더 빠릅니다. 해마다 90억 미터 톤의 이산화탄소가 대기 중으로 방출된다고 말씀 드렸어요, 그렇죠? 음, 이 가운데 약 50억 미터 톤 정도만 소멸됩니다. 전세계의 모든 사람들이 지금 즉시 화석연료의 사용을 덤추다고 해도, 과다한 이산화탄소가 소멸되려면 상당히 긴 시간이 필요할 것입니다. 왜 그런 것일까요…? 음, 이산화탄소가 자연적으로 소멸되는 과정이 매우 느리게 진행되기 때문입니다.

M2 Student: 교수님, 자연적인 소멸 과정에는 어떤 것들이 있나요?

M1: 좋은 질문이에요, *Matt*. 음, 어디 봅시다… 식물은, 음, 학생이 말하려고 했던 것 같은데, 이산화탄소를 들이마시죠. 또한, 이산화탄소는 토양이나 바다에 의해서 흡수되기도 해요. 때때로, 퇴적물이나 암석이 이산화탄소를 흡수해서 탄산염이 되기도 하죠. 실제로 여러 가지 방법들이 있군요.

좀 더 분석적으로 알아보도록 할까요…? 90억 미터 톤 가운데 약 30% 정도가 식물과 토양에 의해 흡수됩니다. 이들은 다른 방법들보다 더 빠르게 이산화탄소를 흡수하지만, 그 능력에는 한계가 있습니다. 물론, 우리가 나무를 심고 도시를 푸르게 가꿈으로써 이산화탄소가 흡수되는 과정을 가속화 시킬 수는 있어요. 하지만 이산화탄소의 양이 너무 많아서 이러한 방법은 완전한 해결책이 될 수는 없죠. 또한, 바다에 흡수되는 이산화탄소의 양은, 오, 25% 정도나 되지만 그 속도가 비교적 느린 편입니다. 바다의 순환을 통해 이산화탄소가 소멸되는 과정에서 한 가지 문제가 되는 것은, 이것이 해수면 아래의 깊은 곳으로 가라앉아야 한다는 사실입니다. 하지만, 제가 아직까지 언급하지 않은 여러 가지 이유로, 이산화탄소가 이렇게 흡수되는 지역은 극지방뿐입니다.

이산화탄소는 침전물과 암석을 통해서 소멸되기도 합니다. 이산화탄소는 침식 현상의 한 종류인 풍화 작용을 통해서 침전물과 암석에 흡수됩니다. 풍화 작용의 영향으로… 음, 이산화탄소가 탄산염 퇴적물과 탄산염암으로 변화하면서, 대기중에서 소멸됩니다. 안타깝게도, 이러한 과정은, 음, 수천 년이나 걸립니다. 그 결과, 90억 톤 가운데 겨우 1% 정도만 이러한 과정을 통해서 소멸됩니다.

나머지 이산화탄소는 대기에 남아있게 됩니다. 많은 사람들은, 몇몇 지역에서 보고된 기온의 상승이 어느 정도는 이러한 이산화탄소 때문이라고 생각하죠. 예를 하나 들어봅시다… 대기를, 음, 커다란 욕조라고 생각해 보죠. 이제, 여러분이 욕조에 물을 채운다고 상상해 보세요. 배수되는 물의 양보다 더 많은 물을 부으면 어떤 일이 발생할까요? 결국, 욕조는 가득 채워져서 넘칠 것입니다. 그렇죠? 자, 우리는 소멸되는 이산화탄소의 양보다 더 많은 이산화탄소를 배출해 내고 있습니다. 기본적으로, 우리는 해마다 40억 미터 톤의 이산화탄소를 배출하고 있죠. 최근에, 대기와 이산화탄소의 비율은 1,000,000:385입니다. 이 비율이 1,000,000:450까지 증가하면, 몇몇 전문가들은 환경에 미치게 될 영향이 수천 년 혹은 수십만 년 동안 돌이킬 수 없을 정도로 될 것이라고 생각합니다. 예, *Matt*?

M2: 교수님, 끼어 들어서 죄송합니다만, 교수님께서 방금 대기와 이산화탄소의 비율이 현재 1,000,000:385라고 하셨죠?

M1: 그렇습니다.

M2: 비율로 따지면, 상당히 적은 수치 아닌가요? 제 말씀은, 그렇게 적은 수치로, 음, 어떻게 대기 전체에 그렇게 막대한 영향을 미칠 수 있을까요? 이해가 되지 않는군요.

M1: 좋은 의견이네요, Matt. 중요한 것은… 우리는 아직 이산화탄소를 온난화의 주범으로 완전하게 확신하고 있지는 않는다는 점입니다. 우리가 알고 있는 것은 대기 중의 이산화탄소 수치가 급격하게 상승하고 있다는 사실이죠. 그와 동시에, 지구는 더워지고 있고요. 그래서, 최근에, 많은 과학자들은 이 둘 사이의 연관성을 찾아보려는 시도를 해 왔어요. 또한, 지구가 오늘날에 비해서 훨씬 더 더웠을 때, 대기 중의 이산화탄소 비율이 더 높았을 것이라고 생각합니다. 하지만, 실제로, 우리가 어떤 결론을 단정짓기 전에, 기후 연구 분야에서의 연구가 더 많이 이루어져야만 합니다.

하지만, 이산화탄소가 지구 온난화의 원인일 수도 있다는 가능성에 대비하여, 대기에 존재하는 너무 많은 이산화탄소를 제거할 방법을, 음, 연구하는 사람들이 많이 있습니다. 사용을 줄이는 것도 도움이 되겠지만, 제거해야 할 이산화탄소의 양이 이미 너무 많습니다. 그러면, 음, 과학자들이 대기 중의 이산화탄소를 제거하는데 활용하는 몇 가지 방법에 대해서 이야기를 해 보도록 하겠습니다.

Actual Test 03

Reading Section   p.33

Answers

1. C [Vocabulary Question]
2. B [Factual Question]
3. B [Vocabulary Question]
4. B [Rhetorical Purpose Question]
5. D [Factual Question]
6. A [Negative Factual Question]
7. A [Vocabulary Question]
8. D [Factual Question]
9. C [Reference Question]
10. C [Factual Question]
11. A [Inference Question]
12. 4th [Insert Text Question]
13.

	Desalination Method
Reverse Osmosis Method	C, F, G
Forward Osmosis Method	B, D

[Fill in a Table Question]

Translation

바닷물의 담수화

물은 지구의 모든 생명체에게 필수적인 것이지만, 안타깝게도, 고르게 분포되어 있지는 않다. 육지의 많은 지역에는 물이 없으며, 다른 지역에는 물이 부족하다. 하지만, 물이 풍부한 지역도 있다: 바로 바다이다. 그러나, 염분 때문에, 바닷물은 식수와 농업용수로 활용될 수 없다. 인간의 능력으로 인해, 바닷물을 사용할 수 있도록 염분을 제거하는 방법이 발견됨으로써 이러한 문제는 해결되고 있다. 가장 널리 사용되는 방법 – 강제 증발법과 역삼투법은 – 비용이 많이 들기 때문에, 기술자들은 새로운 방법을 찾으려 하고 있다. 세 가지 방법이 실험되고 있다: 정삼투법, 탄소나노튜브, 그리고 바이오미메틱스(생체 모방학)가 그것이다. 세 가지 방법 모두 현재는 비용이 많이 들지만, 완성이 되면, 바닷물을 더 저렴하게 담수화 할 수 있는 방법이 나타나게 될 것이라고 기대대고 있다.

최초의 방법이며, 지금까지도 가장 널리 사용되는 담수화 방법은 강제 증발법이다. 이 방법에서는, 많은 양의 바닷물이 수증기가 될 때까지 가열된다. 그리고 나면, 염분만 남게 되고, 수증기는 응축되어 담수가 생산되고 있다. 현재, 대략 85%의 담수화된 물이 이러한 방법을 통해서 생산된다. 두 번째 방법은 역삼투법이다. 담수 시설에서, 고압 펌프가 염분을 걸러낼 수 있는 상당히 얇은 막에 바닷물을 통과시켜, 이를 담수로 변화시킨다. 두 방법 모두 상당한 에너지를 사용해야 하기 때문에 비용이 많이 든다. 사우디아라비아와 같은 석유가 풍부한 페르시아만의 국가에서는 문제가 되지 않지만, 빈곤한 아프리카 해안의 국가들은, 과도한 비용 때문에 담수 시설을 건설할 수 없다. (따라서, 후진국의 많은 사람들이 현재 깨끗한 식수를 이용하지 못하고 있다.)

새로운 세 가지 담수 방법도 비용이 높기 때문에, 감당할 수 있을 정도로 가격을 낮추기 위한 개선책이 필요하다. 세 방법 모두, 역삼투법과 같이 바닷물을 막에 통과시키는데, 몇몇 주요한 차이점이 있다. 정삼투법의 경우, 바닷물을 막에 통과시켜, 바닷물과 다른 종류의 염분을 함유하고 있는 – 유도 용액이라고 불리는 – 염용액으로 흡수시킨다. 유도 용액은 바닷물을 끌어들여, 바닷물이 유도 용액과 바닷물 사이에 위치한 막을 통과하도록 하는데, 이를 통하여 바닷물의 염분이 제거된다. 그리고 나서, 새 용액을 낮은 온도로 가열하여 염분을 제거한다. 바닷물에 들어있는 염분에 비하여 유도용액에 들어있는 염분을 제거하는 것이 더 쉽기 때문에, 이 방법이 효과가 있는 것이다. 정삼투법의 장점은 물을 막에 통과시키는데 필요한 고압 펌프가 필요 없기 때문에, 담수화에 필요한 에너지의 양이 적다는 점이다.

탄소나노튜브와 바이오미메틱스는 막의 중심 부분을 재설계 하는 방법이다. 나노튜브는 탄소로 만들어지며 한 쪽 끝부분이 전기적으로 충전이 되어있는 상태이다. 여러 개의 나노튜브가 막에 설치되어 있는데, 이는 전기적으로 충전되어 있어서, 양성을 띄는 염분 이온은 튕겨나가며, 전기적으로 충전되지 않은 물의 입자들만 막을 통과할 수 있게 된다. 바이오미메틱스 방법의 경우, 아쿠아포린이라는 세포를 막에 갖다 놓는다. 이는 물이 생물의 세포를 통과하도록 해주는 단백질이다. 마찬가지로, 아쿠아포린의 중앙 부분은 전기적으로 충전되어 있기 때문에, 염분 이온은 튕겨나가며 물만 통과할 수 있게 된다.

이러한 세 가지 방법들이 완성되어 언젠가는 사용 가능할 정도로 비용이 낮아지게 되면, 물을 사용하기 힘든 약 10억 명 정도의 사람들이 담수를 공급받게 될 것이라고 기대대고 있다. 현재, 전 세계 3억 명의 사람들이 담수를 사용하기 위해서 담수화 시설에 의존하고 있다. 150개국의 14,500개의 담수화 시설에서는 매일 대략 60억 갤런의 담수가 생산된다. 페르시아만 지역의 국가들과 같은 몇몇 국가들은, 담수의 공급을 오직 담수화 시설에만 의존하고 있다. 하지만, 담수의 생산은 비용이 많이 들기 때문에, 모든 국가에서 사용할 수 있는 해결책이 아니다. 담수화 비용은, 담수를 수입할 수 있는 경우에, 수입하는데 필요한 비용의 거의 두 배에 이른다. 최근에 바닷물의 담수화 비용이 낮아지고는 있지만, 여전히 비싼 편이다. 미래에는, 전세계 인구가 증가함에 따라, 담수와 관련된 문제가 계속 존재하게 될 것이다. 수자원을 보존하고 꼭 필요할 때에만 담수를 사용하는 것이 아마도 진정한 해결책이 될 것이다.

Listening Section p.39

Answers

1. C [Gist-Content Question]
2. A [Understanding Function Question]
3. C [Understanding Organization Question]
4. B [Making Inferences Question]
5. B [Understanding Attitude Question]
6. B [Gist-Content Question]
7. B, D [Detail Question]
8. A [Understanding Organization Question]
9. A [Making Inferences Question]
10. D [Understanding Function Question]
11. C [Understanding Attitude Question]

Script

| 03-02 |

M Professor: Greetings, Jennifer. Did you get my note that I wanted to speak with you?

W Student: Yes, Professor Cornwall. I received the email you sent me.

M: Great. Then you must know what this meeting is about.

W: Er, actually, I'm not sure. You didn't write anything about it in the email. You just mentioned that since I'm a senior and you're my advisor, that, uh, we need to have a chat once the semester starts.

M: Oh, I see . . . I really didn't tell you any more than that?

W: No, sir. You didn't.

M: Goodness, I must be getting forgetful in my old age. Anyway, there's nothing for you to worry about. Just, like you mentioned, you're a senior, and you're my advisee, so the school requires us to have a talk at the start of your senior year. Uh, by the way, all seniors on campus have to do this. The school isn't singling you out.

W: That's good to know. So, uh, what exactly do we need to discuss?

M: Well, basically . . . What are your plans for after you graduate? A job? Graduate school? Travel? Or something else?

W: Hmm . . . That's a good question. I haven't put much thought into it to be honest with you.

M: Well, then . . . It's a good thing that the school insists on these meetings. Wouldn't you agree?

W: Er, yeah. Now that I think about it, you're probably right.

M: So, now that we're, uh, thinking about it, as you say, what would you like to do?

W: Hmm . . . I'm probably leaning toward getting a job.

M: ⁵That's a good choice. I have your transcript here, and I must say that your grades are fairly good. You probably could have done better your freshman year, but lots of students do, uh, poorly their first year away from home.

W: You can say that again. But, in my defense, I made the dean's list every semester during my sophomore and junior years.

M: That's true, and it's quite an impressive accomplishment. Chemistry is not an easy major to do well in, but your grades the past two years have been, well, quite exceptional. In fact, I think they're good enough that some potential employers will, uh, gloss over your grades from your freshman year.

W: That's a relief.

M: So, assuming you do as well this year as you have in the past two years, I imagine you're going to have several companies offering you jobs.

W: Are you serious?

M: Competent chemists are hard to find these days. I fully expect you to get job offers from private industries, universities, and a government organization or two.

W: Of those, I'm most interested in working for a private company. I hope to get some offers from a few pharmaceutical companies. Lots of them are doing cutting-edge research, and I'd love to get involved in that.

M: In that case . . . let me make a few calls. I used to be in that industry before I started teaching here five years ago, and I still maintain a few contacts. If I talk to a couple of people, I should be able to, uh, get the ball rolling for you.

W: You'd do that for me, Professor Cornwall? Wow. How can I ever thank you?

M: Just keep up the good work, and don't let me down this year. That's all the thanks I require.

Translation

M Professor: 안녕하세요, *Jennifer*. 학생과 이야기 하고 싶다는 메모는 받았죠?

W Student: 네, Cornwall 교수님. 보내주신 이메일 받았습니다.

M: 좋아요. 그렇다면 제가 왜 보자고 했는지도 알고 있겠군요.

W: 음, 사실은, 잘 모르겠습니다. 이메일에는 적혀있지 않던걸요. 교수님께서 말씀하신 사항은, 제가 졸업 학년이고 교수님은 저의 지도 교수이며, 음, 학기가 시작할 때 교수님과 제가 이야기를 나눌 필요가 있다는 말씀이셨습니다.

M: 아, 그렇군요… 그것 말고 제가 다른 이야기를 한 것은 없었나요?

W: 네, 교수님, 없었습니다.

M: 이런, 제가 나이가 많아서 잊어버린 것이 분명해요. 어쨌든, 걱정할 필요는 없어요. 단지, 학생이 말한 것처럼, 학생은 졸업 학년이 되었기 때문에, 학교 방침상, 학생과 나는 학생의 졸업 학년이 시작되는 시점에서 이야기를 나눠야 해요. 음, 덧붙여 말하자면, 학교의 모든 졸업 학년 학생들이 다들 그렇게 해야 하고요. 학교에서 학생만 선별해서 이렇게 하는 것은 아니에요.

W: 알려주셔서 감사합니다. 그러니까, 음, 교수님과 제가 어떤 대화를 나눠야 하죠?

M: 음, 기본적으로 … 졸업 이후의 계획이 무엇인가요? 취업인가요? 대학원 진학인가요? 여행인가요? 아니면 다른 무슨 계획이 있나요?

W: 흠 … 좋은 질문을 하셨네요. 솔직히 말씀을 드리자면 아직까지 깊게 고민해본 적은 없습니다.

M: 음, 그렇다면 … 학교에서 이러한 만남을 지속시키는 것은 좋은 일이군요. 그렇지 않나요?

W: 음, 네. 생각해보니, 교수님 말씀이 맞는 것 같아요.

M: 그렇다면, 음, 학생이 말한 대로, 우리가 같이 생각을 좀 해보아야 하니까, 학생은 무엇을 하고 싶나요?

W: 흠… 직장을 얻는게 좋을 것 같습니다.

M: 좋은 선택입니다. 학생의 성적 증명서가 있는데, 학점이 상당히 좋더군요. 1학년 때에도 조금 더 잘 할 수도 있었겠지만, 많은 학생들이 집을 떠난 첫 해에는, 음, 성적이 좋지 않은 경우가 많죠.

W: 옳으신 말씀입니다. 하지만, 변명처럼 들릴지는 몰라도, 2학년 때와 3학년 때에는 매 학기 우등생 명단에 올랐었습니다.

M: 그렇군요. 정말 인상적인 성적이에요. 화학은 전공하기 쉬운 분야가 아님에도 불구하고, 학생의 지난 2년간의 성적은, 음, 정말 훌륭하군요. 실제로, 제 생각에는, 음, 성적이 훌륭해서 채용 담당자가 1학년 때의 성적은 무시하고 넘어갈 수도 있을 것 같아요.

W: 안심이 좀 되는군요.

M: 그리고, 학생이 올해에도 지난 2년 동안 해온 것처럼 잘 해낸다면, 여러 회사에서 입사 제의를 받게 될 것입니다.

W: 정말인가요?

M: 요즘에는 능력 있는 화학 전공자를 찾아보기 힘들거든요. 기업, 대학, 그리고 정부 기관 몇 군데에서 학생에게 입사 제의를 해올 것이 분명해요.

W: 그 중에서도, 저는 기업에서 근무하고 싶어요. 제약 회사 몇 군데에서 입사 제의를 받고 싶어요. 제약 회사에서는 최첨단 연구를 실행하고 있는데, 저는 그런 일들을 좋아하거든요.

M: 그렇다면… 제가 전화를 몇 군데 해볼게요. 이 대학에서 학생들을 가르치기 5년 전에는 제가 그 분야에서 일을 했고, 아직도 몇몇 사람들과는 연락을 유지하고 있죠. 제가 두 세 사람에게 이야기를 해 놓으면, 음, 학생이 일을 시작할 수 있도록 해줄 수 있을 것 같네요.

W: Cornwall 교수님, 정말 그렇게 해 주시겠어요? 와. 너무 감사해서 어쩌죠?

M: 계속 공부 열심히 하고, 올 한 해 저를 실망시키지 마세요. 그것이 저에게 보답하는 길입니다.

Script

| 03-03 |

W Professor: In the realm of design, the form known as Art Deco is one I'm sure you've all seen quite often even if you didn't know its name. There are numerous buildings and products done in the Art Deco style. For instance, in New York City, the Empire State Building and the Chrysler Building are two examples of Art Deco architecture. You can see them both here on the screen . . . Oh, but I'm getting a bit ahead of myself. I apologize. Let me first see if I can describe Art Deco to you.

Well, Art Deco is a design style that was widely popular from before World War I, which started in 1914, and it remained influential until sometime in the 1940s. It started in Europe and then spread elsewhere. Art Deco's roots lie in France. In 1900, a world's fair was held in Paris. After it, some French artists formed a group whose purpose was to exhibit the beauty of French decorative arts. Take a look at some of them here . . . and here . . . It was, however, many years later, in 1925, during an exhibition in Paris . . . the, uh, the Paris Exhibition of Decorative Arts . . . that Art Deco became better known and more popular. The term "Art Deco" is actually derived from the French name for the exhibition. Basically, the term refers to the decorative arts. But the term itself didn't enter widespread use until a book about Art Deco was published in the late 1960s.

So, those are the movement's origins. [10]But what exactly is its style of design? Here's an example . . . and another . . . and yet another. They're all different, right? Well, describing Art Deco is rather, uh, complex since, at that time, no one called it Art Deco, and, depending on a person's opinion, something may be considered Art Deco . . . or it may not. Let me show you some more examples on the screen so that you can see what I mean. To begin with, Art Deco designs are characterized by long slender shapes . . . curved surfaces . . . and geometric patterns. These geometric patterns may be orderly . . . or not . . . Steel, glass, stainless steel, aluminum, and lacquered wood were all common materials used in Art Deco. However, artists weren't limited to those materials. In fact, the more, um, unusual, exotic, or expensive the material, the more likely it is that you'll be able to find it somewhere in an Art Deco design.

In addition, streamlined shapes . . . and the appearance

of sleekness and speed . . . are characteristics of Art Deco, particularly in industrial design. Let's look at some examples of Art Deco industrial design. Ah, here we have some cars . . . Note the use of streamlining to make the cars appear both sleek and fast. Prior to the 1920s and 1930s, most cars had box-like structures. This was characteristic of the horse and buggy that they replaced. See here . . . Yet, once Art Deco began to influence automobile designers, well, uh, cars became more aerodynamically shaped. You should know, however, that many art historians refer to the sleek, aerodynamic industrial designs—which weren't limited to cars—of that age as, uh, Streamline Modern. But, in my opinion, Streamline Modern is clearly a form of Art Deco.

M Student: [11]What made the designers from this period so interested in speed?

W: Hmm . . . That's an interesting query. Part of the reason comes from industrialization and the use of machines, which became more widespread in the early 1900s. You see, French artists in the early 1900s wanted to show the sleekness of machines as well as the speed that their use implied. They also wanted to portray wealth and luxury in their designs. In fact, the first Art Deco designs were found on French luxury goods. It was later that Art Deco spread to different branches of the arts. These include, by the way, painting, industrial design, architecture, decorative arts, interior design, and graphic design. In addition, after the horrors of World War I in the 1910s, people wanted to enjoy their lives and show off their wealth. This led, in part, to the Roaring Twenties, an era of economic expansion and good times that occurred between the misery of World War I and the Great Depression in the 1930s. So, in a sense, Art Deco was a reflection of people's need to, well, to feel free, to have fun, and to enjoy their lives.

Of course, Art Deco didn't develop independently. It was influenced by several other art movements, including . . . hmm . . . Neoclassicism, Cubism, Futurism, Modernism, and Art Nouveau. Art Deco also borrowed from various cultures—particularly old ones—from around the world. These included the ancient Greek, Roman, Egyptian, Mayan, Middle Eastern, and Far Eastern cultures. I think you should be able to understand why Art Deco has so many diverse looks. It just had, well, a ton of influences. Okay, now let me show you some more slides of Art Deco works, and you try to tell me which culture or art movement influenced them.

Translation

W Professor: 디자인 분야에서, 아르데코라는 형태가 있는데, 여러분들은 이 명칭을 모른다고 해도 상당히 자주 봤을 것이라고 확신합니다. 아르데코 형식으로 제작된 수많은 건물과 제품들이 있습니다. 예를 들면, 뉴욕시의 엠파이어스테이트 빌딩과 크라이슬러 빌딩이 아르데코 건축의 두 가지 사례이죠. 이 건물들을 화면에서 보실 수 있는데… 아, 제가 너무 앞서 나갔네요. 미안합니다. 여러분들에게 먼저 아르데코에 대해서 설명하도록 하겠어요.

자, 아르데코는 1914년에 발발했던 제1차 세계 대전 이전에 폭넓게 인기를 끌었던 디자인 양식인데, 1940년대까지 영향력이 있었습니다. 이는 유럽에서 시작하여 여러 지역으로 확산되었죠. 1900년, 파리에서 세계 박람회가 개최되었어요. 그 후, 프랑스의 몇몇 예술가들이 프랑스의 아름다운 장식 예술품들을 전시할 목적으로 모임을 결성하게 되었죠. 여기를 잘 보세요… 그리고 여기… 하지만, 몇 해가 지난 1925년, 파리에서 박람회가… 그, 음, 파리 장식 예술 박람회가 열렸던 기간 동안… 아르데코가 더 잘 알려지고 더 많은 인기를 끌게 되었죠. "아르데코"라는 용어는 실제로 프랑스의 박람회 명칭에서 유래되었습니다. 기본적으로, 이 용어는 장식 예술을 의미합니다. 하지만, 1960년대 후반 아르데코와 관련된 책이 출판되었을 때 비로소 이 용어가 사용되었습니다.

그래서, 이러한 일들이 아르데코 운동의 기원이 됩니다. 하지만 이러한 디자인 양식은 정확히 무엇일까요? 여기 그 예가 있습니다… 그리고 또 하나… 여기 또 하나 있군요. 이들은 서로 다릅니다. 그렇죠? 음, 아르데코를 설명한다는 것은 상당히, 어, 어려운데, 당시에는, 이러한 양식을 아르데코라고 부르는 사람이 아무도 없었고, 어떤 예술 작품이 아르데코 형식인지… 혹은 아닌지는, 작품에 대한 개개인의 의견에 달려있었기 때문이었죠. 제 말이 무슨 말인지 여러분들에게 이해시키기 위해, 화면을 통해서 더 많은 사례를 보여드리도록 할게요. 우선, 아르데코 디자인의 특징은 길고 가는 외형과… 곡선 형태의 표면… 그리고 기하학적 패턴입니다. 기하학적 패턴은 질서를 이루고 있거나… 그렇지 않은 경우도 있었죠… 강철, 유리, 스테인리스강, 알루미늄, 그리고 옻칠 목재 등이 아르데코에 사용되었던 흔한 재료들이었습니다. 하지만, 예술가들이 이러한 재료들만 사용한 것은 아니었죠. 사실, 좀 더, 음, 좀 더 흔하지 않고, 독특하거나, 비싼 재료들일수록, 아르데코 디자인에서는 찾아보기가 더 쉽습니다.

또한, 유선형의 외형과… 매끄러움과 속도감이… 아르데코의 특징인데, 산업디자인 분야에서 더욱 그렇습니다. 아르데코의 산업디자인 분야의 사례들을 보도록 하죠. 아, 여기 자동차들이 있군요… 자동차의 맵시와 속도감을 표현하기 위해서 유선형을 사용한 것을 보세요. 1920년대와 1930년대 이전에는, 대부분의 자동차들이 상자처럼 생긴 구조였어요. 이는 자동차에 의해 대체된 말과 2륜 마차의 특징적인 모습이었죠. 여기를 보세요… 하지만, 디자이너들이 아르데코의 영향을 받기 시작하자, 음, 어, 자동차의 모양이 더욱 공기 역학적으로 변했죠. 하지만, 여러분들이 알아야 할 사실은, 많은 예술 사학자들은 이 시대의 자동차에만 적용된 맵시, 공기 역학적인 산업 디자인을, 음, 유선형 근대 양식 이라고 부릅니다. 하지만, 제 의견으로는, 유선형 근대 양식은 분명히 아르데코의 한 형태입니다.

M Student: 이 시기의 디자이너들이 속도에 관심을 가지게 된 계기는 무엇일까요?

W: 흠… 흥미로운 질문이군요. 이유는 산업화와 기계의 사용 때문인데, 이는 1900년대 초반에 널리 보급되었죠. 아시다시피, 1900년대 초반의 프랑스 예술가들은 기계의 맵시를 보여주고 싶어했을 뿐 아니라, 기계를 사용함으로써 얻을 수 있는 속도를 표현하고 싶어했어요. 그들은 자신들의 디자인을 통해서 부

유함과 호화로움을 표현하고 싶어하기도 했죠. 실제로, 최초의 아르데코 디자인은 프랑스의 사치품에서 찾아볼 수 있어요. 아르데코가 서로 다른 예술 분야로 갈라진 시기는 그 이후입니다. 덧붙이자면, 이 분야에는 그림, 산업 디자인, 건축, 장식 예술, 인테리어 디자인, 그리고 그래픽 디자인 등이 있습니다. 게다가, 1910년대에 끔찍했던 제1차 세계 대전이 끝난 후, 사람들은 삶을 즐기고자 했으며 자신들의 부를 드러내고 싶어했죠. 부분적으로는 이 때문에, 불행했던 제1차 세계 대전과 1930년대의 대공황 사이에, 경제적으로 성장하던 행복했던 시기, 즉, 광란의 20년대가 도래하게 된 것입니다. 그래서, 어떤 의미에서는, 아르데코가 사람들이 자신을 드러내며, 자유를 만끽하고, 흥겨워하며, 자신들의 삶을 즐기려는 사람들의 욕구를 반영했다고 볼 수 있습니다.

물론, 아르데코가 독자적으로 발달되지는 않았어요. 이는 여러 다른 예술 운동의 영향을 받았는데… 흠… 신고전주의, 입체파, 미래파, 현대주의, 그리고 아르누보 등의 영향을 받았어요. 아르데코는 또한 다양한 문화, 특히 전세계의 오래된 문화의 개념들을 차용했죠. 그리스, 로마, 이집트, 마야, 중동, 그리고 극동 지역의 문화가 이러한 문화들입니다. 아르데코가 왜 그렇게 다양한 모습을 보이고 있는지 여러분들이 이해할 수 있으리라고 생각해요. 이는, 음, 상당한 영향을 미쳤죠. 좋아요, 이제 아르데코 예술품들의 슬라이드를 더 보여드리도록 하죠. 그리고 여러분들은 어떤 문화와 예술 운동이 아르데코에 영향을 미쳤는지 저에게 말할 준비를 해주세요.

Actual Test 04

Reading Section   p.45

Answers

1. Ⓒ [Vocabulary Question]
2. Ⓐ [Vocabulary Question]
3. Ⓐ [Factual Question]
4. Ⓒ [Reference Question]
5. Ⓓ [Negative Factual Question]
6. Ⓑ [Inference Question]
7. Ⓐ [Factual Question]
8. Ⓓ [Vocabulary Question]
9. Ⓓ [Rhetorical Purpose Question]
10. Ⓑ [Factual Question]
11. Ⓓ [Vocabulary Question]
12. Ⓒ [Reference Question]
13. Ⓑ [Sentence Simplification Question]
14. Ⓐ, Ⓑ, Ⓔ [Prose Summary]

Translation

폼페이와 헤르쿨라네움의 재발견

서기 79년, 이탈리아 남부의 베수비우스 화산이 폭발하여 폼페이와 헤르쿨레나움이 파괴되었다. 이 지역과 인근 지역의 수천 명의 사람들이 재난으로 인해 사망했고, 화산 주변의 전 지역이 뜨거운 화산재와 암석의 두터운 층에 의해 뒤덮여 졌다. 1,500년 이상의 기간 동안, 폼페이와 헤르쿨라네움은 뒤덮인 채로 남아있었으며, 사람들의 기억에서 서서히 사라져갔다. 그 후, 1599년에 발견되기 시작하여, 그 후 1730년대와 1740년대에, 두 도시가 재발견되었다. 놀랍게도, 뜨거운 재에 의해 두 도시는 그대로 보존되어서 수많은 유물들이 발견되었으며, 심지어 그림까지도 원형 그대로 보존되어 있었다. 이로 인하여, 역사학자들과 예술가들은 1세기 무렵의 로마 제국의 독특한 삶의 모습들을 관찰할 수 있었다. 학자들이 연구를 통해, 두 고대 도시에 대해 습득한 지식을 전파시키면서, 유물들과 도시의 발견은 유럽의 예술과 건축에도 상당한 영향을 미쳤다.

베수비우스 화산 폭발은 기록적인 사건이었지만, 폼페이와 헤르쿨라네움의 존재와 위치는 오랫동안 알 수 없었다. 1599년, 이 지역에 운하를 건설하면서 폼페이의 일부가 발견되었지만, 몇몇 벽들만 발굴되었을 뿐이었고, 이 지역은 곧바로 다시 흙으로 덮여졌다. 몇몇 역사학자들은 이를 고대의 검열 때문이라고 생각하는데, 이 벽들에서는 벽화들과 프레스코화가 잘 보존된 채로 발굴되었기 때문이었다. 종교적인 도덕성이 엄격했던 분위기 속에서, 수 세기 전 로마인들이 성적으로 개방적이었던 관습을 드러내는 것은 지속한 일이라고 생각되었다. 이 벽들이 다시 가려지고 나서 재발굴되는데 거의 140년이라는 시간이 필요했다. 우선, 1738년, 새로운 장소를 발굴하던 사람들은 헤르쿨라네움의 유물들을 발견했다. 그 후, 1748년, 적극적으로 폼페이를 발굴하던 팀이 드디어 성과를 이루었다.

그 때부터 현재까지, 수많은 전문가들의 광범위한 고고학적 발굴 작업이 이 지역에서 이루어지고 있다. 이 지역이 유명해진 한 가지 원인은, 1세기 무렵 로마의 사실적인 귀중한 유물들이 이곳에서 발굴되었다는 사실이다. 로마인들의 모습과 의복, 보석을 묘사한 수많은 벽화와 프레스코화가 발견되었다. 성적인 그림들과 관련하여, 예술 사학자들은 이 그림들이 다산 의식과 관련이 있으며 풍기문란의 의도는 없었다고 생각한다. 게다가, 로마인들이 사용했던 수많은 일상 용품들이, 도시의 여러 건물들과 마찬가지로 잘 보존되어 있었다. 이러한 정보를 통해, 학자들은 서기 79년 베수비우스 화산이 폭발할 때까지 로마인들의 사회생활, 예술, 그리고 건축에 대해서 많은 것들을 알아낼 수 있었다. 특히, 보존 상태가 뛰어난 수많은 예술 작품들 덕분에, 학자들은 고대 대가들의 작품 형식과, 그들이 사용했던 재료와 기법, 그리고 시간이 흐르면서 형식이 변화했던 방향에 대해 연구할 수 있는 기회를 얻었다.

로마시대의 그림은 – 고대 그리스의 그림은 사실상 하나도 남아있지 않다 – 거의 남아있지 않기 때문에, 폼페이와 헤르쿨라네움의 재발견은 고대 세계를 관찰할 수 있는 유일한 방법을 제공해주고 있다. 폼페이에서 발견된 그림들은, 재발견된 후 수십 년 동안 그대로 복제되어 유럽 전역에 전파되었다. 폼페이는 고대 로마인들에 대해서, 가능한 많은 것들을 알고 싶어했던 초기의 예술가들과 고고학자들에게 중요한 거점지가 되었다. 폼페이와 헤르쿨라네움의 발견은 신고전주의에 중요한 영향을 미쳤는데, 신고전주의는 18세기 중반에 시작된 운동으로서, 고대 로마와 그리스의 예술과 건축에 대한 관심을 불러 일으켰다.

비록 폼페이와 헤르쿨라네움의 사람들은 거의 2,000년 전에 갑자기 사라져버렸지만, 이 도시들의 재발견을 통하여 우리는 과거 특정 시기의 삶의 모습을 관찰할 수 있다. 아테네와 로마와 같은 다른 고대 도시들에는, 과거의 영광과 위엄을 엿볼 수 있는 장소가 보존되어 있지만, 폼페이와 헤르쿨라네움과는 다르다. 아테네와 로마인들의 삶은 계속되었기 때문에, 많은 변화를 겪었다. 그 결과, 이들의 수많은 고고학적 비밀들은 현대적인 삶에 의해 가려질 수밖에 없다. 그러나 폼페이와 헤르쿨라네움의 경우는 그렇지 않다. 순간적으로, 두 도시가 사라졌고, 그 도시에 살던 사람들도 사라졌지만, 동시에, 이들은 화산재에 의해서 너무나도 보존이 잘 되었기 때문에, 오늘날의 역사학자들은, 다른 어떤 고대의 발굴장소보다 이 두 지역에 살던 사람들에 대해 더 많은 것을 알고 있다.

Listening Section

p.51

Answers

1. Ⓐ [Gist-Content Question]
2. Ⓒ [Gist-Purpose Question]
3. Ⓐ, Ⓓ [Detail Question]
4. Ⓑ [Understanding Function Question]
5. Ⓒ [Understanding Attitude Question]
6. Ⓐ [Gist-Content Question]
7. Ⓒ [Gist-Purpose Question]
8. Ⓑ, Ⓒ [Detail Question]
9. Ⓐ [Understanding Function Question]
10.

	Penguins	Whales
Ⓐ		X
Ⓑ		X
Ⓒ	X	
Ⓓ	X	

[Connecting Content Question]

11. Ⓑ [Understanding Function Question]

Script

| 04-02 |

W **Student Housing Office Employee:** Hello. You must be Brad Crawford, right?

M **Student:** Yes, ma'am. That's me. I called you about ten minutes ago to see if I could come in and have a chat with you. You're available now, right?

W: Yes, I am, Mr. Crawford, so why don't you have a seat and make yourself comfortable?

M: Thank you very much, ma'am. I appreciate it.

W: Now . . . You seemed to be a little upset when you were talking to me over the phone. Why don't you tell me exactly what the problem with your room is?

M: Okay. So, um, I just checked into my dorm room about an hour ago. I'm in Deerfield Hall by the way.

W: Okay.

M: Anyway, everything . . . and I mean everything . . . is totally messed up with my room.

W: Such as?

M: First, I was supposed to be given a double room. I just transferred here from a college out of state, so I don't have any friends on campus yet. That means that the school assigned me a roommate for my sophomore year. But, uh, when I got to my room, imagine my surprise when I saw that I had not one but two roommates. I definitely didn't sign up for that. But, uh, come to think of it . . . I thought that triples were only for freshmen, not for upperclassmen.

W: ⁴As a general rule, you're right. But some sophomores get assigned to triples. Was that the only problem with your room?

M: **Not by a long shot.**

W: Okay. Go on then.

M: Like I said, I've been assigned to a triple, but the room is set up for a double.

W: Meaning that . . . ?

M: There are two beds, two dressers, and two desks. And since I was the third person to check in to the room—the other two guys got there early in the morning before my plane arrived—well, let's just say that I guess I'll be sleeping on the floor tonight. And I can't even unpack my bags since, well, there's nowhere to put my clothes.

W: Goodness, that is an awful situation.

M: So, uh, can you help me? This is my first day at a new school, and I have to say that I'm not very impressed.

W: Mr. Crawford, I completely understand how you feel. First, let me start by apologizing to you for this massive mistake. None of this should have happened.

M: Okay.

W: Now, this is what I'm going to do . . .

M: Yes?

W: Here at the student housing office, we anticipate things like this happening every year. It's a big school. Mistakes happen. So we leave some rooms empty to compensate for these mistakes. ⁵If you don't mind moving to a different dorm—that would be Victory Hall by the way—I can get you a single room. So you'd have a place all to yourself at no extra charge. How does that sound?

M: **Like I won the lottery.**

W: I thought you might say that. In that case, let me set up your room transfer. It'll take a couple of minutes. Then you can go back to your dorm, get your stuff, and move into your new place.

Translation

W Student Housing Office Employee: 안녕하세요. *Brad Crawford* 학생 맞죠?

M Student: 네, 그렇습니다. 저 맞는데요. 선생님과 이야기를 나눌 수 있는지 10분 전에 전화했었어요. 지금은 이야기 나눌 수 있죠?

W: 네, 그래요. *Crawford*씨, 이쪽에 앉아서 마음을 좀 가라앉히지 그래요?

M: 고마워요, 선생님. 감사합니다.

W: 음… 전화상으로 이야기 할 때 보니 조금 흥분한 것 같던데요. 방에 정확히 어떤 문제가 생겼는지 말해줄 수 있나요?

M: 네, 그러니까, 음, 저는 한 시간 전에 제 방에 도착했죠. 그리고 저는 *Deerfield Hall*에 살고 있어요.

W: 네.

M: 어쨌거나, 모든 것이… 그러니까 제 말은 모든 것이… 제 방과 관련된 모든 것이 다 엉망이 되어버렸어요.

W: 예를 들면요?

M: 우선, 저는 2인실을 사용하게 될 거라고 생각했어요. 제가 다른 주에서 이사 온지 얼마 안되었기 때문에, 대학에 친구가 한 명도 없거든요. 그래서 2학년 때에는 학교에서 저한테 룸메이트를 한 명 배정해 주기로 했어요. 그런데, 음, 제가 방에 갔더니 룸메이트가 한 명이 아니고 두 명이었다는 사실을 알게 되었을 때, 제가 얼마나 놀랐는지를 상상해보세요. 저는 분명히 그렇게 신청하지 않았거든요. 하지만, 그러고 보니… 3인실은 신입생들에게만 할당이 되고, 상급생들에게는 할당이 안 되는 줄 알았는데요.

W: 일반적으로는 그래요. 하지만 몇몇 2학년 학생들도 3인실에 배정되는 경우가 있죠. 학생의 방과 관련된 문제는 그것 뿐인가요?

M: 아니오, 그렇지 않아요.

W: 좋아요. 계속 이야기 해보세요.

M: 말씀 드린 것처럼, 3인실에 배정된 것인데, 그 방은 2인실이예요.

W: 무슨 얘기죠…?

M: 침대도 두 개, 옷장도 두 개, 그리고 책상도 두 개예요. 제 비행기가 도착하기도 전에 아침 일찍 두 사람이 방에 들어와서 제가 세 번째 사람이 되어 버렸기 때문에, 오늘 밤에 저는 바닥에서 잠을 자게 될 수도 있어요. 제 옷장도 없어서, 음, 저는 짐도 풀지 못했어요.

W: 저런, 정말 좋지 않은 상황이네요.

M: 그래서 말인데, 음, 저를 도와주실 수 있나요? 새 학교의 첫날인데, 좋은 인상을 받지 못했다고 말씀드릴 수밖에 없네요.

W: 기분이 어떨지 전적으로 이해해요, *Crawford*씨. 너무 큰 실수를 저지른 것에 대해서 사과 드릴게요. 있어서는 안될 일이었는데요.

M: 네.

W: 음, 제가 이렇게 해 드리죠…

M: 어떻게요?

W: 학생주거 사무소에서는, 해마다 이러한 일이 발생할 것을 예상하고 있어요. 규모가 큰 학교이기 때문에, 실수도 많이 발생하죠. 우리는 이러한 실수에 대비해서 비어있는 방을 몇 개 남겨둔답니다. 학생이 *Victoria Hall*에 있는 다른 방으로 옮기는 것이 싫지 않으면, 1인실을 드리겠어요. 추가 비용 없이 혼자만의 공간이 생기는 것이죠. 어떻게 생각하세요?

M: 복권에 당첨된 기분이네요.

W: 그러실 줄 알았어요. 그러면, 학생의 방을 변경 하도록 할게요. 몇 분 정도 걸릴 거예요. 그리고 나서, 학생은 방으로 돌아가서 짐을 가지고 나온 뒤, 새 방으로 옮기면 되겠군요.

Script

| 04-03 |

M Professor: Today, I'd like to examine an ocean ecosystem, so I've selected South Georgia Island for us to study. South Georgia Island is located deep in the South Atlantic Ocean near South America and north of Antarctica. It's a rugged land of mountains and harbor inlets and has some of the wildest weather in the world. It—the weather I mean—changes at an almost hourly rate. What makes South Georgia Island special is its diverse marine animal life. In fact, when many species there are mating, the island has more marine mammals and birds than, uh, than any other place in the world.

The bulk of these animals are penguins, elephant seals, and fur seals. Tens of thousands of them live there, and tens of thousands more migrate there to breed. Some scientists estimate that perhaps 300,000 penguins reside in just one area around the island during their mating season. And it's not just on land that massive numbers of animals may be found. The cold waters around South Georgia Island are also teeming with life. Large numbers of whales—but not as many as in years past—make the area their home. One reason there are fewer whales there now is that, for almost a century, South Georgia was the site of one of the largest whaling and sealing operations in history. For most of the nineteenth century and parts of the early twentieth century, seals and whales were killed there in record numbers. Most tragically, blue whales were massacred almost to extinction. Although some whale species and seal populations have rebounded, the blue whale is still struggling to increase its numbers.

I'm sure you're all wondering what makes South Georgia Island so special that all these animals live there, right? Well, first, it's far enough north of Antarctica that sea ice doesn't form around it in winter. As a result, its waters are open all year round. Having open water is necessary for seals and penguins to be able to swim and feed and for whales to be able to surface to breathe. But, more important is that the area around the island has an important food source for all these animals. I'm talking about krill, which is a small marine creature eaten by many animals. It's a, uh, a type of crustacean that resembles a small shrimp. It's found all around the world, but it thrives in nutrient-rich cold waters. South Georgia Island is in a unique position as far as krill goes. Cold currents from Antarctica bring huge masses of krill there. [11]**So the waters around South Georgia have one of the highest krill densities anywhere. Here's an interesting tidbit for you: It's estimated that the mass of all the krill in the waters surrounding Antarctica is greater than the combined mass of every human on Earth. Ponder that for a moment . . .**

Krill is a crucial part of the ocean ecosystem. It feeds on another small species called phytoplankton, and the krill, in turn, gets consumed by larger animals such as whales, seals, and penguins. In addition, fish that marine mammals and birds eat consume krill. Yet scientists have noticed a disturbing trend in recent years. In some seasons, the amount of krill is not as high as it was before. This occurred in both 2004 and 2009. Some believe there's a cycle and that the long-term effects are negligible. But others think that this is an issue we should be concerned about. You see, krill go through several life stages, one of which is the larva stage. They're often born under the ice shelves in Antarctica, which reach out far into the ocean. Under the ice, krill larvae have time to mature since they don't get consumed by predators there. When the larvae mature, they emerge from the ice shelves and are carried by the currents to South Georgia Island and other places. But, in recent years, large portions of the ice shelf have been disappearing. This is making it harder for large numbers of krill larvae to reach the adult stage.

W Student: Professor, is this because of global warming?

M: We're not sure about that. You see, the overall amount of ice in Antarctica is actually, uh, increasing. But, in some places, it's not growing but is simply disappearing. In the area called the Antarctica Peninsula, large amounts of ice are vanishing. Take a look at the map up here on the wall . . . Here's the peninsula . . . And here's South Georgia Island almost due north of it . . . Get the connection . . . ? In this particular area, there's less surface ice than there was before. Of course, in other areas of Antarctica, such as here . . . here . . . and here . . . the amount of ice is increasing. What's probably going to happen is something that has been occurring for thousands—no, millions—of years: Species will have to adapt to the changes in their environment. Those that can will survive. Those that can't, uh, won't.

Translation

M Professor: 오늘은, 해양 생태계에 대해서 알아보도록 할 텐데요. 오늘의 수업을 위해서 남 조지아 섬을 선택해 보았습니다. 남 조지아 섬은 남아메리카와 남극대륙의 북쪽 지역 사이 남대서양의 한 가운데에 위치해 있습니다. 이 섬의 지형은 산이 많고 바위투성이고, 만이 형성되어 있으며, 섬의 기상 상황은 전세계에서 가장 험난합니다. 기상 상황이 거의 한 시간마다 변화할 정도죠. 남 조지아섬이 특별한 이유는 이 섬에 다양한 해양 동물이 살고 있기 때문입니다. 실제로, 짝짓기를 할 때가 되면, 이 섬에는 바다 포유 동물과 조류가, 음, 전 세계 어느 지역보다도 더 많아집니다.

대부분의 이러한 동물들은 펭귄, 바다 코끼리, 그리고 물개입니다. 수십만 마리의 동물들이 이곳에 살고 있으며, 또 다른 수십만 마리의 동물들이 이곳으로 새끼를 낳기 위해 모여듭니다. 몇몇 과학자들은, 짝짓기 시기 동안, 이 섬의 한 지역에 대략 300,000마리의 펭귄이 서식하는 것으로 추정하고 있습니다. 수많은 동물들이 발견되는 지역은 육지뿐만이 아닙니다. 남 조지아 섬 인근의 차가운 바닷물 속에도 생명체가 매우 많습니다. 이 지역에 서식하는 고래의 수가 상당히 적은 이유는, 100년 정도의 기간 동안 남 조지아 섬에서 고래잡이와 바다표범잡이가 역사상 가장 성행했기 때문이죠. 19세기 대부분의 기간과 20세기 초반에 바다표범과 고래는 기록적인 수치를 보이며 죽었습니다. 가장 끔찍한 것은, 대왕고래가 거의 멸종할 정도로 죽었다는 사실이죠. 몇몇 고래와 바다표범의 수가 회복되기는 했지만, 대왕고래의 수는 여전히 증가하지 않고 있습니다.

여러분들은 모두 남 조지아 섬의 어떤 특별한 점 때문에 이러한 동물들이 그 곳에서 서식하는지 궁금해할 것입니다, 그렇죠? 음, 우선, 이 섬은 남극대륙에서 멀리 떨어져 있기 때문에, 겨울에도 바다가 얼지 않습니다. 그렇기 때문에, 이 지역의 바다는 일년 내내 녹아있는 상태죠. 개빙 구역(떠다니는 얼음이 수면의 10분의 1 이하인 지역)이 있기 때문에 바다표범과 펭귄이 수영을 하며 먹이를 구할 수 있고, 고래들도 수면에 나와 호흡을 할 수 있습니다. 하지만, 이 섬의 주변 지역에는 모든 동물들에게 중요한 식량 자원이 있다는 사실이 더 중요합니다. 많은 동물들의 먹이가 되는 작은 바다 생물인 크릴에 대해서 이야기 해보도록 하죠. 크릴은, 음, 작은 새우처럼 생긴 갑각류 입니다. 이것은 전 세계에서 찾아볼 수 있지만, 양분이 풍부한 냉수해 지역에서 잘 자랍니다. 남 조지아 섬은 크릴에게는 이상적인 장소죠. 남극대륙에 흘러 들어오는 한류와 함께 엄청난 양의 크릴이 이 지역으로 이동해 옵니다. 그래서 남 조지아 섬 주변의 바다에는 어떤 지역보다도 크릴이 더 많이 살고 있습니다. 여러분들이 흥미를 가질만한 이야기가 있습니다: 남극대륙 주변에 서식하는 크릴의 수가 지구상의 인류를 모두 합한 수 보다 더 많다고 합니다. 잠시 생각을 해 보세요…

크릴은 해양 생태계에 있어서 중요합니다. 크릴은 플랑크톤이라는 작은 종을 먹고 살며, 그리고 나서, 고래, 바다표범, 그리고 펭귄과 같은 자신보다 더 큰 동물들에게 잡아 먹힙니다. 게다가, 해양 포유류와 조류들의 먹이가 되는 물고기들이 크릴을 먹습니다. 하지만, 과학자들은 최근 몇 년 동안 불안한 경향을 감지해왔습니다. 어떤 해에는, 크릴의 개체수가 예전만큼 풍부하지 않았던 것이죠. 2004년과 2009년에 그러했습니다. 몇몇 과학자들은 이러한 현상이 단지 주기적인 것이며 그 장기적인 영향은 무시해도 좋다고 생각하고 있습니다. 하지만 다른 과학자들은 이러한 현상을 우리가 걱정해야만 하는 문제라고 생각합니다. 그러니까, 크릴은 여러 생애 단계를 거치는데, 유충 단계가 그 중 하나입니다. 이들은 남극 대륙의 빙붕(빙상의 가장자리가 바다에 돌출되어 떠 있는 부분)의 아래에서 태어나는데 이는 해양의 멀리 떨어진 곳에 있습니다. 얼음 아래에서, 크릴의 유충들은 포식자들에게 잡아 먹히지 않기 때문에 완전히 성장할 수 있습니다. 유충이 완전히 성장하면, 이들은 빙붕에서 나와 해류를 타고 남 조지아 섬 및 다른 지역들로 이동합니다. 하지만, 최근 몇 년 동안, 많은 빙붕이 사라지고 있습니다. 이 때문에 많은 수의 크릴들이 유충 단계에서 완전히 성장하는데 어려움을 겪고 있는 것이죠.

W Student: 교수님, 그러한 현상은 지구 온난화 때문인가요?

M: 확신할 수는 없습니다. 그러니까, 남극대륙의 얼음의 양은 실제로, 음, 증가하는 추세입니다. 하지만, 몇몇 지역에서는, 얼음이 천천히 사라지고 있어요. 남극 반도라 불리는 지역에서는, 많은 양의 얼음이 사라지고 있죠. 벽에 있는 지도를 보세요… 이곳이 남극 반도예요… 그리고 이곳이 남극대륙의 거의 정북방향에 위치한 조지아 섬 이고요… 연관성을 이해할 수 있겠지요…? 이 특정한 지역에서, 수면의 얼음이 예전보다 줄어들었어요. 물론, 이쪽 지역과 같은 남극대륙의 다른 곳에서는… 여기… 그리고 여기… 얼음의 양이 증가하고 있죠. 이러한 현상은 아마도 수천, 아니 수백만 년 동안 계속해서 일어날 것입니다: 생물들은 환경의 변화에 적응해야만 하겠죠. 그렇지 못한 종들은, 음, 살아남지 못할 것이고요.

Actual Test 05

Reading Section p.57

Answers

1. C [Vocabulary Question]
2. B [Inference Question]
3. B [Sentence Simplification Question]
4. A [Factual Question]
5. A [Vocabulary Question]
6. C [Factual Question]
7. C [Vocabulary Question]
8. D [Reference Question]
9. D [Rhetorical Purpose Question]
10. B [Factual Question]
11. C [Vocabulary Question]
12. A [Rhetorical Purpose Question]
13.

	Type of Guitar
Electric Guitar	A, C, F
Acoustic Guitar	D, E

[Fill in a Table Question]

Translation

전자기타

전자기타는 로큰롤 뿐만 아니라 다른 여러 음악 장르에서 가장 흔히 사용되는 악기이다. 이 악기는 어쿠스틱 기타에 기초하고 있지만, 전기에 의해 작동되며, 증폭 장치에 의해 소리가 증폭된 후 스피커를 통해서 소리를 낸다. 이로 인하여 전자 기타는 어쿠스틱 기타에 비해 더 큰 소리를 낼 수 있다. 지난 수십 년 동안, 전자 기타는 성능을 향상시키고, 더 다양한 기타를 만들기 위해 꾸준히 변화되었지만, 1930년대와 1940년대에 미국에서 처음으로 개발된 이래로, 기본적인 특징은 크게 변화하지 않았다.

몇 가지 확연한 차이점을 제외하면, 전자 기타는 일반적인 기타와 비슷하다. 첫째로, 전자 기타는, 몸통의 가운데가 비어있지는 않지만, 어쿠스틱 기타처럼 솔리드 바디 형태를 가지고 있다. 전자 기타의 몸통에는 텅 빈 부분이 없어서 음향 집음이 필요하기 때문에, 전기선을 사용해서 기타를 증폭기와 스피커에 연결한다. 음향 집음은 소리를 내기 위해서 필요한데, 집음 과정을 통해 기타 줄의 진동이 앰프에 전달되는 신호로 변화되어, 이로써 신호가 증폭되고 스피커를 통해 소리가 전달된다. 연구와 실험을 통해서, 전자 기타는 음질 및 증폭의 측면에서 향상되었고, 기타에 장착된 장비들이나 바닥에 있는 음향 페달과 같은 외부 장치를 통해 음향 효과를 만들어낼 수 있게 되었다.

역사적으로, 전자 기타는 전적으로 미국의 발명품이다. 조지 뷰챔프가 1931년 최초의 상업적인 전자 기타를 발명한 것으로 인정을 받고 있다. 그가 발명한 기타의 별칭은 "프라이팬" 이었는데, 그 모양이 마치 조리 기구처럼 생겼기 때문이었다. 뷰챔프는 하와이 음악을 연주했던 음악인이었는데, 하와이 음악은 당시에 매우 인기가 좋았다. 당시 거의 모든 하와이 음악들은 어쿠스틱 무릎 철강 기타로 연주되었는데, 이 기타는 연주자의 무릎이나 받침대에 올려져서 연주되었다는 점 이외에는 일반적인 기타와 같은 형태였다. 기타 연주자는 피크를 이용하여 오른손으로 기타 줄을 튕기고, 음정을 변화시키기 위해 왼손으로는 금속관을 사용하여 기타의 목 부분에 있는 줄을 문질렀다. 이러한 개념으로부터, 뷰챔프는 현의 진동을 증폭기에 전달하는 금속 무릎 기타의 자기 음향 집음 원리를 발전시킬 아이디어를 떠올렸는데, 이를 이용하여 스피커에 전달되기 전에 소리를 향상시킬 수 있었다.

1932년, 뷰챔프와 제조업자였던 아돌프 리첸바커는 프라이팬 기타를 생산하기 위해서 회사를 설립했다. 안타깝게도, 그들은 1937년 까지 뷰챔프의 발명에 대한 특허권을 획득하지 못했다. 그 사이에, 다른 발명가들과 회사들이 자신들만의 개조된 전자 기타를 만들기 위해서 애를 썼다. 그 후, 1940년, 레스 폴이 가장 인기 있는 전자기타를 만들었다. 다재다능한 어쿠스틱 기타 연주자였으며 컨츄리 가수였던 폴은 1930년대에 더 큰 소리를 내는 전자 기타에 관심을 갖게 되었다. 상업적인 판매에 있어서 만족할 만한 수준은 아니었지만, 폴은 "통나무"라고 불렸던 자신만의 전자 기타를 만들었다. 기본적으로, 이 기타는 기타 줄이 달려있는 긴 나무였으며, 음향 집음 장치가 모두 증폭기와 스피커에 연결되어 있었다. 마침내, 폴은 가운데 홈이 없는 기타의 몸통을 개발해냈고, 이로 인해서 로그 기타는 비로소 기타의 모습을 띄게 되었다. 기타가 제작되면서, 로그 기타는 최초의 솔리드 바디 전자기타가 되었다. 폴은 결국 깁슨 기타 회사에 자신이 발명한 기타를 판매했다. 로그 기타는 레스 폴 깁슨 이라고 불렸으며, 지금까지도 사상 최초의 고전적인 전자 기타로 인정 받고 있다.

전자 기타가 발명되었을 때, 이는 주로 하와이 음악의 연주에 사용되었고, 그 후, 재즈, 블루스, 그리고 로커빌리 음악의 연주에도 사용되었다. 그리고 나서, 1950년대 무렵, 전자 기타는 로큰롤 음악의 기초가 되었다. 초기의 로큰롤 음악은 컨츄리, 블루스, 그리고 로커빌리 음악의 영향을 받았다. 전자 기타가 없다면 로큰롤 음악이 존재할 수 없다고 말할 수는 없지만, 전자 기타 없는 로큰롤 음악은 상상하기 힘들다. 레스 폴과 다른 미국의 발명가였던 레오 펜더의 기타는 당시 로큰롤 음악의 표준이 되었다. 1950년대 이후, 대부분의 기타 제조업자들은 로큰롤 장르와 헤비메탈과 같은, 로큰롤에서 파생된 여러 장르에 적합한 제품들을 생산해 오고 있다.

Listening Section   p.63

Answers

1. B [Gist-Content Question]
2. D [Gist-Purpose Question]
3. C [Understanding Attitude Question]
4. A [Making Inferences Question]
5. B [Understanding Function Question]
6. A [Gist-Purpose Question]
7. B [Detail Question]
8. C [Detail Question]
9. A [Understanding Question]
10. D [Understanding Function Question]
11. C [Making Inferences Question]

Script

| 05-02 |

M1 Student: Professor Malkin, I just ran into my TA, uh, David Proctor, in the hall. He told me that you wanted to speak to me about something. So, uh, here I am.

M2 Professor: Ah, hi, Charles. I'm so glad you got here right now. I was getting ready to leave for the day, and I don't have any contact information for you.

M1: Oh, yeah. Sorry about that.

M2: Anyway, I wanted to speak with you about the paper you just turned in this morning.

M1: You've already got it graded? Wow. That's incredible. So, um, how'd I do on the paper?

M2: Actually, I don't have the papers graded yet. It would take an, uh, an incredibly superhuman effort to get forty papers graded in five hours you know.

M1: Yeah, right. So then . . .

M2: ⁵Well, I didn't grade the papers. But I did glance through all of them. It's a habit I've gotten into lately since, every semester, some students, uh . . . how should I say this . . . misinterpret my instructions on how to write their papers.

M1: Uh-oh.

M2: Yeah. Uh-oh.

M1: Um . . . How badly did I mess up?

M2: Not as badly as I've seen in the past. But you still pretty much failed to follow my precise instructions.

M1: Okay. Uh . . . Is there any way that I can, you know, rewrite my paper? Please?

M2: Of course, Charles. That's why I go over the papers as soon as I get them. I'm here to help students, not to give out low grades.

M1: Thank you so much.

M2: Oh, it's not that big of a deal. And you still have to resubmit your work . . . by this Friday.

M1: That's all right. That gives me three days. Okay, so let's get down to business. What did I do wrong, and how can I fix it?

M2: Good attitude, Charles.

M1: Thanks, Professor.

M2: All right. Now, here's your paper. Please notice that I mentioned that this was supposed to be a research paper, so . . . Yes?

M1: But I did research on it. I was in the library for three days getting the information I used to write this paper.

M2: Charles, I think I see how you misunderstood my instructions. When I said, "Write a research paper," I meant that you needed to include footnotes and a bibliography with your paper. You know, you need to cite all of your sources. I believe I mentioned in class that you had to have at least five different sources. You did hear that, didn't you?

M1: Yes, sir. I did. I just, er, wasn't sure what you meant by that.

M2: Charles, the next time you don't understand something that I say, either ask me in class right then and there or talk to me after class. Now, look . . . I know you might not want to ask me in front of the class. You might be embarrassed because you think that you're the only one who doesn't understand. But let me fill you in on something . . . If you don't know or understand something, chances are that a lot of other students feel the same way. They'll be thanking you—albeit silently—if you speak up and ask a question.

M1: Okay, Professor. I'll keep that in mind for the future.

Translation

M1 Student: *Malkin* 교수님, 제가, 음, 학과 건물에서 *David Proctor* 조교를 우연히 만났는데요. 교수님께서 저에게 하실 말씀이 있다고 해서요. 그래서, 음, 이렇게 찾아왔습니다.

M2 Professor: 아, 안녕, *Charles*. 이렇게 찾아와 줘서 반갑네요. 지금 막 퇴근 준비를 하던 참이었어요. 학생에 대해서 아무런 얘기도 듣지 못했거든요.

M1: 아, 예. 죄송합니다.

M2: 어쨌든, 학생이 오늘 아침에 제출한 보고서와 관련해서 이야기를 좀 나눌까 해서요.

M1: 벌써 성적을 매기셨나요? 와. 정말 놀랍군요. 그러면, 음, 제가 보고서를 잘 썼나요?

M2: 사실, 아직 보고서의 성적을 매기지는 않았어요. 5시간 동안 40편의 보고서의 성적을 매기려면, 음, 어, 엄청난 초인적인 노력이 필요하겠죠.

M1: 네, 그렇죠. 그러면 …

M2: 보고서에 성적을 매기지는 않았지만 대강 훑어보기는 했어요. 최근에 생긴 버릇인데, 매 학기마다, 몇몇 학생들이, 음… 어떻게 말을 해야 좋을지… 제가 보고서 작성 방법에 대해 설명한 것을 제대로 이해하지 못하는 것 같더군요.

M1: 아! 이런.

M2: 그래요. 아! 이런.

M1: 음… 제가 얼마나 엉망으로 쓴 것인가요?

M2: 예전에 보았던 보고서들만큼 나쁘지는 않아요. 하지만 학생은 제가 자세히 설명한대로 쓰지 않은 부분이 많더군요.

M1: 네. 음 … 무슨 방법이 없을까요. 그러니까, 제가 보고서를 다시 작성해도 될까요? 부탁 드려도 될까요?

M2: 물론이죠, Charles. 그래서 제가 보고서들을 받자 마자 한 번 훑어보는 거예요. 저는 학생들을 돕기 위해서 이 자리에 있는 것이지, 낮은 점수를 주려고 이 자리에 있는 것은 아니니까요.

M1: 정말 감사합니다.

M2: 아, 별 일도 아닌걸요. 그리고 학생이 보고서를 다시 제출해야 할 기한은… 이번 주 금요일까지예요.

M1: 상관 없습니다. 3일이나 여유가 있는걸요. 좋아요, 즉시 본격적으로 보고서 작성을 시작하겠습니다. 어느 부분이 잘못 되었고, 제가 어떻게 고칠 수 있을까요?

M2: 좋은 태도군요, Charles.

M1: 감사합니다, 교수님.

M2: 좋아요. 자, 여기 학생의 보고서가 있어요. 이 보고서는 연구 보고서가 되어야 한다고 말했던 것에 주목해야 해요. 그래서… 예?

M1: 하지만 저는 그것에 대해서 조사를 했는걸요. 이 보고서에 필요한 정보를 찾기 위해서 3일 동안 도서관에 있었어요.

M2: Charles, 학생이 내 설명을 왜 잘못 이해했는지 이제 알겠네요. 내가, "연구 보고서를 쓴다."라고 말한 것은 학생의 보고서에 각주와 참고 문헌 목록을 적어야 한다는 의미였어요. 사용한 자료의 출처를 모두 밝혀야 한다는 얘기죠. 제가 수업 시간에 최소한 다섯 가지 정도의 자료를 활용해야만 한다고 말했던 것으로 기억합니다. 분명히 들었죠?

M1: 네, 교수님. 들었습니다. 저는 단지, 어, 그것이 무슨 의미인지 확실히 못 알아들었던 것 같네요.

M2: 내 말이 이해가 되지 않으면, 수업 시간 중이나 수업이 끝나고 나서 내게 물어보도록 해요. 자, 그러니까… 학생은 아마도 다른 학생들 앞에서 질문하는 것을 원하지 않는군요. 학생 혼자만 이해하지 못했다고 생각해서 부끄러워하는 것 같아요. 하지만 학생에게 한 가지 알려줄 것이 있는데… 학생이 무엇인가를 이해하지 못하거나 모른다면, 다른 많은 학생들도 그럴 가능성이 높죠. 학생이 용기를 내어 질문을 한다면, 그러한 학생들이 말은 하지 않겠지만 고마워할 것 같아요.

M1: 네, 교수님. 앞으로는 명심하겠습니다.

Script

| 05-03 |

M Professor: After King Henry VII's death in 1509, his son Henry VIII became the king of England. Henry VIII is one of the most famous of all English rulers. His fame rests on two main things: his six wives and his break with the Catholic Church. Both are closely connected as it was his desire to end his first marriage and to marry his second wife that led to him splitting with the Church. From his six marriages, Henry VIII had three surviving legitimate children: Mary, Elizabeth, and Edward.

Like many kings, Henry had one overriding obsession: He required a male heir. His first marriage was to Catherine of Aragon, a princess from the Spanish court. There were a few, uh . . . complications for Henry to marry Catherine. First and foremost was that she had previously been married to Arthur, Henry's, um, older brother. Arthur died in 1502 after he'd only been married for seven days. The marriage had been intended to create an alliance between England and Spain. In fact, the Spanish encouraged Henry to marry Catherine to maintain the alliance. Yet, at that time, most people considered it bad luck and against the teachings of the Church for someone to marry his brother's wife. Eventually, a special papal bull . . . uh, that's a decree . . . was granted to permit the marriage, after which Henry and Catherine wed in 1509.

They had five children together, but four—two boys and two girls—died in infancy, something that was, sadly enough, common at the time. Only one child— their daughter Mary—reached adulthood. Yet Henry desired a male heir. He mostly wanted to avoid any claims on the throne by outsiders, something that had occurred before and had resulted in warfare between England's noble houses.

W Student: Um, Professor White, was it against the law for a woman to be the ruler of England?

M: Not at all. There was no such law, but Henry believed a female heir wouldn't have as, er, as legitimate a position as would a male heir. Now, Henry had his eye on many other women, including two sisters, Mary and Anne Boleyn. Henry may have had an affair with Mary Boleyn, but he ultimately chose Anne to be his next bride. [10]From 1525 to 1533, Henry tried to get either an annulment or a divorce from Catherine, but he failed. The reasons for this are somewhat complicated and relate to the pope and other key figures, and, well . . . uh, it's explained very well in your textbook. So, let's get back to our story. In 1533, Henry secretly married Anne Boleyn. Shortly afterward, he arranged to have an English archbishop—Thomas Cranmer was his name—annul his marriage to Catherine and legitimize his marriage to Anne.

The split from the Catholic Church was the result of this. Almost immediately, the pope excommunicated both Henry and Thomas Cranmer. Being excommunicated is basically like being banned from church. However, should the person, uh, see the error of his ways and be penitent, he can be allowed back into the church. Henry, however, was too strong willed to beg the pope for anything. Oh, yes, at the same time, the pope declared that Henry was still married to Catherine, so he annulled Henry's marriage to Anne. Anyway, none of that mattered to Henry since, over the next few years, a series of laws were enacted in England that made him the supreme head of the Church of England. This led to a complete split with the Catholic Church. But keep in mind that this was more of a power struggle with the pope and Rome than it was a dispute over religious doctrine.

Anyway, Henry's actions were all for naught since Anne failed to produce a male heir. She miscarried several male children and gave birth to Elizabeth. Henry eventually grew tired of Anne, so she was accused of treason and of having affairs with several men. The evidence was, uh, quite frankly, weak, but Henry had already acquired a new mistress, so Anne was executed in May 1536. Henry, not one to wait around, married his mistress, Jane Seymour, ten days later. Jane produced a male heir—Edward—in 1537, but she died from complications during the birth.

Henry went through a few more wives until he died in 1547, whereupon Edward succeeded him. Edward's rule was short. [11]**It was marked by the growth of Protestantism in England as well as attempts to, um, eradicate the Catholic Church from the country.** Edward, however, died in 1553 from an illness believed to be pneumonia or tuberculosis. He had no heir, so his older sister Mary became queen. **Does that answer your question, Cathy . . . ?** Mary was a devout Catholic who promptly began a restoration of the Catholic Church. She failed though, due both to popular resistance and to her own early death in 1558. Elizabeth then succeeded Mary to the throne. It was Elizabeth who ultimately fulfilled her father's wish for a strong monarch on the English throne. Let's talk about how she accomplished this.

Translation

M Professor: 1509년에 헨리 7세가 사망한 뒤, 그의 아들 헨리 8세가 잉글랜드의 왕이 되었습니다. 헨리 8세는 잉글랜드의 모든 통치자들 가운데 가장 유명합니다. 그는 두 가지 사실 때문에 유명하죠: 부인을 6명 두었으며 로마 가톨릭 교회와 단절했다는 사실 때문입니다. 두 사건은 서로 밀접한 연관성이 있는데, 그가 첫 번째 결혼을 파기하고 두 번째 부인을 맞이하고자 했던 사건 때문에 로마 가톨릭 교회와 단절하게 되었습니다. 헨리 8세는 6번의 결혼을 통해서 세 명의 적자를 얻었습니다: 메리, 엘리자베스, 그리고 에드워드가 그 세 명입니다.

다른 왕들과 마찬가지로, 헨리에게는 가장 우선적인 강박관념이 있었습니다: 그는 남자 후계자를 원했습니다. 그는 아라곤의 캐서린과 첫 번째 결혼을 했는데, 그녀는 스페인 왕가의 공주였죠. 헨리와 캐서린의 결혼에는, 음…몇 가지 복잡한 문제들이 있었습니다. 가장 중요한 문제는 그녀가, 음, 헨리의 형인 아더와 결혼을 했다는 사실입니다. 아더는 1502년에 사망했는데, 결혼한지 겨우 7일만이었죠. 그 결혼은 잉글랜드와 스페인 간의 동맹 관계를 위한 것이었어요. 실제로, 스페인은 동맹 관계를 유지하기 위해서 헨리와 캐서린을 결혼시키려고 했던 것이었죠. 하지만, 그 당시에, 대부분의 사람들은 이러한 사실을 불운이라 여겼고, 형수와의 결혼은 가톨릭의 가르침에 어긋난다고 생각했습니다. 결국, 1509년에 헨리와 캐서린이 결혼을 한 후, 혼인을 승낙한다는 교황의 인장… 음, 칙령이…내려졌습니다.

그들 사이에는 5명의 자식이 있었으나, 두 명의 아들과 두 명의 딸들은 아기였을 당시 사망했는데. 이는 슬픈 일이지만, 당시에는 흔한 일이었어요. 오직 한 명, 그들의 딸 메리 만이 장성했습니다. 하지만 헨리는 남자 후계자를 원했어요. 그는 외부 인물이 왕위 계승을 주장하는 것을 차단시키려고 했는데, 예전에도 이러한 일 때문에 잉글랜드의 귀족 가문들 사이에 전쟁이 일어났기 때문이었죠.

W Student: 음, White 교수님. 잉글랜드에서는 여성이 통치자가 되는 것을 법으로 금지하고 있었나요?

M: 그렇지는 않았어요. 그러한 법은 없었지만, 헨리는 여자 후계자에게는, 음, 남자 후계자와 동일한 수준의 정통성이 없다고 생각했어요. 그리고 나서, 헨리는 다른 여자들에게 눈을 돌리기 시작했는데, 두 자매였던, 메리와 앤 볼린이 그들이었죠. 헨리는 메리 볼린과 과거가 있었지만, 그는 결국 두 번째 부인으로 앤을 선택했어요. 1525년부터 1533년까지, 헨리는 캐서린과 이혼을 하거나 결혼을 취소하려고 애썼지만, 실패했죠. 그 이유는 다소 복잡하고 교황을 비롯하여 다른 주요 인물들과 관련이 있는데, 그리고, 음… 어, 여러분들의 교과서에 설명이 잘 되어 있습니다. 그러니, 하던 이야기로 되돌아 갑시다. 1533년, 헨리는 앤 볼린과 비밀리에 혼인을 하게 됩니다. 혼인 후 얼마 지나지 않아서, 헨리는 잉글랜드의 대주교 토마스 크랜머가 캐서린과의 결혼을 무효화하고 앤과의 결혼을 인정해 주도록 일을 꾸몄습니다.

로마 가톨릭 교회와의 단절은 바로 이 사건 때문이었습니다. 이 사건 직후에, 교황은 헨리와 토마스 크랜머를 파문했습니다. 파문을 당한다는 것은 기본적으로 교회와의 단절을 의미합니다. 그러나, 파문을 당했던 사람이, 음, 자신의 과오를 뉘우치면 다시 교회에 속할 수 있었습니다. 하지만, 헨리는 자신의 의지가 워낙 확고해서 교황에게 고개를 숙이지 않았어요. 오, 그래요, 동시에, 교황은 헨리와 캐서린의 혼인 상태가 여전히 유효하다고 선언하면서, 헨리와 앤의 결혼을 무효화했죠. 어쨌든, 이러한 사건들은 헨리에게 문제가 될 것이 없었는데, 그 후로 몇 년 동안, 헨리를 영국 국교회의 수장으로 정하는 여러 법안이 제정되었기 때문이었어요. 이로 인하여 로마 가톨릭 교회와는 완전히 단절하게 되었음은 물론이고요. 그러나 이 사건은 종교적인 교리를 주제로 한 논쟁이라기 보다는 교황과 로마에 맞선 권력 투쟁의 성격이 더 강했음을 기억해 주시기 바래요.

어쨌든, 이러한 헨리의 행동은 아무런 소득이 없었는데, 앤이 남자 후계자를 낳지 못했기 때문이었죠. 그녀는 여러 명의 남자 아이를 유산한 끝에 엘리자베스를 낳았습니다. 헨리는 결국 앤에게 지쳐버려서, 그녀에게 반역과 불륜의 죄를 덮어 씌웠습니다. 이 죄목에 대해서는, 음, 솔직히 말해서, 근거가 부족했지만, 헨리는 이미 새 정부를 두고 있었기 때문에, 1536년 5월에 앤을 처형했습니다. 헨리는, 주저하지 않는 성격이었기 때문에, 앤을 처형한지 불과 열흘이 후에, 그의 정부, 제인 세이무어와 결혼을 했습니다. 제인은 1537년에 남자 후계자인 에드워드를 낳았지만, 출산의 합병증으로 인해 사망했습니다.

헨리는 1547년 사망하기 전까지 몇 명의 부인을 더 얻었고, 에드워드가 헨리를 계승했습니다. 이 시기는 영국 개신교의 성장기였던 동시에, 음, 잉글랜드와 로마 가톨릭 교회 사이의 관계를 완전히 근절하려 했던 시기이기도 했습니다. 하지만, 에드워드는 폐렴과 결핵으로 인해 1553년에 사망하게 됩니다. 그에게는 왕위 계승자가 없었기 때문에, 장녀였던 메리가 여왕이 되었죠. 질문에 대한 답변이 됐나요, Cathy…? 메리는 즉시 로마 가톨릭 교회와의 관계 복원을 시도했던 독실한 가톨릭 신자였습니다. 하지만 그녀는 결국 실패했는데, 민중의 반란이 한 가지 이유였고, 1558년에 그녀가 일찍 사망했던 것이 두 번째 이유였습니다. 그 후 엘리자베스가 메리의 뒤를 이어 권좌에 올랐죠. 잉글랜드에 강력한 왕권을 확립하려 했던 자신의 아버지의 열망을 마침내 충족시켰던 인물이 바로 엘리자베스였습니다. 그녀가 어떻게 이를 성취할 수 있었는지에 대해서 이야기 해보도록 하죠.

Actual Test 06

Reading Section p.69

Answers

1. Ⓑ [Vocabulary Question]
2. Ⓒ [Vocabulary Question]
3. Ⓒ [Factual Question]
4. Ⓓ [Rhetorical Purpose Question]
5. Ⓓ [Sentence Simplification Question]
6. Ⓑ [Negative Factual Question]
7. Ⓒ [Factual Question]
8. Ⓒ [Inference Question]
9. Ⓐ [Factual Question]
10. Ⓓ [Vocabulary Question]
11. Ⓑ [Factual Question]
12. Ⓓ [Inference Question]
13. 2nd [Insert Text Question]
14. Ⓒ, Ⓓ, Ⓔ [Prose Summary]

Translation

하드자 부족

인류가 처음 진화했을 때, 그들은 주변의 동·식물 덕분에 생존할 수 있는 수렵 채집자였다. 그 후, 약 10,000년 전, 인류는 농업과 가축 사육 방법을 알아냈다. 이때에, 오늘날까지 존재하고 있는 문명이 탄생하게 된 것이다. 하지만, 지구상의 몇몇 오지에는, 여전히 현대 문명의 혜택을 누리지 않고 살아가는 소수 집단들이 있다. 탄자니아의 하드자 부족이 바로 이러한 집단이다. 그들은 농사를 짓지 않으며, 영구적인 거주지도 없고, 가지고 다닐 수 있는 것 이상의 소유물도 없다. 그들은 사실상 석기시대에 살고 있는 것과 마찬가지로, 수렵 채집한 것들만 먹는다.

하드자 부족은 아프리카 동부의 탄자니아 북쪽 지역에 살고 있는데, 이 지역은 음불루 고원과 에야시 호수의 해안 사이에 위치한 혹독하고, 건조한 평원 지대이다. 하드자 부족의 많은 사람들은 현대 세계에 동화되었지만, 대략 1,000명 정도의 사람들이 여전히 전통적인 방식을 따르고 있다. 그들은 30명을 넘지 않는 소규모 집단생활을 하는데, 구성원들의 대부분은 친족 관계이다. 하지만, 집단은 유동적인데, 사람들은 원할 때 집단에 소속되었다가 탈퇴할 수 있고, 다른 집단에 속하고 싶을 때에는 마음대로 이동할 수 있으며, 우연히 발견한 집단에서 먹고 자는 경우가 많기 때문이다. 갈등이 생기면, 관련된 한 집단이나 두 집단 모두가 갈라져서 새로운 집단을 형성한다. 이렇게 해서, 하드자 부족은 전쟁과 내부적인 갈등을 피해 왔다. 인구 밀도가 상당히 낮기 때문에, 하드자 부족은 대규모의 전염병에 감염되는 것을 피할 수 있었다.

대부분의 다른 사회와 마찬가지로, 하드자 부족의 가족은 아버지, 어머니, 그리고 아이들로 구성된다. 하드자 부족에게는 결혼이라는 개념이 없고, 남자와 여자가 서로에게 이끌리면, 곧바로 부부가 된다. 그들은 평생 함께 살면서 아이들을 키우기도 하며, 다른 짝을 찾아서 헤어지기도 한다. 헤어지는데 있어서 중요한 역할을 하는 것은 여성인데, 여성들은 사냥을 더 잘하여, 식량을 잘 구할 수 있는 남성을 찾는 경우가 많기 때문이다. (이러한 점 때문에, 대부분의 부족 남성들은 여성에게 자신의 잠재적인 가치를 보여주기 위하여 열심히 일을 한다.) 일반적으로, 하드자 부족의 남성들은 사냥을 하며, 여성들은 주로 과일이나 먹을 수 있는 식물을 채집한다. 하지만, 하드자 부족에는 지도자나 권력자가 없으며, 남성이 여성보다 우월한 위치에 있어야 한다는 개념도 없다. 몇몇 하드자 부족의 여성은 다른 집단 – 대개 다른 탄자니아인 부족의 – 남성과 결혼을 하는 경우도 있지만, 대부분의 여성은, 그들을 지배하려는 다른 아프리카 부족의 남성들의 대우를 견디지 못하고, 몇 년 후 되돌아 온다.

하드자 부족은 외부 세계에 거의 알려져 있지 않다. 그 결과, 그들 대부분은 자신들의 방언을 사용하고, 몇몇은 스와힐리어를 사용하지만, 아프리카 언어 이외의 언어를 구사할 수 있을 정도로 교육받은 사람은 거의 없다. 이 때문에 인류학자들은 이들을 연구하는데 어려움을 겪는데, 그들의 말을 해석하는 것도 어렵지만, 외부인들이 그들과 함께 생활할 수 있도록 하드자 부족을 설득하는 것도 쉽지 않기 때문이다. 이러한 만남을 준비하는 과정 조차도 쉽지 않은데, 하드자 부족은 대부분 자신들의 나이도 모르며, 다른 세상의 사람들과 달리 시간에 대해서도 신경을 쓰지 않기 때문이다. 하지만, 하드자 부족은 현대적인 옷을 입고, 도끼와 칼과 같은 금속 도구를 사용하며, 금속 냄비를 이용하여 음식을 만드는 등, 현대 문명에 완전혀 적응하고 있다. 그러나 이러한 것들을 제외하면, 그들은 기술적으로 진보한 문명을 전혀 활용하지 않는다. 예를 들면, 하드자 부족에게는 걸어 다니는 것 이외의 어떠한 교통 수단도 없으며, 일하는데 사용되는 기계도 없고, 영구적인 주거 시설도 없다. 그들은 필요할 때 이동하며, 배가 고플 때 사냥이나 채집을 하고, 대부분의 남는 시간은 유유자적하며 보낸다.

인류학자들은 하드자 부족에 큰 관심을 가지고 있다; 그들의 생활양식은 초기 인류의 생활양식과 비슷하기 때문에, 그들과 초기 인류 사이에 연관성이 있다고 생각한다. 하드자 부족이 거주하는 혹독한 환경은, 그들이 수십만 년 동안 비교적 평화롭게 살아올 수 있었던 이유가 된다. 토양은 농사를 지을 수 없을 정도로 척박하고, 깨끗한 물도 거의 없으며, 걷기는 6개월이나 지속된다. 하지만, 탄자니아의 인구가 증가하면서, 사람들이 하드자 부족의 영토를 침범하고 있어서, 이 지역에 거주하는 하드자 부족민의 수는 60년 전과 비교하면 4분의 1수준이다. 아마도 언젠가는, 하드자 부족의 생활양식이 사라지게 될 것이다.

Listening Section   p.75

Answers

1. Ⓐ [Gist-Purpose Question]
2. Ⓒ [Detail Question]
3. Ⓓ [Understanding Function Question]
4. Ⓒ [Making Inferences Question]
5. Ⓐ [Understanding Attitude Question]
6. Ⓐ [Gist-Content Question]
7. Ⓒ [Gist-Purpose Question]
8. Ⓑ [Detail Question]
9.

	Before	After
Ⓐ	X	
Ⓑ		X
Ⓒ		X
Ⓓ	X	

[Connecting Content Question]

10. Ⓓ [Understanding Attitude Question]
11. Ⓐ [Understanding Function Question]

Script

| 06-02 |

M Librarian: Good evening. You're going to check out all five of these books, right?

W Student: I sure am. Uh, wait a minute. That's not going to be a problem, is it? I mean, um, we're allowed to check out five books at once, aren't we?

M: Absolutely. Actually, the computer system permits you to check out more than one hundred books. I think the number is somewhere around 150, but I can't recall exactly.

W: Are you serious?

M: Sure. But the only people whom I've ever seen with even close to a hundred books checked out are graduate students. And I've only seen that a couple of times. Anyway, so, may I see your ID card, please?

W: Sure . . . Here you are.

M: Thank you very much. Let me just scan it into the computer, and . . . hmm . . .

W: Hmm? What do you mean by that?

M: There seems to be some kind of problem with your file.

W: Oh yeah? That's weird. Do you know what it is?

M: Not yet, but let me take a closer look here for a second . . . I've been working at the library for a couple of years, so I can figure out what most of the usual problems are.

W: You're not a regular employee?

M: Not at all. I'm a graduate student. Uh, I'm actually one of those graduate students with more than a hundred books checked out.

W: Nice one. So, uh, about my books?

M: Yeah, right. Okay, it seems that you have an unpaid fine from a book that you returned late last semester. Since you didn't pay the fine during the break, a lock has been put on your account until you pay it off.

W: A fine? That's odd. I thought that I had taken care of renewing all of my books.

M: I don't know. I guess you must have missed one.

W: Well, okay. Those things happen. So how much is it? I don't know if I've got enough money on me to pay it off right now though. I sure hope I don't owe too much.

M: ⁵I don't think you'll have too much of a problem with this fine. You owe a grand total of . . . one dollar and twenty-five cents.

W: Get out of here.

M: Seriously. You can take a look at the screen right here . . . See. It's for the book *Psychology and You*, which you apparently turned in five days too late last December.

W: Oh, I remember that book. I even knew that I owed money on it. I really meant to pay the fine sometime before I went home for the semester. I guess it must have slipped my mind though.

M: So, do you want to pay it off right now? If you do, you'll be able to check out these books once I clear the fine from your account.

W: That sounds perfect to me. I've got the money right here. Here you go . . . Okay, so I can take these books with me now, right?

M: Yeah. Totally. Just give me a couple of minutes, and I will have everything all taken care of for you.

Translation

M Librarian: 안녕하세요. 책 다섯 권 모두 대출하려는 것 맞죠?

W Student: 네, 맞아요. 음, 잠시만요. 별 문제될 것 없겠지요? 제 말은, 음, 한 번에 다섯 권의 책을 빌리는 것이 가능한 것 같은데, 맞죠?

M: 물론이죠. 사실은, 컴퓨터 시스템 덕분에 학생은 백 권 이상의 책을 빌려갈 수도 있어요. 제 생각에는 150권 정도의 책도 가능할 것 같은데, 정확한 수는 기억이 나지 않는군요.

W: 정말인가요?

M: 그럼요. 하지만 백 권 가까이 대여했던 학생들은 대학원생들 밖에 없어요. 그러한 경우가 두 세 번 정도 있었던 것 같군요. 그건 그렇고, 자, 학생증 좀 보여주시겠어요?

W: 네… 여기 있습니다.

M: 감사합니다. 컴퓨터에서 검색을 좀 해보도록 할게요, 그런데… 흠…

W: 흠? 왜 그러세요?

M: 학생의 자료에 문제가 조금 있는 것 같아서요.

W: 예? 이상한데요. 무슨 문제인지 아시겠어요?

M: 아직 잘 모르겠지만, 조금 더 자세히 살펴보도록 할게요… 제가 이 도서관에서 근무한지 2년 정도 되어서, 통상적인 문제들은 거의 다 해결할 수 있어요.

W: 정식 직원이 아니신가요?

M: 물론 아니죠. 저는 대학원생이에요. 음, 사실은 제가 백 권 이상의 책을 대여했던 그 대학원생들 중 한 명이랍니다.

W: 훌륭하시군요. 그러면, 음, 제 책은요?

M: 네, 됐어요. 이제 알겠네요. 학생이 지난 학기 말에 반납했던 책에 부과된 연체료를 납부하지 않은 것 같네요. 방학 동안에 이 연체료를 납부하지 않아서, 완료될 때까지 학생의 계정을 막아둔 것 같아요.

W: 연체료라고요? 말도 안돼요. 저는 대출했던 책들의 기한 연장에 상당히 신경을 많이 썼는데요.

M: 저야 잘 모르지요. 아마도 한 권에 대해서는 신경을 못썼던 것 같군요.

W: 음, 알겠습니다. 그랬군요. 그러면, 연체료가 얼마예요? 지금 바로 연체료를 납부할 수 있을 만큼 저에게 돈이 있는지 모르겠네요. 액수가 너무 크지 않았으면 좋겠어요.

M: 연체료가 그렇게까지 큰 부담이 되지는 않을 것 같아요. 연체료는 다 해서… 1달러 25센트 입니다.

W: 장난치지 마세요.

M: 정말이에요. 여기 화면에서 확인하실 수 있어요… 보세요. *심리학과 당신*이라는 책이 있는데, 학생이 이 책을 12월 말에 분명히 5일 늦게 반납했네요.

W: 아, 이 책 기억나네요. 이 책에 부과된 연체료에 대해서도 알겠어요. 집에 돌아가기 전, 학기 중에 이 연체료를 납부하기로 되어있었어요. 잊어버렸던 것 같기는 하지만요.

M: 그러면, 지금 바로 납부 하시겠어요? 그렇게 하시면, 제가 학생의 계정에 등록된 연체료 정보를 지우고 난 후, 이 책들을 대출해 드릴 수 있어요.

W: 정말 잘 됐군요. 그 정도의 돈은 지금 가지고 있어요. 여기 있습니다… 됐네요. 이제 이 책들을 가져가도 되죠, 그렇죠?

M: 네. 물론이죠. 잠깐만 기다려 주세요. 그러면 제가 처리해 드릴게요.

Script

| 06-03 |

W Professor: Now that we've gone over the physical characteristics and habits of wolves, I'd like to discuss one particularly controversial issue concerning them. I'm referring to the reintroduction of wolves into Yellowstone National Park during the mid-1990s. As I mentioned earlier, by the 1930s, virtually all of the wolves in the U.S. had been killed. There were only a few living in, um, Minnesota and Michigan. Most of them were killed by people who feared that the wolves would eat their livestock and attack humans. This was erroneous thinking since, well, those actions aren't in a wolf's nature. Yes, wolves will kill livestock when it's available, but they prefer to hunt wild game. Also, they rarely attack humans. Basically, wolves have a bad reputation that's not entirely deserved.

Nevertheless, that didn't stop most wolves in the country from being eliminated. Then, in the 1980s, a few wolves crossed the border from Canada and wandered into Montana and Idaho in the northwest part of the country. Those wolves bred, and their babies formed new packs. Soon, their numbers slowly began growing. Then, in 1995, the government took the controversial step of introducing several pairs of wolves into Yellowstone National Park in Wyoming. These wolves, which had been captured in Canada, established new packs. The packs expanded, so today there are around . . . hmm, about 1,600 or so wolves in the U.S., mostly in Wyoming, Montana, and Idaho.

The government reintroduced the wolves for two main reasons. First, naturalists wanted an opportunity to study them more closely and to see how they'd adapt to a new environment. Second, the absence of wolves from Yellowstone for several decades had a clear effect on the park's ecology. The biggest one was the growing elk population. Many wolves hunt elk as a primary food source. An elk is like a deer yet is often much bigger. In Yellowstone, the large elk populations ate the grasses, small shrubs, and trees that grew near streams. This let the steams' waters spread out, so they became both broader and shallower. The waters also became warmer due to a lack of shade from overhanging trees. As a result, many of the fish populations in the streams died. This negatively affected animals that depended on fish as a source of food. The elk also ate new sprouts of aspen trees, thereby preventing these trees from growing to full height. And, finally, the number of coyotes began to grow out of hand since wolves were not around to compete with them for food. Now do you see how a single animal's presence—or absence in this case—can affect an entire ecosystem?

However, since 1995, there has been a great change. Let's see . . . With wolves in the park, the elk population has been brought under control. The streams are narrower, deeper, and full of fish, birds, and beavers. More aspen trees are growing to maturity. There are fewer coyotes. And, finally, the wolves help supply other animals with food since wolves simply leave a dead animal where it is once they've eaten their fill. Other animals, such as eagles and bears, then usually consume the remains of the dead animals after the wolves leave.

M Student: [10]Professor Logan, I thought you said that the move was controversial. **But, um, it sounds to me like the wolves have been good for the area. Is that not true?**

W: You're right on both counts, Josh. In fact, there are estimates that tourists are spending an additional $35 million a year to visit Yellowstone just to see the wolves. But there really is a controversy. It comes mostly in the form of protests by locals. First, they believe the wolves pose a danger to their livestock and children. But these worries are mostly unfounded. For example, out of all the sheep that died in the area two years ago, a mere, uh, one percent were killed by wolves. And there have been no reported cases of wolves attacking humans. It's my opinion that these protests were covers for the locals' main concern: hunting. Many locals are avid outdoorsmen and love hunting. Now that they have to compete with the wolves for elk, many have become upset.

So, because of the protests and the growing wolf population, the government permits hunters to kill some wolves. Farmers have always had the right to kill wolves that are on their property or are attacking their livestock. [11]But now there's a wolf quota. Each year, a certain number of wolves—I think it's around 200—are killed. This helps control the population, and, in some ways, it's good for the wolves. **Uh, the ones that aren't killed, that is.** Every wolf pack has a territory, and it's within this territory that they find all of their food. If there are too many wolves, some will starve to death while others will get attacked by other wolves when they enter a new pack's territory in search of food. It's all about keeping a balance of nature. When animals don't do it, humans have to, uh, lend a helping hand.

Translation

W Professor: 지금까지 우리는 늑대의 신체적 특성과 습성에 대해서 알아보았는데요. 이제부터는 늑대와 관련하여 특히 논란이 되고 있는 한 가지 문제에 대해서 논의해볼까 합니다. 1990년대 중반에 옐로우스톤 국립 공원에 늑대를 다시 받아들였다는 사실을 이야기하는 것입니다. 앞서 말씀 드렸던 바와 같이, 1930년대에, 사실상 미국의 모든 늑대들이 죽었습니다. 겨우 몇 마리만, 음, 미네소타와 미시간 주에 살아 남아 있었죠. 대부분의 늑대들은, 이들이 가축을 잡아먹거나 사람을 공격하는 것을 두려워했던 사람들에 의해 죽었습니다. 이는 잘못된 생각인데, 음, 그러니까, 이러한 행동은 늑대의 습성이 아니기 때문이죠.

그렇습니다. 늑대는 가축이 주변에 있을 때에는 사냥을 하지만, 대개 야생 동물을 사냥하는 것을 더 좋아합니다. 또한, 이들은 사람을 공격하는 경우가 거의 없습니다. 기본적으로, 늑대는 받지 않아도 될 좋지 않은 평판을 받고 있는 것이죠.

그럼에도 불구하고, 미국의 늑대들은 계속해서 죽어 나갔습니다. 그 후, 1980년대, 몇몇 늑대들이 캐나다 국경을 지나서 미국의 북부 지역인 몬태나와 아이다호 지역으로 이동해 왔습니다. 이 늑대들이 새끼를 낳았고, 이들은 새로운 무리를 형성했죠. 곧, 그 수가 천천히 증가하기 시작했어요. 그리고 나서, 1995년, 정부는 몇 쌍의 늑대를 와이오밍 주의 옐로우스톤 국립공원으로 들여왔는데, 이는 논란을 일으켰습니다. 캐나다에서 붙잡힌 이 늑대들은 새로운 무리를 형성했습니다. 이 무리가 더 커져서, 오늘날에는… 음, 대략 1,600마리 정도의 늑대가 미국에 서식하고 있으며, 대부분이 와이오밍, 몬태나, 그리고 아이다호 지역에서 살고 있습니다.

정부가 늑대를 다시 들여왔던 데에는 두 가지 이유가 있습니다. 첫째로, 박물학자들이 늑대를 더 가까이에서 연구하고 싶어했고, 이들이 어떻게 새로운 환경에 적응하는지 알아보고자 했습니다. 둘째로, 수십 년 동안 옐로우스톤에 늑대가 없었다는 사실이 공원의 생태계에 분명히 영향을 주었던 것입니다. 가장 큰 영향은 엘크 개체수의 증가 였습니다. 많은 늑대들이 먹이로서 주로 엘크를 사냥합니다. 엘크는 사슴과 비슷하지만 훨씬 더 큽니다. 옐로우스톤에서, 수많은 엘크들은 풀, 작은 관목, 그리고 근처 시냇가에서 자라는 나무들을 뜯어 먹습니다. 이로 인하여 물이 옆으로 넓게 퍼져서, 시냇물의 폭이 넓어지고 깊이는 얕아지게 되었죠. 또한 시냇물을 뒤덮고 있던 나무의 그늘이 없어졌기 때문에, 수온이 상승하게 되었습니다. 그 결과, 시냇물의 물고기들이 많이 죽었습니다. 따라서, 물고기를 먹고 사는 동물들에게도 부정적인 영향이 미치게 되었죠. 엘크들은 또한 포플러 나무의 새싹도 뜯어 먹었는데, 이렇게 되면 이 나무들은 완전히 자라나지 못하죠. 그리고, 마지막으로, 코요테의 개체수가 손쓸 수 없을 정도로 많아졌는데, 이는 먹이를 놓고 경쟁 관계를 형성하는 늑대가 없었기 때문입니다. 이제 여러분들은 한 동물의 존재가 – 이 경우에는 부재가 – 전체적인 생태계에 영향을 미칠 수 있다는 사실을 잘 아시겠죠?

하지만, 1995년부터, 상황이 많이 변했습니다. 어디 봅시다… 공원의 늑대들 덕분에, 엘크의 개체수가 통제 가능한 정도의 수준으로 하락했습니다. 시냇물의 폭도 좁아지고, 깊이는 더 깊어져서, 현재 수 많은 물고기, 새, 그리고 비버들이 서식하고 있죠. 보다 많은 포플러 나무들이 완전히 성장할 수 있습니다. 코요테의 수도 줄어들었고요. 그리고, 마지막으로, 늑대 덕분에 다른 동물들이 먹이를 확보할 수 있게 되었는데, 늑대들은 배불리 먹고 나서 죽은 동물들을 남겨 두기 때문이죠. 그리고 나면, 독수리나 곰과 같은 다른 동물들은 늑대들이 남겨 둔 죽은 동물들을 먹습니다.

M Student: *Logan* 교수님, 교수님께서 조금 전에 늑대의 이주가 논란이 되었다고 하셨던 것 같은데요. 하지만, 음, 늑대들은 이 지역에 이로운 영향을 미치고 있는 것 같은데요. 그렇지 않나요?

W: 두 가지 측면에서는 맞는 말이예요, *Josh*. 실제로, 관광객들이 늑대를 보기 위해서 옐로우스톤을 방문해서 소비한 금액은 일 년에 3천 5백만 달러에 이르는 것으로 추정되고 있죠. 하지만 실제로 논란의 여지가 있어요. 이는 주로 지역 주민들의 항의에

의한 경우가 많죠. 우선, 그들은 늑대가 가축들과 어린이들에게 위험하다고 생각해요. 하지만 이러한 우려는 그 근거가 없어요. 예를 들어, 2년 전에 이 지역에서 죽은 모든 양들 가운데, 음, 단지 1퍼센트 정도만 늑대에게 죽었어요. 그리고 늑대가 사람을 공격했다는 사건이 기록된 적은 단 한 번도 없었죠. 제 생각으로는, 이 지역의 주민들의 항의는 지역 주민들의 주된 관심사와 관련된 핑계에 불과합니다: 바로 사냥이죠. 이 지역의 많은 주민들은 야외 활동을 상당히 즐기며 사냥을 좋아합니다. 이제 그들은 엘크를 놓고 늑대와 경쟁을 해야 하기 때문에, 기분이 나빠진 것이죠.

그래서, 이러한 저항과 늑대 개체수의 증가 때문에, 정부에서는 사냥꾼들이 약간의 늑대들을 죽이는 것을 허가해 주었습니다. 농부들에게는 자신의 토지 안에 있거나 가축을 공격하는 늑대들에 대해서는 항상 늑대를 죽일 수 있는 권리가 있습니다. 하지만 죽일수 있는 늑대의 수는 정해져 있죠. 해마다, 일정한 수의 늑대들이 - 제 생각에는 대략 200마리 정도인 것 같은데 - 죽임을 당합니다. 이는 늑대 개체수의 조절에 도움이 되며, 어떤 면에서는, 늑대들에게도 도움이 됩니다. 음, 죽임을 당하지 않은 늑대들에게 그렇긴 하겠지만요. 모든 늑대 무리들은 그들만의 영역을 확보하고 있고, 그 영역 내에서만 먹이를 찾습니다. 늑대의 수가 너무 많으면, 몇몇 늑대들은 굶어 죽을 것이며, 반면에 어떤 늑대들은, 먹이를 찾아 그들의 영역으로 침입해 온 다른 늑대들에게, 공격을 받게 될 것입니다. 이 모든 것이 자연의 균형을 유지하기 위해 일어나는 현상입니다. 동물들 사이에 이러한 일이 발생하지 않는다면, 음, 사람들이 인위적으로 도와줄 수 밖에 없습니다.

Actual Test 07

Reading Section   p.81

Answers

1. Ⓐ [Vocabulary Question]
2. Ⓐ [Inference Question]
3. Ⓑ [Factual Question]
4. Ⓒ [Rhetorical Purpose Question]
5. Ⓐ [Reference Question]
6. Ⓓ [Vocabulary Question]
7. Ⓒ [Factual Question]
8. Ⓒ [Rhetorical Purpose Question]
9. Ⓐ [Vocabulary Question]
10. Ⓒ [Factual Question]
11. Ⓓ [Sentence Simplification Question]
12. Ⓒ [Vocabulary Question]
13. 1st [Insert Text Question]
14. Ⓐ, Ⓒ, Ⓔ [Prose Summary]

Translation

월리스 선

찰스 다윈은, 자신의 발견을 발표하지 않은 채, 20년 동안 진화에 대하여 연구했다. 하지만, 1858년, 또 다른 박물학자, 알프레드 러셀 월리스의 편지를 받은 후, 획기적인 저서인 종의 기원을 통해서 자신의 이론을 서둘러 발표하게 되었다. 그 편지의 내용에는 윌리스의 진화 이론이 포함되어 있었는데, 이는 다윈의 이론과 상당히 비슷했다. 다윈이 유명했던 반면, 월리스의 이름은 과학계 외부에는 거의 알려져 있지 않았다. 하지만 현대에는, 그가 생물지리학의 아버지로서 뿐만 아니라 역사상 가장 위대한 표본들을 수집했던 업적으로 어느 정도의 명성을 얻었다. 게다가, 월리스는 월리스 선으로 가장 잘 알려져 있는데, 이 선은 동남아시아, 뉴기니, 그리고 오스트레일리아의 동물군을 구분하는 깊은 바다 밑의 경계선에 대한 이론으로서, 진화에 대한 그의 생각의 근간을 이루고 있다.

알프레드 러셀 월리스는, 다윈과 마찬가지로, 영국인이었으며 박물학자였지만, 두 사람의 공통점은 이 두 가지가 전부였다. 월리스는 다윈보다 젊었고, 부유한 집안에서 태어나지 못했기 때문에, 14세 이후로는 정식 교육을 받지 못했다. 그는 독학을 했으며 토지 측량사로 일하면서 영국에서 취미 삼아 식물학을 공부했다. 그 후, 모험심에 이끌린 월리스와 그의 친구는, 1848년에 아마존 밀림을 찾아가 4년이라는 시간을 그곳에서 보냈다. (그곳에서, 월리스는 재미있기도 하고 돈도 벌 수 있는 일을 찾게 된다.) 곤충, 동물, 그리고 식물의 표본을 영국 박물관으로 보냄으로써 그의 비용이 충당되었다. 월리스가 그의 대부분의 경력에 있어서, 자신의 연구에 사용할 기금을 마련했던 방식은 이러한 것이었다. 그의 광범위한 연구와 수집된 표본의 대부분은 동남아시아에서 얻어진 것이었는데, 대부분이 말레이 반도와 현재 인도네시아의 여러 섬에서 이루어 졌으며, 1854년에 그가 연구를 시작한 이후 8년이라는 시간을 그는 그곳에서 보냈다.

이렇게 끊임없이 표본을 수집하던 중, 월리스는, 다윈에게 보냈던 유명한 편지에 설명되어 있는, 진화에 대한 생각을 가지게 되었다. 월리스는, 그가 수집했던 종들 가운데, 개별적인 종들 내에 다양한 종자들이 존재한다는 사실을 알게 되었다. 그는 또한 동물들의 분포에 있어서 지리가 매우 중요한 역할을 한다는 사실도 알게 되었다. 월리스는 바다 깊은 곳의 선에 의해서, 인도네시아 제도의 동쪽 지역, 뉴기니, 그리고 오스트레일리아의 동물군과, 인도네시아의 서쪽과 말레이 반도의 동물군이 구분된다는 사실을 알아냈다. 이 선은 셀레베스 해에서 시작하여 서쪽으로는 보르네오 섬과 동쪽으로는 셀레베스 섬을 두고 그 가운데를 지나, 다시 서쪽으로는 발리 섬과 동쪽으로는 롬복 섬의 가운데에 위치한 좁은 해협을 지나간다. 마침내, 박물학자들이 이 선에 월리스 선이라는 이름을 붙였다.

월리스는 딱따구리, 코뿔새, 그리고 꿩을 포함하여 177종의 새들이 이 선의 서쪽 지역에서 주로 발견된다는 사실을 알아냈다. 또한, 코뿔소, 오랑우탄, 호랑이, 그리고 긴팔원숭이를 포함한 215종의 포유류들은 이 선의 서쪽 지역에서만 발견되며, 동쪽 지역에서는 발견되지 않는다는 사실도 알아냈다. 월리스는 선의 서쪽지역에서는 거의 알려지지 않은 종들을 선의 동쪽 지역에서 발견했다. 캥거루와 같은 유대류, 코알라, 그리고 극락조, 앵무새, 그리고 화식조와 같은 수많은 새들이 그러한 동물들이었다. 모두 다 해서, 그는 선의 서쪽 지역에서는 존재하지 않으며, 동쪽 지역에서만 존재하는 241종의 조류, 79종의 포유류를 발견했다. 선의 양쪽 지역에 존재하는 대부분의 동물들은, 그 지역의 외부에는 비교적 알려지지 않았다.

월리스 선은 현재 생물지리학이라는 분야의 한 가지 사례인데, 월리스는 이 분야의 아버지라고 여겨진다. 월리스는 어떠한 힘에 의해서 이러한 동물들이 특정 지역에는 존재하고, 다른 지역에는 존재하지 않게 되었으며, 두 지역 사이에 위치한 바다 깊은 곳의 선 때문에, 두 지역에 존재하는 종들이 서로 이동하지 못하게 되었을 것이라는 결론을 내렸다. 각각의 지역 내에서, 자신이 발견한 다양한 표본들이 비슷한 여러 종으로 분류될 수 있다는 사실을 토대로, 그는 각각의 종이 예전부터 존재해왔던 공통된 여러 종들로부터 갈라져 나왔을 것이라는 결론을 내릴 수 있었다. 다시 말해서, 이들은 진화했다는 것을 의미한다. 하지만, 월리스는 그 용어를 사용하지 않았다. 다윈은 월리스의 생각이 자신의 생각과 비슷하다는 것을 알게 되었고, 1858년 7월에 자신의 이론을 발표하였으며, 월리스에게도 동등한 공로가 있다고 인정했다. 하지만 진화론을 최초로 주장했으며 처음으로 이론을 발표한 것으로 인정받은 인물은 다윈이었다. 이들의 지속적인 신뢰를 바탕으로, 두 사람은 계속해서 친구로 남았으며, 월리스는 다윈의 명성을 시기하지 않았고, 다윈은 월리스가 진화론에 기여했다는 사실에 대해서 결코 부인하지 않았다.

Listening Section   p.87

Answers

1. Ⓐ [Gist-Purpose Question]
2. Ⓓ [Understanding Attitude Question]
3. Ⓐ [Understanding Organization Question]
4. Ⓒ [Connecting Content Question]
5. Ⓒ [Making Inferences Question]
6. Ⓓ [Gist-Content Question]
7. Ⓑ [Detail Question]
8. Ⓓ [Understanding Organization Question]
9. Ⓒ [Understanding Attitude Question]
10. Ⓑ [Making Inferences Question]
11. Ⓑ [Understanding Function Question]

Script

| 07-02 |

W Professor: Hi, Greg. If you're here, then it must be two thirty, right?

M Student: Yes, Professor Thompson. That's right. I'm here for my appointment.

W: Great, great. Okay, so do you have your schedule for next semester all worked out? What classes are you interested in taking this time?

M: I think that I've got most of my schedule figured out. I'm still trying to decide on a couple of things though, so perhaps you'll be able to help me a bit.

W: All right. May I see your schedule, please?

M: Of course you may. Here you are . . .

W: All right . . . So, you're going to take two economics courses next semester. The introduction to international finance course is a good one. I believe Professor Martin is teaching that next semester. You'll enjoy his class a lot.

M: Great. I'm really looking forward to it. What about the advanced microeconomics class? Do you know anything about that one?

W: I believe it will be taught by a visiting professor next semester. As far as I know, that person hasn't been selected yet, so I can't help you out there. But I'm sure that our department will get a competent professor, so don't worry about it.

M: Okay. That's not a problem then. And what about the other two classes I've chosen?

W: Hmm . . . You're taking a marine biology course. I assume that you're getting a science credit out of the way. But, if I may ask, why marine biology? That class has a lab, and you don't need to take a lab class to fulfill your science requirement. That is going to mean extra work for you, you know.

M: Ah, right. Well, actually, my father, um, is encouraging me to take that class. That's his line of work, and I suppose he's hoping that I'll switch majors or something.

W: Okay, I understand. He pays the bills, so you might as well humor him. Besides, I have lunch with Professor Drake every week, and he's quite an entertaining speaker. You'll have a good time in his class.

M: Great.

W: And your last class looks fine, too. Spanish 3 will complete your language requirement. But, um, you still need to take one more class.

M: That's right. And I can't choose between the two that I'm considering. That's why I could use some guidance.

W: What are your options?

M: I'm trying to decide between an American history course and one in the English Department. That would be a course in, uh, medieval poetry.

W: Er . . . Why are you taking either of those? You've already taken all of the humanities classes that you need to graduate.

M: I know, but, uh, both of those topics are actually personal interests of mine.

W: Really? I had no idea.

M: Yeah, so, um, I thought it might be a good thing to get

some, uh, you know, formal training in them.
- **W:** Okay. I see your point. After all, you're here to learn and to get a broad education. Only taking classes in your major would be pretty boring. So, which one are you leaning toward?
- **M:** I think the history class would be a lot more fun.
- **W:** Then sign up for it. Okay, I'd say that we're pretty much all done here, right?

Translation

W Professor: 안녕, *Greg*. 여기 도착한 것을 보니, 2시 30분이 되었나 보군요. 그렇죠?

M Student: 네, *Thompson* 교수님. 그렇습니다. 교수님과 면담 약속이 있어서 왔습니다.

W: 좋아요, 좋아요. 그러면, 완성된 다음 학기 시간표는 가지고 있나요? 이야기 하고 싶은 과목은 어떤 과목인가요?

M: 시간표 문제는 대부분 해결한 것 같습니다. 두 세 가지 더 결정을 해야 하지만요. 그래서 교수님의 도움이 조금 필요합니다.

W: 좋아요. 시간표를 좀 볼 수 있을까요?

M: 물론이죠. 여기 있습니다…

W: 좋아요… 음, 다음 학기에 경제학 수업을 두 과목이나 수강하는군요. 국제금융학 개론은 좋은 과목인 것 같네요. *Martin* 교수님께서 다음 학기에 강의를 하실 것입니다. 재미있는 강의가 될 거예요.

M: 잘됐네요. 정말 기대가 되는군요. 고급 미시경제학 수업은 어떤가요? 이 수업에 대해서 알고 계신 것이 있나요?

W: 다음 학기에 이 수업은 초빙 교수님께서 강의를 해 주실 것 같군요. 제가 알기로, 강의를 하실 교수님은 아직 결정 되지 않았어요. 그래서 별 도움을 못 주겠네요. 하지만 우리 학과에서는 분명히 유능한 교수님을 모실 테니, 걱정할 필요 없어요.

M: 알겠습니다. 그렇다면 문제될 것이 없군요. 제가 선택한 나머지 두 과목은 어떤가요?

W: 흠… 해양생물학 수업을 선택했네요. 과학 학점을 이수하기 위해서 수강하려는 것 같군요. 하지만, 왜 하필 해양생물학이죠? 이 과목은 실험실에서 진행되는 수업인데, 과학 필수 학점을 이수하기 위해서라면, 실험실에서 진행되는 수업을 들을 필요는 없을 텐데요. 알고 있겠지만, 수업 이외에 해야 할 성가신 것들이 많을 거예요.

M: 아, 맞습니다. 음, 사실은, 아버지께서, 음, 이 수업을 추천해 주셨어요. 해양생물학은 아버지께서 일하시는 분야이기도 하고, 제 생각에 아버지께서 제가 전공을 바꾸기를 원하시는 것 같아요.

W: 그렇군요, 알겠어요. 아버지께서 학비를 내주시니, 만족시켜드리는 편이 좋겠죠. 그건 그렇고, 내가 *Drake* 교수님과 매 주 점심식사를 같이 하는데, 그 분은 설명을 아주 재미있게 하신답니다. 정말 재미있을 거예요.

M: 잘됐네요.

W: 마지막으로 선택한 과목도 괜찮은 것 같아요. 스페인어3을 수강하면 언어 필수 과목들은 모두 충족되겠군요. 하지만, 음, 한 과목을 더 수강해야 할 듯 한데요.

M: 맞습니다. 생각하고 있는 두 과목 중에서 선택을 하기가 힘들더라고요. 그래서 상담을 받으려고 하는 것입니다.

W: 선택할 수 있는 과목이 어떤 것들이죠?

M: 미국의 역사나 영문학과 수업 중 한 과목을 놓고 고민하고 있습니다. 영문학 과목은, 음, 중세시대의 시와 관련된 수업입니다.

W: 음… 왜 그 두 과목들을 중 한 과목을 수강하려 하는 것이죠? 졸업에 필요한 인문학 수업은 이미 모두 이수한 것 같은데.

M: 저도 알고 있습니다만, 음, 둘 다 제가 관심을 가지고 있는 주제라서요.

W: 정말인가요? 몰랐군요.

M: 네, 그래서, 음, 저에게는 이 과목이, 음, 그러니까, 정식으로 교육을 받을 수 있는 좋은 기회라고 생각합니다.

W: 좋아요. 무슨 의미인지 알겠어요. 결국, 학생은 폭넓은 교육을 배우고 익히려는 것이군요. 전공 수업만 수강한다는 것이 지루하겠네요. 그래서, 어떤 과목을 수강할 생각인가요?

M: 제 생각에는 역사 과목을 수강하는 것이 더 재미있을 것 같습니다.

W: 그러면 수강신청을 하도록 해요. 좋아요, 그러면 우리 얘기는 잘 마무리 된 것 같군요, 그렇죠?

Script

| 07-03 |

M Professor: So, as you can see, it has been proven that Cro-Magnon man first appeared in the Tanzania region of East Africa about 200,000 years ago. Please take into account that the Cro-Magnons weren't the first humanoids to appear, but they are the direct ancestors of modern-day humans. The next question we shall endeavor to answer is how humans spread from East Africa to the rest of the world. Through archaeological fieldwork and research on DNA from people around the world, we think we've compiled a pretty good idea about the path of human migration.

First, how did humans migrate? Mostly by walking. Thousands of years ago, there were no tame beasts of burden to carry people, and there's no evidence of people using ships until more modern times. Instead, people used their, um, feet to take them wherever they wanted to go. What for us is an eight- or nine-hour-long plane ride to Europe or Asia took early humans tens of thousands of years and countless generations to accomplish. Second, why did humans migrate? The obvious answer is necessity. In many cases, they were pursuing food sources or looking for new supplies of meat and wild fruits and vegetables. Additionally, population pressures were responsible for some migrations. When one area had too many people to support, some of them simply moved away in search of, uh, greener pastures. Wars and natural disasters may have accounted for some migrations as well. Oh, and climate change such as, uh, the ice ages that were prominent on the planet thousands of years ago, definitely caused people to move to new lands.

It was around 70,000 years ago that the first humans left Tanzania and began to spread throughout the African continent. About 50,000 years ago, modern humans arrived in the Middle East. From there, various groups of people ventured to India, Southeast Asia, and even Australia. It's now believed that they reached many of these places during an ice age, when, um, sea levels were lower. For instance, there's speculation that humans crossed the Red Sea in the Middle East during a cold period. Also, many anthropologists believe that people made it to Australia and other nearby islands either by walking across land bridges or by sailing on small rafts across waters that were much narrower compared to today. Oh, and from Southeast Asia, humans moved northward into East Asia and Siberia around 30,000 years ago.

As for Europe, it took much longer for humans to migrate there. You see, um, Neanderthals already lived there, so they served as competition for resources with the Cro-Magnons. Eventually, however, Cro-Magnons outlived the Neanderthals, who disappeared from history.

W Student: [11]Professor Moody, don't some people believe that Neanderthals and Cro-Magnons, uh, crossbred and that the end result was modern humans?

M: There have been some studies that have looked into that, but, so far, there isn't any convincing proof. The problem is that no remains of people exhibiting characteristics of both Neanderthals and Cro-Magnons have been unearthed. Perhaps, however, some may be found in the future.

Now, it was around 12,000 to 15,000 years ago when, during yet another ice age, the sea level became low enough for a land bridge to appear between Asia and North America. This enabled people in Siberia to cross over to Alaska—well, the land that's Alaska today—and then go down into the Americas. 1,000 years after that event happened, humans reached the southern tip of South America.

The final burst of human migration occurred in the Pacific Ocean during more modern times. It's believed that sometime between 3000 and 1000 B.C., people living in Taiwan began sailing to various Pacific islands. Over a very long period, they managed to reach numerous islands. In fact, they got as far east as, uh, Easter Island near South America. They also made it to the Hawaiian Islands and traveled southward to New Zealand. Extensive DNA testing of many Pacific islanders has proven that almost all of them originated from people who lived on western islands and then moved eastward. How these people accomplished this is one of the marvels of human migration. They traveled on ships on the open ocean out of sight of land. This was made possible by their exceptional navigational skills.

Ultimately, human migration took people everywhere on Earth with, uh, the exception of Antarctica. But, despite having originated in Africa, these people all developed into distinct races. This was the result of slight changes in their DNA across countless generations of people. Interestingly, human migration has not ended and can actually be considered to be, well, ongoing. Think about it . . . People are still moving to new lands all the time. The biggest of these migrations—after the Pacific islanders—was the migration of people from the Old World to the New World that began in 1492. But that's a story for another class since our time is up. Be sure to read chapter twelve before the start of our next class, all right?

Translation

M Professor: 음, 여러분들도 아시다시피, 크로마뇽인은 약 200,000년 전에 아프리카 동부 탄자니아에서 처음으로 등장했다는 사실이 판명되었습니다. 크로마뇽인이 최초로 등장했던 원인(原人)은 아니라는 사실을 다시 한번 상기해 주셨으면 합니다. 하지만, 그들은 현생 인류의 직접적인 선조입니다. 우리가 알아내야 하는 다음 문제는, 어떻게 인류가 아프리카 동부에서 전세계 여러 지역으로 퍼져 나갔는가 하는 것입니다. 고고학적 현장 조사와 전세계 사람들의 DNA 분석을 통해, 우리는 인류의 이주 경로에 대한 상당히 그럴듯한 의견들을 수집해 왔습니다.

첫째로, 인류의 이주 방법은 무엇이었을까요? 주로 도보를 이용했을 것입니다. 수천 년 전에는, 사람이 타고 다닐 정도로 길들여진 가축도 없었고, 현대에 더 가까운 시대가 되기 전까지는 사람들이 배를 이용했다는 증거도 없습니다. 그 대신, 사람들은, 음, 그들이 원하는 곳에 가려면 걸어갈 수밖에 없었죠. 우리가 유럽이나 아시아로 이동하려면 8시간에서 9시간 정도 비행기를 타야 하지만, 초기의 인류에게는 끝없이 여러 세대에 걸쳐진 수만 년의 시간이 필요했습니다. 둘째로, 인류의 이주 원인은 무엇이었을까요? 명확한 답변이 필요합니다. 많은 경우에, 그들은 식량 자원을 찾아 다녔거나, 육류, 과일, 그리고 야채의 새로운 공급원을 찾아 다녔을 것입니다. 게다가, 인구가 증가한 사실도 어느 정도는 이주의 원인이 되었습니다. 한 지역에 부양해야 할 사람들이 너무 많아지면, 이들 가운데 몇몇 사람들은, 음, 미지의 장소를 찾아서 떠났을 것입니다. 전쟁과 자연재해 또한 어느 정도는 이주에 대한 설명이 되기도 했습니다. 아, 그리고 예를 들면, 음, 수천 년 전에 지구상에 존재했던 빙하 시대와 같은 기후의 변화 역시 사람들이 새로운 지역으로 이동했던 원인이 되었죠.

인류가 탄자니아 지역을 떠나 아프리카 대륙 전체로 이동했던 시기는 약 70,000년 전 이었습니다. 약 50,000년 전, 현생 인류는 중동 지역에 도착했습니다. 그곳에서, 다양한 집단의 사람들이 인도, 동남 아시아, 그리고 심지어 오스트레일리아까지 이동했죠. 그들은 빙하 시대에 이러한 지역으로 이동했던 것으로 추정되는데, 음, 이 시기에는 해수면이 낮았죠. 예를 들면, 인류는 추웠던 시기에 홍해를 건너 중동 지역으로 이동했다는 가설이 있습니다. 또한, 많은 인류학자들은 사람들이 육교를 통해서 걸어갔거나, 혹은 작은 뗏목으로 오늘날에 비해서 훨씬 좁았던 해로를 건너서 오스트레일리아와 그 주변의 섬들로 이동했다고 생각합니다. 아, 그리고 대략 30,000년 전에, 인류는 동남아시아로부터 동아시아와 시베리아 지역으로 이동했습니다.

유럽의 경우, 인류가 이 지역으로 이주하는데 더 긴 시간이 필요했습니다. 그러니까, 음, 이 지역에는 이미 네안데르탈인이 살고 있었기 때문에, 크로마뇽인과 자원을 두고 경쟁하게 되었죠. 하지만, 결국, 크로마뇽인이 네안데르탈인보다 오래 살아남았고, 네안데르탈인은 역사에서 자취를 감추게 되었습니다.

W **Student**: *Moody* 교수님, 몇몇 사람들은 네안데르탈인과 크로마뇽인들 사이에, 음, 서로간의 교배에 의해서 현생인류가 탄생했다고 생각하고 있지 않나요?

M: 그에 관한 연구가 어느 정도 이루어 지기는 했지만, 지금까지는, 어떠한 설득력 있는 근거도 전혀 존재하지 않습니다. 문제는 네안데르탈인과 크로마뇽인의 특성을 알려주는 유물이 발굴되지 않는다는 사실이죠. 하지만, 아마도, 미래에는 몇몇 유물들이 발견될 수도 있을 것입니다.

자, 약 12,000년에서 15,000년 전, 또 다른 빙하 시대에, 해수면이 낮아져서 아시아와 북아메리카 사이에 육교가 생겼습니다. 이로 인해서 시베리아 지역의 사람들이 알래스카로 건너갈 수 있었고 – 음, 오늘날의 알래스카를 말하는 것입니다 – 그리고 나서 아메리카대륙 전체로 이동했죠. 이로부터 1,000년이 지난 후, 인류는 남아메리카의 최남단까지 도착했습니다.

인류의 마지막 폭발적인 이주 현상은 보다 현대에 태평양 지역에서 발생했습니다. 대략 기원전 3000년에서 1000년 사이에, 타이완에 거주하던 사람들이 태평양의 여러 섬들로 항해를 시작했던 것으로 보입니다. 오랜 기간에 걸쳐서, 그들은 여러 섬에 그럭저럭 도착할 수 있었죠. 실제로, 그들은, 음, 남아메리카 인근의 이스터섬에 이르기까지, 동쪽으로 멀리 이동했어요. 그들은 또한 하와이 제도에 도착하기도 했으며, 남쪽으로는 뉴질랜드까지 이동하기도 했죠. 태평양 지역의 섬에 살고 있는 사람들의 DNA를 광범위하게 분석해본 결과, 이 지역의 거의 모든 사람들의 뿌리는 서쪽 지역의 섬에 살던 사람들이며, 이들이 동쪽으로 이동해왔다는 것을 증명해 주었습니다. 이 사람들이 이동했던 방법은 인류의 이주에 있어서 경이로운 사건들 중 하나입니다. 그들은 육지가 보이지 않는 광활한 대양을 배를 타고 이동했던 것이죠. 이는 그들의 뛰어난 항해 기술 덕분에 가능했던 것입니다.

결국, 인류의 이주에 의하여, 사람들은, 음, 남극 대륙을 제외한 지구상의 모든 지역으로 퍼져 나가게 되었어요. 하지만, 비록 인류의 발상지는 아프리카지만, 이 사람들은 서로 다른 인종으로 진화했습니다. 이는 셀 수 없이 여러 세대에 걸쳐 DNA가 조금씩 변화하여 생긴 결과죠. 흥미롭게도, 인류의 이주는 아직 끝나지 않았고, 실제로는, 음, 아직도 계속되고 있다고 할 수 있습니다. 생각해보세요… 사람들은 아직도 항상 새로운 지역으로 이동합니다. 이러한 이동 중 가장 큰 이동은 – 태평양의 여러 섬들로의 이주 이후 – 1492년에 시작된, 구대륙 사람들의 신대륙으로의 이주입니다. 하지만 오늘 수업 시간이 다 끝나서 이 내용은 다음 시간에 이야기를 해 보도록 합시다. 다음 수업을 시작하기 전에 12장을 꼭 읽어오세요, 아시겠죠?

Actual Test 08

Reading Section p.93

Answers

1. Ⓑ [Factual Question]
2. Ⓓ [Vocabulary Question]
3. Ⓓ [Reference Question]
4. Ⓐ [Rhetorical Purpose Question]
5. Ⓒ [Factual Question]
6. Ⓑ [Factual Question]
7. Ⓒ [Inference Question]
8. Ⓓ [Reference Question]
9. Ⓐ [Vocabulary Question]
10. Ⓑ [Vocabulary Question]
11. Ⓐ [Inference Question]
12. Ⓑ [Vocabulary Question]
13. Ⓐ [Negative Factual Question]
14. Ⓒ, Ⓓ, Ⓔ [Prose Summary]

Translation

고대 이집트의 동물 미라 제작

사후 세계를 위해서 사람을 보존해야 한다는 믿음 때문에 고대 이집트인들이 시신을 미라로 만들었다는 사실에 대해서는 널리 알려져 있지만, 고대 이집트인들이 동물들도 미라로 만들었다는 사실은 잘 알려져 있지 않다. 고고학자들은 이집트 전역에서 수십만 마리의 동물 미라를 발견했다. 이렇게 보존된 동물들에는 고양이, 악어, 황소, 뱀, 새, 물고기, 비비, 개, 가젤, 사자, 그리고 심지어는 코끼리도 있다. 동물들을 미라로 만들었던 주된 이유는, 죽은 사람이 사후 세계에서 이들을 반려동물로 삼을 수 있도록 하기 위함이었다. 미라화된 동물들은 특별한 날에 이집트의 신들에게 바쳐지기도 했으며, 좋은 날씨와 풍년을 염원하기 위해 신들에게 제물로 바쳐지기도 했다. 광범위한 조사 덕분에, 고고학자들은 이집트인들이 동물을 미라로 제작하는데 사용했던 방법을 알아낼 수 있었다.

이집트에 대한 고고학적 탐사가 절정에 이르렀던 19세기 후반과 20세기 초반에 동물의 미라가 발견되었지만, 인간의 미라의 발견과, 함께 발굴되었던 여러 유물들 때문에, 동물의 미라는 그다지 중요하게 여겨지지 않았다. 최근에는 동물 고고학자라고 불리는 전문가들에 의해서 동물 미라들이 더 광범위하게 연구되고 있다. 전문가들은 동물 미라 제작의 비밀을 알아냈다. 일반적으로, 동물의 장기는 손으로 제거되거나, 장기를 녹이는 테레빈유와 시더유의 혼합물로 추출된다. 그 후, 미라 제작자는 천연 탄산소다 – 고대부터 이집트에서 채굴된 소금의 종류 – 가 들어있는 작은 아마포 주머니를 동물 몸 속에 넣어 동물이 건조될 때 내부의 수분과 지방을 흡수하도록 했다. 동물의 시신이 건조되면, 미라 제작자는 그것을 아마포로 감싸고, 그 위에 종교적인 상징을 써 넣었다. 어떤 동물의 미라들은 나무나 돌로 만든 관에 넣어지기도 했다.

미라는 부유층과 빈곤층의 무덤에서 모두 발견되기 때문에, 미라가 파라오나 상류층의 전유물은 아니었다. 일반적으로, 미라화된 동물들은 죽은 사람들이 귀여워하던 애완동물들이었다. 어떤 사람이 죽으면, 사후 세계에서도 반려동물로 삼을 수 있도록 애완동물도 같이 죽여서 미라 제작했던 경우가 많았다. 파라오와 상당히 부유한 사람들의 경우, 이러한 애완동물들은 색다른 동물들인 경우가 많았지만, 평범한 사람들의 무덤에서는 일반적으로 개와 같은 평범한 동물들이 발견되었다. 파라오가 죽으면, 수천 마리의 동물들이 도살되어 미라로 제작된 후 장례 의식에 사용되었다. 동물들 이외에도, 그 사람이 사후에 식량으로 사용할 수 있도록 보존된 고기를 붕대에 감아서 놓아두기도 하였다.

아피스 소나 악어와 같은 몇몇 동물들은 신으로 여겨졌기 때문에, 이들을 달래기 위한 목적으로 이들은 미라로 만들어졌다. 종종, 아피스 소는, 평생 동안 보살핌을 받았으며, 신성시 되었다. 이 동물이 죽으면, 미라화 할 수 있도록 그 시체를 특별한 돌에 놓아두어 건조시켰다. 그 후, 성직자, 귀족, 그리고 일반 시민들은 그 소를 잃은 것에 대해서 통곡하면서, 소를 기리는 성대한 행진 의식을 열었다. 이 소가 매장되어 있는 무덤에는 약탈자들이 그냥 지나칠 수 없을 만큼 값어치 있는 보물들이 상당히 많이 있었기 때문에, 동물 고고학자들은 아직까지 완전한 형태의 아피스 소 미라를 발견하지 못했다. 이집트인들은 또한, 악어들이 나일강의 홍수를 예측할 수 있다고 믿었기 때문에, 악어를 숭배했고 미라로 만들었다. 이곳에 서식하는 악어들은 본능적으로 나일강의 범람 수위보다 더 높은 곳에 알을 낳았기 때문에, 이집트인들은 홍수가 날 경우 그 수위가 어느 정도인지를 악어가 경고해 준다고 생각했다.

동물 미라 제작은 고대 이집트의 중요한 사업이었다. 축제 기간과 애도의 시기에는, 이집트인들이 신들을 기쁘게 하기 위하여 신들에게 동물 미라를 바쳤다. 신에게 바칠 제물을 제작하기 위해서 사원으로부터 먼 지역까지 이동해야 했던 순례자들에게 미라화된 제물을 판매하는 사업이 생겨났다. 이렇게 미라화된 동물들은 몸집이 작은 곤충이나 뒤쥐에서 고양이나 새와 같이 몸집이 큰 동물에 이르기까지 매우 다양했다. 일반적으로, 가격은 미라의 크기에 달려 있었다. 동물 고고학자들은 일부 동물 미라 판매업자들이 부정한 방법을 사용했다는 사실을 알아냈다. 고대 사원에서 발견된 아마포로 감아놓은 몇몇 미라에는 뼈만 있는 것도 있었고, 동물의 깃털만 있는 것도 있었으며, 진흙이나 돌만 있는 것도 있었다. 그럼에도 불구하고, 대부분은 제대로 제작된 동물 미라였다. 결과적으로, 이집트인들은 수십만 구의 미라를 남겨 두었는데, 이로써 동물 고고학자들은 고대 이집트 대해서 더 많은 것들을 알아내기 위한 연구를 할 수 있었다.

Listening Section

p.99

Answers

1. Ⓑ [Gist-Purpose Question]
2. Ⓒ [Detail Question]
3. Ⓐ [Understanding Attitude Question]
4. Ⓒ [Making Inferences Question]
5. Ⓓ [Understanding Function Question]
6. Ⓒ [Gist-Content Question]
7. Ⓓ [Detail Question]
8. Ⓐ [Understanding Attitude Question]
9.

	Elastic Deformation	Ductile Deformation	Brittle Deformation
Ⓐ		X	
Ⓑ	X		
Ⓒ			X
Ⓓ		X	

[Connecting Content Question]

10. Ⓑ [Making Inferences Question]
11. Ⓐ [Understanding Function Question]

Script

| 08-02 |

W Student: Pardon me, but are you Mr. Mullen?

M Student Housing Office Employee: No, I'm afraid that I'm not. Mr. Mullen is currently out of the office and won't be back until next week.

W: Next week? Oh no. I really need to speak with him as soon as possible. It's rather important.

M: May I ask what this is about? I work for Mr. Mullen, so perhaps I can assist you.

W: I sure hope that you can. You see, my roommate is driving me nuts, and I absolutely have to get out of my current situation. Today. Immediately. Now.

M: Whoa there. Slow down and take a deep breath . . . There, that's much better. Now, why don't you start from the beginning and tell me what's going on?

W: All right. Well, I'm a freshman, so I didn't get to choose my roommate for this year.

M: That's right. The only times that freshmen choose their roommates are when they actually have a friend from high school that is coming here with them. But I must say that that doesn't happen too often.

W: I didn't know anyone coming here, so I just let the school choose for me.

M: Did you fill out the form we sent that asked about your preferences in a roommate?

W: I sure did, and it seemed like the school went out of its way to give me someone who is my complete opposite.

M: How so?

W: Okay . . . I wrote down that I am an early riser. I get up at six every morning. But that's about when my roommate goes to bed. I also noted that I am a nonsmoker, but my roommate smokes in the room all the time. I'm allergic to smoke, so that's causing huge problems for me.

M: Oh my.

W: Oh, I'm not done yet.

M: Go on then.

W: I wrote down that I am a quiet person who doesn't drink or party. But my roommate has her friends over all the time and seems to be a nonstop partier. Because of her, I have to go to the library to get any studying done, and it's on the other side of campus from my dorm. And I simply don't feel safe walking home alone from the library late at night.

M: Yes, I know what you mean.

W: So, basically, my roommate and I are complete opposites. Because of her, I can't get any work done. I'm worried that my grades are going to be awful, and that will disappoint my parents and me.

M: All right. There is still time for you to change dorms rooms.

W: Thank goodness.

M: [5] And, this time, before you move into a new room, we'll let you talk to your potential roommate. That way, you can see if the two of you will get along well with one another.

W: You know, you ought to do that for all students.

M: We'd love to, but, logistically, it just wouldn't be possible.

W: Yeah, I see your point. That really wouldn't be possible, would it? Okay, what do you need me to do now? Fill out some paperwork or something?

Translation

W Student: 실례합니다만, *Mullen* 선생님이시죠?

M Student Housing Office Employee: 아니오, 제가 아닌데요. *Mullen* 선생님께서는 부재중이셔서, 다음주까지 안 계실 거예요.

W: 다음주라고요? 아, 안돼요. 그 분과 가능한 빨리 얘기를 해야 해요. 상당히 중요한 문제라서요.

M: 무슨 일인지 저한테 알려주시겠어요? 저는 *Mullen* 선생님 밑에서 일을 하고 있어서, 학생을 도와줄 수 있을지도 몰라요.

W: 도와주실 수 있었으면 좋겠군요. 그러니까, 제 룸메이트 때문에 미칠 것 같아서, 정말이지 이 상황에서 벗어나고 싶어요. 오늘. 지금. 당장이요.

M: 진정해요. 마음을 좀 가라앉히고 심호흡을 좀 해봐요… 그렇게, 좀 나아질 거예요. 이제, 무슨 일인지 처음부터 자세히 얘기해줄 수 있나요?

W: 좋아요. 음, 저는 신입생이고요, 그래서 올해에는 룸메이트를 선택할 수 없었어요.

M: 그렇죠. 신입생이 룸메이트를 선택할 수 있는 경우는 같은 고등학교에서 함께 진학한 경우 이외에는 없죠. 하지만 그런 경우는 드물죠.

W: 저는 같이 진학한 학생이 없었기 때문에 학교에서 정해주는 대로 따를 수 밖에 없었어요.

M: 선호하는 룸메이트에 대한 질문지 작성을 했었나요?

W: 물론 했죠, 그런데 학교에서는 마치 일부러 저와 완전히 반대인 사람을 정해준 것 같아요.

M: 어떻게 그럴 수 있죠?

W: 틀림없어요… 저는 일찍 일어나는 편이라고 작성했어요. 제가 6시에는 일어나거든요. 하지만 제 룸메이트는 그 시간에 잠자리에 들어요. 뿐만 아니라 저는 비흡연자라고 작성했는데, 제 룸메이트는 항상 방에서 담배를 피워요. 저는 담배연기를 정말 싫어해서, 그것 때문에 정말 문제가 심각하다고요.

M: 저런.

W: 아, 아직 더 남았어요.

M: 계속 해보세요.

W: 저는 술을 마시거나 파티를 좋아하지 않는 조용한 사람이라고 작성했어요. 하지만 제 룸메이트는 항상 친구들을 초대해서 끊임없이 파티를 열어요. 그녀 때문에, 공부를 하려면 항상 도서관에 가야만 하는데, 도서관은 기숙사의 반대편에 있어요. 그래서 밤 늦게 도서관에서 방으로 걸어오는 것이 불안하기도 하고요.

M: 네, 무슨 말인지 잘 알겠군요.

W: 그래서, 근본적으로, 제 룸메이트와 저는 완전히 반대예요. 그녀 때문에, 아무것도 할 수 없어요. 형편없는 성적을 받게 될까 두렵기도 하고, 부모님과 저 자신을 실망시킬 것 같아서 걱정이네요.

M: 알겠어요. 기숙사를 바꿀 시간이 아직 있어요.

W: 정말 다행이예요.

M: 그리고, 이번에는, 새 방으로 옮기기 전에, 룸메이트가 될 학생과 이야기할 수 있도록 해줄게요. 그렇게 하면, 서로 잘 지낼 수 있을지를 알 수 있게 될 거예요.

W: 있잖아요, 모든 학생들한테 그렇게 해 주셔야 한다고 생각해요.

M: 우리도 그렇게 하고 싶지만, 현실적으로, 그렇게 하는 것은 불가능하겠죠.

W: 네, 무슨 말씀인지 알겠어요. 정말로 불가능하겠죠, 그렇죠? 좋아요, 저는 이제 어떻게 해야 하나요? 서류 같은 것을 더 작성해야 하나요?

Script

| 08-03 |

M Professor: Take a look at the picture in page 271 of your books, everyone. Notice how the rocks appear to be in, um, layers. However, the layers aren't straight but, rather, curve and bend. This is an example of rock deformation. These rocks were once layers, or strata, of sediment on the ocean floor. It was only after a very long time—and because of lots of stress—that these rocks came to be located on mountaintops and in very new shapes. So, what causes rocks to deform like this

... ? What forces are at work, and what factors influence how rocks are deformed . . . ? That's what I'd like to discuss with you now.

Rocks get deformed by stress that is applied to the rock. This stress is mostly the result of the movement of the earth—I mean the ground, not the planet—and the pressure that this creates. Think of the stress as being, uh, as being akin to pressure. If a rock is exposed to uniform stress, which we geologists call confining pressure, it undergoes no changes. Confining pressure occurs when the pressure, or stress, is equal on every side of the rock. However, if this, uh, situation changes, the rock can get deformed. There are three types of stress that can result in rock deformation. They are tension, compression, and shear stress. Tension can cause the rock to be pulled and stretched. Compression, as you can probably imagine, causes the rock to be squeezed, which decreases its volume. And shear stress acts by pushing parts of a rock in opposite directions. As a result, the rock may bend, fold, or break.

Also, rock deformation can occur in three ways. We call these methods elastic deformation, ductile deformation, and brittle deformation. Elastic deformation happens when the change in a rock is not permanent. In other words, when the stress is removed, the rock returns to its original shape. Think of, um . . . an elastic band that you stretch. Of course, like an elastic band, a rock also has its limits, so it may break or change shape once its elastic limit is reached. The second type, ductile deformation, is the result of stress that pushes a rock beyond its elastic limit. So the deformation is permanent. Rocks that have undergone ductile deformation often appear to be flowing or bending, just like the ones in the picture you saw. And the last type of deformation, brittle deformation, happens when rocks break and undergo a permanent change. Yes? You have a question?

W Student: What's the difference between ductile and brittle deformation?

M: Well, first, they're both permanent changes. But, in brittle deformation, the rock breaks. In ductile deformation, the rock either bends or folds, yet it doesn't break. [11]Got it . . . ? Good. Now, there are four major factors that influence rock deformation. They are . . . please write this down because you will be tested on this . . . the temperature of the rock, the amount of confining pressure, the strain rate, and the composition of the rock.

The temperature of the rock determines whether it will be more ductile or brittle. As a general rule, the higher the temperature, the more ductile the rock becomes. Think of glass. It's very brittle at room temperature and thus breaks easily. But, when glass is heated, it becomes ductile, so it bends and folds. This enables glassmakers to make various shapes out of it. Well, you may be surprised by this, but rock acts in a similar manner. The depth of the rock helps determine its temperature. Deeper in the Earth, temperatures are higher. Thus, rocks near the surface tend to have lower temperatures and thus are brittle while rocks at greater depths have higher temperatures and are therefore more ductile.

Confining pressure is the next factor. A rock with a high confining pressure is surrounded by equal pressure on all sides. This reduces its brittleness because it's difficult for fractures to occur in the rock. So, a high confining pressure makes rocks more ductile. Again, depth is important. Pressure is greater at deeper depths while it's lower near the surface. The third factor is the strain rate, which refers to how quickly or slowly stress is applied to the rock. If a rock's strain rate is fast, the rock will fracture easily. Consider the results of hitting a rock with a sledgehammer . . . But, if a rock's strain rate is low, it will, over thousands or millions of years, bend and fold but not break. Strain rates are typically higher nearer the surface since rocks there are exposed to weathering factors such as wind, water, and ice.

Okay. Let me sum up what I just said. Rocks near the surface tend to be fairly brittle because they're exposed to low temperatures, low confining pressures, and high strain rates. Meanwhile, rocks deep within the Earth are more ductile since they're exposed to high temperatures, high confining pressures, and low strain rates. Now, let's move on to the last factor and examine the composition of rocks to see how that influences whether they are brittle or ductile.

Translation

M Professor: 모두들, 교과서 271페이지의 그림을 보세요. 암석들의 단층이, 음, 어떤 모양을 나타내는지에 주목해 주세요. 하지만, 이 단층들은 곧은 모양이 아니며, 휘거나 굽은 형태를 띠고 있죠. 이는 암석이 변형된 사례입니다. 이 암석들은 지층, 즉, 단층이었거나 해저의 퇴적층을 구성하고 있었습니다. 이는 상당히 오랜 시간이 흐르면서 생성된 것인데 – 응력이 엄청나기 때문에 – 암석들은 산 정상에서 이동한 것이며, 새로운 형태를 띠게 되었습니다. 그렇다면, 무엇이 암석을 이렇게 변형시켰을까요…? 어떠한 힘이 작용하며, 어떠한 요인이 암석의 변형에 영향을 주는 것일까요…? 이러한 문제들에 대해서 이제 여러분들과 논의해보려고 합니다.

암석에 가해진 응력에 의해서 암석은 변형됩니다. 이러한 응력은 대부분 땅의 움직임 때문에 발생하며 – 지구가 아니라 땅을 의미합니다 – 이러한 움직임에 의해서 응력이 생깁니다. 응력을, 음, 압력과 동일한 종류라고 생각해 봅시다. 지질학자들이 균등 응력이라고 부르는, 균일한 응력에 암석이 노출되면, 암석은 변화하게 됩니다. 균등 응력은 압력, 즉 응력의 세기가 암석 주변의 모든 방향에서 균등할 때의 경우를 말합니다. 하지만, 이러한 상황이, 음, 변화하면, 암석은 변형될 수 있습니다. 암석의 변형을 야기하는 응력의 종류에는 세 가지가 있는데, 이는 인장 응력, 압축 응력, 그리고 전단 응력입니다. 인장 응력은 암석을 잡아당겨 늘어나게 합니다. 압축 응력은, 여러분들이 상상할 수 있듯이, 암석을 짓누릅니다. 그리고 전단 응력은 암석을 서로 다른 방향에서 누르는 힘을 말합니다. 그 결과, 암석이 휘어지거나, 구부러지거나, 혹은 부서지게 됩니다.

또한, 암석의 변형은 세 가지 방식으로 일어날 수 있습니다. 우리는 이러한 방식들을 탄성 변형, 연성 변형, 그리고 취성 변형 작용이라고 부릅니다. 탄성 변형은 암석의 변화가 영구적이지 않을 때 발생합니다. 다시 말해서, 응력이 사라지면, 암석이 원래의 형태로 되돌아 오는 것을 의미하죠. 여러분들이… 음, 탄성이 있는 끈을 잡아 늘였다고 생각해 봅시다. 물론, 탄성이 있는 끈과 마찬가지로, 암석도 한계점이 있어서, 탄성 한계에 도달하면 암석은 부서지거나 변형됩니다. 두 번째 유형은, 연성 변형인데, 이는 탄성 한계 수준까지 응력이 가해질 때 발생합니다. 따라서, 변형의 결과는 영구적이죠. 연성 변형 과정을 거친 암석들은 구부러지거나 휘어진 모습을 보이는데, 여러분들이 사진에서 볼 수 있는 그대로입니다. 그리고, 마지막 유형의 변형인, 취성 변형 작용은, 암석이 부서져서 영구적으로 변화할 때 발생합니다. 예? 질문이 있나요?

W Student: 연성 변형과 취성 변형의 차이점은 무엇인가요?

M: 음, 첫째로, 둘 다 영구적인 변형을 일으킵니다. 하지만, 취성 변형 작용을 거치면 암석이 부서지죠. 연성 변형 작용을 거치면 암석이 휘어지거나 구부러질 뿐, 부서지지는 않고요. 아시겠지요…? 좋습니다. 자, 암석의 변형에 영향을 주는 주요한 요인은 네 가지가 있습니다. 이들은… 이에 대해서 시험을 볼 예정이니 필기해 주세요… 암석의 온도, 균등 응력의 크기, 변형률 속도, 그리고 암석의 구성요소 입니다.

암석의 온도에 따라서 연성 변형 작용이 발생할지, 혹은 취성 변형 작용이 발생할지가 결정됩니다. 일반적으로, 온도가 더 높을수록 암석의 연성이 커집니다. 유리를 생각해 보세요. 유리는 상온에서 부서지기 쉬워서 쉽게 깨지죠. 하지만, 유리가 가열되면, 연성이 생겨서, 휘어지거나 구부러질 수 있습니다. 그렇기 때문에 유리 제조업자가 다양한 형태의 유리 제품을 만들 수 있는 것이죠. 음, 이러한 사실에 놀랐을지 모르겠지만, 암석도 이와 비슷합니다. 암석이 존재하는 깊이에 따라서 그 온도가 결정되죠. 땅 속 깊은 곳의 온도가 더 높습니다. 그렇기 때문에, 표면 가까이에 있는 암석은 온도가 더 낮아서 깨지기 쉽지만, 상당히 깊은 곳에 있는 암석은 온도가 높아서 연성이 더 높습니다.

균등 응력이 그 다음 요인입니다. 높은 균등 응력을 받는 암석은 모든 방향으로부터 똑 같은 정도의 응력을 받습니다. 이로 인하여 취성이 낮아지게 되는데, 암석에 균열이 잘 생기지 않기 때문입니다. 높은 균등 응력에 의해서 암석의 연성이 증가하게 되는 것이죠. 또 다시, 깊이가 중요합니다. 깊은 곳에서는 응력이 높지만 표면 근처에서는 응력이 낮죠. 세 번째 요인은 변형률 속도인데, 이는 암석에 응력이 얼마나 빠르게, 혹은 천천히 영향을 미치는지를 의미합니다. 암석의 변형률 속도가 빠르다면, 그 암석에는 쉽게 균열이 생길 것입니다. 큰 망치로 암석을 내리치는 결과를 생각해 봅시다… 그러나, 암석의 변형률 속도가, 수천 년에서 수백만 년 정도로 느리다면, 그 암석은 부서지지 않고 휘어지거나 구부러집니다. 변형률 속도는 일반적으로 표면에 가까울수록 높은 편인데, 이는 암석이 바람, 물, 그리고 얼음과 같은 풍화작용을 일으키는 요인에 노출되기 때문입니다.

좋습니다. 제가 했던 말들을 요약해 보도록 하죠. 지표면 근처의 암석들은, 낮은 온도, 낮은 균등 응력, 그리고 높은 변형률 속도에 노출되므로 깨지기 쉽습니다. 반면에, 땅속 깊은 곳에 있는 암석들은, 높은 온도, 높은 균등 응력, 그리고 낮은 변형률 속도에 노출되므로 연성이 높습니다. 자, 이제 마지막 요인으로 넘어가서, 암석의 구성요소가 암석의 취성과 연성에 어떻게 영향을 주는지에 대하여 알아보도록 합시다.

Actual Test 09

Reading Section p.105

Answers

1. B [Sentence Simplification Question]
2. A [Vocabulary Question]
3. A [Reference Question]
4. B [Vocabulary Question]
5. C [Factual Question]
6. D [Reference Question]
7. C [Inference Question]
8. A [Factual Question]
9. C [Vocabulary Question]
10. D [Rhetorical Purpose Question]
11. D [Vocabulary Question]
12. B [Factual Question]
13. 4th [Insert Text Question]
14. A, D, F [Prose Summary Question]

Translation

완벽주의

무엇인가를, 혹은, 여러 경우에, 모든 것을 완벽하게 하려는 욕구를 완벽주의라고 한다. 완벽주의는 개인이 완벽해지려고 하는데 너무 몰두하거나, 실수를 저지르는 것에 대해 너무 많은 걱정을 하게 되어, 위험을 감당하는 것을 두려워하게 되어서, 적응성, 창조력, 그리고 성취도의 수준이 감소하게 되는 심리적인 상태를 말한다. 심리학자들은 완벽주의가 어린 시절에 발생한다고 생각한다. 주된 원인은 부모들인데, 부모들은 아이들이 학교 공부나 운동을 완벽하게 하려는 것이나 여러 가지 다른 노력을 하는 것을 부모로부터의 인정, 사랑과 동일시 하도록 만드는 상황을 조성하기 때문이다. 완벽주의자들이 보여주는 몇몇 증상들로는, 실수에 대해서 과도하게 걱정을 하며, 개인적인 기준을 너무 높게 설정하고, 부모의 기대와 비판에 대해서 너무 많은 걱정을 하며, 스스로의 행동을 의심하여 아무것도 할 수 없는 지경에 이르게 되고, 순서에 과도하게 집착하는 점 등을 들 수 있다.

완벽주의는 일반적으로 어린 시절에 시작된다. 부모들은 아이들에게 다른 아이들보다 더 뛰어나야 한다는 압박감을 심어주게 되고, 계속해서 자신의 욕망과 욕구를 아이들의 삶에 투영시키려는 행동을 계속하게 된다. 아이들은 자신들이 무엇인가를 완벽하게 해냄으로써 부모를 기쁘게 할 수 있다는 사실을 알게 된다. 여기에는 높은 성적을 받고, 대회에서 우승을 하며, 그리고 운동을 잘하는 것 등이 포함된다. 부모들이 성공에 대해서 칭찬을 하고 실패에 대해서 비판하거나 꾸짖는 것을 통해서 이를 강화한다면, 그들은 아이들을 완벽주의자로 만들고 있는 것이다. 점차적으로, 아이들은 실패를 피하려 할 뿐 아니라 실수를 저지르는 것에 대해서 과도한 두려움을 가지게 된다. 아이들은 결국, 자신이 실수를 할 경우, 다른 사람들이 자신을 하찮게 여길 것이라고 믿게 된다. 불안한 느낌은 종종 이 아이들이 어른이 될 때까지 이어진다. (일부 완벽주의자들은 이러한 감정 문제를 극복해내지만, 그렇게 하는 데에는 종종 많은 노력과 긴 시간이 소비된다.)

부모들이 아이들에게 이렇게 하는 이유는 서로 다른 두 가지 심리적 상황 때문에서이다. 첫째로, 부모들 스스로가 완벽주의자여서, 이러한 태도를 자신들의 아이들에게 물려주려 하는 경우이다. 이 부모들이 인생에 성공을 했거나 그렇지 못했을 수도 있지만, 그들은 자신들이 다름 아닌 완벽한 것만을 인정할 것이라는 생각을 아이들에게 전달한다. 이러한 상황은 부모가 성공을 했을 경우에 더 심할 것이다. 몇몇 아버지들은 아들이 학업, 운동, 혹은 사업에서 크게 성공해 주기를 기대하기 때문에, 아들들은 자신들이 원하지 않지만 오직 아버지가 원하는 방향으로 인생의 경로를 선택하도록 강요 받는 경우가 많다. 두 번째로 관련된 심리학적인 측면은 분리 불안이다. 분리 불안을 느끼는 부모들 하에서는 아이들이 부모에게 의존하며, 부모 가까이에 머무르는 범위에서만 아이들의 행동이 허락된다. 아이들이 어떤 식으로든 독립된 행동을 하려고 하면 – 심지어 아주 어릴 때에도 – 부모는 그들을 과소평가하며 비판한다. 그렇게 되면, 아이들은 부모와 가까이 있으면서 부모의 눈에 완벽하게 보일 때에만 그들에게 인정받고 사랑받는다는 것을 깨닫게 된다.

이러한 두려움의 결과는 상당히 부정적이다. 몇몇 완벽주의자들은 어떤 일도 마무리하지 못하게 되는데, 그들은 자신들이 한 일이 충분하게 완벽하지 않으면 어떻게 될 지를 두려워하며, 일을 완성하기 위해서 더 많은 행동을 해야 한다고 생각하기 때문이다. 다른 이들은 실패를 두려워해서 아무것도 시작하지 못한다. 게다가, 완벽주의자들은 자신들의 삶에 순서를 정해놓음으로써, 완벽하고자 하는 욕구에 혼란을 일으킬 수 있는 어떠한 불확실한 요인들도 모두 통제할 수 있다. 이로 인하여, 몇몇 완벽주의자들은 그들의 삶에 일어나는 어떠한 변화도 견디지 못하는, 만사를 자기 뜻대로만 하려는 사람이 된다. 완벽주의자들은 자신의 실수를 숨기려는 경향이 있는데, 이 또한 부정적인 측면이다. 그들은 실수에 대한 반발의 가능성을 몹시 두려워하여, 그들의 실수에 대해서 남을 탓하게 된다. 이러한 성향 때문에, 완벽주의자들은 그들의 실수를 극복하고 목표를 달성하는데 필요한 피드백을 받기 힘든 상황에 처하게 된다. 이상하게도, 완벽함을 추구하는 완벽주의자들은 성공하기 위해서 필요한 것들을 차단하는 경우가 많다.

완벽하고자 하는 욕구는 어린이들의 – 이후에는 어른이 되었을 때의 – 자기감에 대한 시각과 관련이 있다. 완벽주의자들은 그들이 성취하는 업적 이외에는 자신이 아무것도 아니라고 생각하기 시작한다. 이러한 생각은, 실수를 두려워함으로써 아무것도 하지 못하게 되는 상황과 함께, 극도의 근심과 좌절감을 불러 일으킨다. 이러한 압박감 때문에, 부모의 높은 기대감에 부끄럽지 않게 살아갈 자신이 없다고 생각하는 10대와 젊은이들이 자살을 하는 경우도 있다. 그들은 완벽해지려는 스트레스를 더 이상 견디지 못하고 삶을 마감하게 되는 것이다.

Listening Section p.111

Answers

1. D [Gist-Content Question]
2. A [Detail Question]
3. B [Understanding Organization Question]
4. C [Understanding Function Question]
5. D [Making Inferences Question]
6. B [Gist-Content Question]
7. D [Detail Question]
8. D [Understanding Function Question]
9. A [Understanding Organization Question]
10. C [Connecting Content Question]
11. B [Understanding Attitude Question]

Script

| 09-02 |

M1 Professor: Jason, would you mind stepping into my office for a few moments? I'd like to have a word with you if you've got the time.

M2 Student: ⁴Sure, Professor Pierson. I don't have anything to do until later in the afternoon.

M1: That's great. Oh, would you mind closing the door? I'd like for this to be a private conversation.

M2: ⁵Uh, sure. Say . . . I'm not in any kind of trouble or anything, am I?

M1: Trouble? You? That'll be the day.

M2: Well, I'm relieved to hear you say that.

M1: Yes, but this is something rather serious, so that's why I don't want anyone hearing what I'd like to talk to you about.

M2: Go ahead.

M1: Jason, I've noticed that your grades in physics are only in the B and C range. As your advisor, I need to know if there is something going on that I, uh, need to know about.

M2: No, there's nothing unusual going on in my life.

M1: Well, you're about to finish your sophomore year here, and, thus far, you've failed to get an A in any of your physics classes. Your grades continue to be rather, uh, middling. I had hoped that you would show some improvement in your major by now, but that just hasn't been the case.

M2: Yeah, I guess that physics is a little tougher than I had imagined it would be . . . Uh, wait a minute.

M1: Yes?

M2: You already know about my grades for this semester? How'd you pull that off?

M1: Jason, your professors and I are all in the same department. It's not like we don't talk about our students. And I always take an interest in my advisees and try to monitor their progress.

M2: Oh, all right. That makes sense.

M1: There is one thing that I've noticed though . . .

M2: What's that?

M1: You've taken three psychology courses in your time here, and you've gotten A's in all three of them. Uh, actually, you got an A+ in one. You seem to have a, uh, a certain aptitude for that field.

M2: Oh, psychology? It's just a hobby really. I read a lot of psych books in my free time. You know, uh, Jung, Freud, and some other writers.

M1: That's interesting. So, um, Jason, if you don't mind my asking . . . Have you ever considered switching majors from physics to psychology?

M2: Uh, wow. No, I haven't.

M1: You might want to give it some thought. You seem to do much better in psychology than you do in physics, and there is enough time for you to switch majors and still graduate in four years. Now that I know you read psychology books in your free time, I'm even more convinced that this is something you should think long and hard about.

M2: You know . . . you may be right, Professor Pierson. But I'd need to think about this . . . oh, and discuss the matter with my parents, too.

M1: Of course. I totally understand. Anyway, summer vacation is coming soon, so you've got a couple of months to think about it. But consider making that change. If you do, you can reorganize your schedule for the fall semester and get started on your new major then.

Translation

M1 Professor: Jason, 잠시 내 사무실에 들르지 않겠나? 시간이 괜찮다면 자네와 몇 마디 나누고 싶은데.

M2 Student: 물론이죠, Pierson 교수님. 오후 늦게까지 별 다른 일 없습니다.

M1: 잘됐군. 오, 문을 좀 닫아 주겠나? 사적인 대화를 나눠야 할 것 같아서.

M2: 아, 알겠습니다. 그렇다면… 저에게 무슨 문제가 생긴 것은 아니죠, 그렇죠?

M1: 문제? 자네에게? 그럴 리가 있나.

M2: 음, 그렇게 말씀하시니 마음이 놓이네요.

M1: 그래, 하지만 이것은 좀 진지한 이야기라네. 그래서 자네와 내가 나누는 이야기를 남들이 듣지 않았으면 하는 것이고.

M2: 말씀하세요.

M1: Jason, 자네 물리학 과목들의 학점이 B학점과 C학점 밖에는 없더군. 나는 자네의 지도 교수로서, 자네에게, 음, 뭔가 문제가 있는지 알아야 할 필요가 있다네.

M2: 아니오, 저에게 별로 특별한 문제는 없습니다.

M1: 음, 이제 곧 2학년 생활이 끝나는데, 이제까지, 물리학 과목에서 한번도 A학점이 없다니. 자네의 성적은 계속해서, 음, 중간 정도로군. 이제 자네도 전공과목에서 향상된 모습을 보여줄 때가 된 것 같은데, 그렇지 못하군.

M2: 네, 물리학은 제가 생각했던 것보다 좀 더 어려운 것 같습니다… 잠시만요.

M1: 응?

M2: 저의 이번 학기 학점도 이미 알고 계신가요? 어떻게 아셨어요?

M1: 자네의 교수님들과 내가 같은 학과에 소속되어있지 않은가. 우리가 학생들에 대해서 이야기를 하지 않을 리가 없지. 그리고 나는 언제나 내가 지도하는 학생들에게 관심을 가지고 있고, 그들의 학업 성취 과정을 지켜보려 한다네.

M2: 아, 그렇군요. 이해가 가네요.

M1: 내가 알아낸 것이 한 가지 있네만…

M2: 그게 무엇이죠?

M1: 자네는 지금까지 심리학 수업을 세 과목 수강했는데, 모든 과목에서 A 학점을 맞았더군. 음, 그 중 한 과목은 A+를 받았고. 자네는, 음, 이 분야에 소질이 있는 듯 하네만.

M2: 아, 심리학이요? 사실은 심리학이 제 취미입니다. 여가 시간에 심리학 서적을 많이 읽습니다. 그러니까, 음, 융, 프로이드, 그리고 몇몇 다른 분들의 책을 읽죠.

M1: 그것 참 흥미롭군. 그러니까, 음, Jason, 내 질문이 기분 나쁘지 않다면 말일세… 자네의 전공을 물리학에서 심리학으로 변경해 보는 것을 생각해 본 적이 있는가?

M2: 아, 이런 아니오, 그런 적은 없습니다.

M1: 아마 생각해보고 싶어질 걸세. 자네는 물리학 보다는 심리학을 더 잘하는 것 같고, 전공을 변경할 시간도 충분하고 4년 내에 졸업도 할 수 있지. 게다가 여가 시간에 심리학 서적을 읽는다고 하니, 나는 자네가 이 문제에 대해서 긴 시간 동안 심사숙고 해보아야 한다고 생각하네.

M2: 음… 교수님 말씀이 옳을 것 같기도 하네요. 하지만, 생각을 좀 해 봐야 할 것 같습니다… 아, 그리고 부모님과도 상의를 해 봐야 할 것 같네요.

M1: 물론 그렇지. 전적으로 이해한다네. 어쨌든, 곧 여름방학이니, 두 달 정도 생각 할 시간이 있군. 하지만, 변경하는 방향으로 생각해 보게나. 만약 그렇게 한다면, 자네는 가을학기 시간표를 다시 작성해야 할 것이고, 그러면 새로운 전공을 시작하게 될 것이야.

Script

| 09-03 |

W Professor: From very humble beginnings, Christianity

spread, first throughout parts of the Middle East and the Roman Empire and then, eventually, to pretty much the entire world. One odd thing about Christianity is that its birthplace today has fewer Christians than almost any other place in the world where it's a major influence. The Middle East—and Israel, the homeland of Christianity—in particular has seen a decline in the number of Christians living there since the nineteenth century. The reasons for this are legion, but here are some of the major ones: the spread of Islam, Muslim Arabs perceiving Christian Arabs as being allied with Christians in Western countries, which Muslim Arabs believe are making war on them, the rise of Israel as an independent state, and the emigrating of Christian Arabs to other lands to escape these problems.

Let's turn our attention first to the numbers of Christian Arabs in the Middle East. And when I say the Middle East, I'm talking about the Levant. This is the area around the western part of the Mediterranean Sea. It includes Egypt, Jordan, Israel, Lebanon, and Syria. Other parts of the Middle East, such as Iraq, Saudi Arabia, and the Persian Gulf states, haven't had significant Christian populations in centuries, uh, if ever. So, uh, why don't I just say "Levant" instead of "Middle East" to avoid confusion? Okay . . . ? In the nineteenth century, approximately 25% of the population of the Levant was Christian. On the eve of World War I in 1914, it rose slightly to around 28%, but, since then, there has been a steady decline in the number of Christians there. By 1945, 19% of the Levant was Christian, and a survey in 2007 estimated that only nine percent of the area was Christian. These Christians are divided into numerous sects. Egypt has the most—around eight million. But they live in a nation with tens of millions of Muslims. Lebanon has around 1.5 million Christians, which is about 40% of the country's population. Syria is next at one million Christians, Jordan has around a quarter of a million, and Israel has the smallest at around 120,000.

Christianity actually thrived in the Levant during the early years of the Byzantine Empire. But, it began losing adherents when the teachings of Mohammad spread throughout the region in the seventh and eight centuries. During that time, many Christian Arabs converted to Islam either by choice or out of a need to survive. Yet Christianity didn't disappear in the region, and Muslim and Christian Arabs lived side by side with few disturbances between them for centuries. Yet, in recent times, there have been clashes between Christians and Muslims as well as between various Christian sects in the Levant. Many have taken place in Lebanon. For instance, from 1975 to 1990, a civil war between different Christian sects took place there. Even today, armed militias hold a lot of power in Lebanon despite their having been driven almost completely underground.

Today, the biggest danger for Christian Arabs is that many Muslim Arabs lump them together with Christians in the West, particularly American Christians. Many Muslim Arabs don't consider American involvement in the Middle East—especially in Iraq and Afghanistan—in terms of global strategy or as defensive measures against terrorism. Instead, they regard these wars as attacks by Christian nations upon Muslim nations. Therefore, many vent their anger against the only Christians that they see: their Christian Arab neighbors. While there have been occasional outbreaks of violence between the two sides, there have not yet been any large-scale disruptions. Interestingly, many Christian Arabs frequently get upset because of the views of Christians from around the world rather than those of their Muslim Arab neighbors. The reason is that many Western Christians believe that all Arabs are Muslims. Thus Christian Arabs resent being connected with terrorism and the violence that Muslim Arabs are often responsible for.

The last major problem for Christian Arabs lies with Israel. Since Israel became a state in the 1940s, it has been threatened by war by much of the Arab world. The Israelis often regard all Arabs as potential enemies. Therefore, their policies are directed at Arabs and fail to distinguish between Muslim and Christian Arabs. For example, all Arabs in Israeli territory are subjected to restrictions related to employment and travel since Israel is so frequently targeted by terrorist attacks from Muslims. In Israel, many Arab settlements have been bulldozed and rebuilt as Israeli settlements. This has fueled intense hatred between the Israelis and Arabs of all religions. For many Christian Arabs, the best solution has been to move to another land. This has accounted for most of the decline in the number of Christian Arabs in the Levant. And, sadly, it's often the best and the brightest of them who migrate in the hope of finding and making better lives for themselves somewhere else.

Translation

W Professor: 초라하게 시작했던 때부터, 기독교는, 처음에는 중동의 여러 지역과 로마 제국으로, 그 후에는 결국 전세계의 상당히 여러 지역으로 전파되었습니다. 기독교의 한 가지 이상한 점은, 크리스트교 발상지의 교인들의 수가, 주요한 영향을 받은 세계의 다른 지역들의 교인들의 수에 비해서 더 적다는 사실입니다. 특히 중동에서는 - 기독교의 발상지인 이스라엘을 포함해서 - 19세기 이래로 기독교도의 수가 계속해서 감소해왔습니다. 그 이유는 여러 가지이지만, 주요한 이유들이 몇 가지 있습니다: 이슬람교의 확산, 기독교계 아랍인들이 서양 국가들과 동맹을 맺어 현재 자신들과 전쟁을 벌이고 있다고 믿는 이슬람계 아랍인들, 이스라엘이 독립 국가를 건국한 사실, 기독교계 아랍인들이 이러한 문제들을 피하기 위해서 자신들의 영토 밖으로의 이주하고 있는 사실이 그 원인들입니다.

중동 지역의 기독교계 아랍인들의 수에 대해서 우선 집중해 보도록 합시다. 그리고 제가 중동이라고 일컫는 지역은 레반트 지역을 말합니다. 레반트 지역이란 지중해의 서부 연안이며, 이집트, 요르단, 이스라엘, 레바논, 그리고 시리아를 말합니다. 이라크, 사우디 아라비아, 그리고 페르시아만의 국가들과 같은 다른 중동 지역 국가들의 경우에는, 기독교도의 수에 있어서, 음, 혹시 있다 하더라도, 그다지 중요하지 않습니다. 그러니, 음, 혼란을 피하기 위해서 "중동"이라는 용어 대신 "레반트"라는 용어를 사용하도록 할까요? 괜찮겠지요…? 19세기, 레반트 지역 인구의 약 25% 정도가 기독교도였습니다. 제1차 세계 대전 직전이었던 1914년, 그 수가 28% 정도로 소폭 상승했지만, 그 이후로, 이 지역의 기독교도 수는 꾸준히 감소해 왔습니다. 1945년 무렵, 레반트 지역 인구의 19%가 기독교도였고, 2007년의 조사 결과에 따르면 이 지역 인구의 겨우 9% 만이 기독교도로 추정되고 있습니다. 이 기독교도들은 여러 지역에서 살고 있습니다. 이집트에 가장 많이 있는데 - 대략 8백만 명 정도가 있습니다. 하지만 그들은 천만 명 정도의 이슬람교도들과 한 나라에서 살고 있죠. 레바논에는 백 5십만 명의 기독교도들이 있으며, 이들은 전체 인구의 약 40%를 구성하고 있습니다. 시리아에는 백만 명 남짓의 기독교도가 있으며, 요르단에는 대략 25만 명 정도, 그리고 이스라엘에는 가장 적은 수인 12만 명이 있습니다..

기독교는 비잔틴 제국 초기에 레반트 지역에서 번성했습니다. 하지만, 마호메트의 가르침이 7, 8세기 무렵 이 지역에 전파되면서 기독교 신자들의 수가 줄어들기 시작했죠. 이 시기에, 기독교계 아랍인들은 자신들의 선택에 의해서, 혹은 살아남기 위해서 이슬람교로 개종했습니다. 그러나 이 지역에서 기독교가 사라지지는 않았으며, 이슬람교도와 기독교도들은 수백 년 동안 큰 갈등 없이 함께 살아왔습니다. 하지만, 최근, 레반트 지역에서는 기독교도와 이슬람교도 사이에서 갈등이 발생하고 있을 뿐만 아니라, 기독교도들 사이에서도 충돌이 일어났습니다. 예를 들면, 1975년부터 1990년까지, 이 지역의 기독교도 분파들 사이에 내전이 발생했습니다. 오늘날에도, 무장한 민병대들이, 거의 전적으로 지하조직이기는 하지만, 레바논에서 상당한 권력을 유지하고 있습니다

오늘날, 기독교계 아랍인들이 직면하고 있는 가장 큰 위험요소는, 많은 이슬람계 아랍인들이 그들을 서양의 기독교인들, 특히 미국의 기독교인들과 같은 부류로 취급한다는 사실입니다. 많은 이슬람계 아랍인들은, 미국이 중동에 개입하는 것을 – 특히 이라크와 아프가니스탄에 개입하는 것을 – 테러에 대한 방어 수단이라는 국제적인 전략으로 바라보고 있지 않습니다. 대신, 그들은 이러한 전쟁을 기독교 국가들이 이슬람교 국가를 공격한 것이라고 생각합니다. 그렇기 때문에, 많은 이슬람교도들이 그들의 눈에 보이는 기독교도들에게 분노를 표출하고 있습니다: 이들이 바로 주변에 살고 있는 기독교계 아랍인들인 것이죠. 양쪽의 폭력적인 충돌이 간헐적으로 발생하기는 하지만, 대규모의 혼란은 아직까지 없었습니다. 흥미롭게도, 많은 기독교계 아랍인들은 주변 지역의 이슬람계 아랍인들의 시각보다는 전세계 기독교인들의 시각 때문에 당혹스러워 하고 있습니다. 서양의 많은 기독교인들은 모든 아랍인들을 이슬람교도라고 생각하기 때문이지요. 그래서 이슬람계 아랍인들이 종종 일으키는 테러와 폭력 사태를 자신들과 연관시키는 것에 대해서 분개하고 있습니다.

기독교계 아랍인들에게 마지막으로 중요한 문제는 이스라엘입니다. 1940년대에 이스라엘이 건국한 이래로, 이 나라는 아랍 세계와의 전쟁 위협에 시달려 왔습니다. 이스라엘인들은 종종 모든 아랍인들을 잠재적인 적으로 간주합니다. 따라서, 그들의 정책은 아랍인들과 관련되어 결정되는데, 그들은 이슬람계 아랍인과 기독교계 아랍인을 따로 구분하지 않습니다. 예를 들면, 이스라엘 영토에 거주하는 모든 아랍인들은 취업과 여행에 제한을 받는데, 이는 이스라엘이 이슬람교도들의 테러 공격의 대상이 되는 경우가 많기 때문입니다. 이스라엘에서는, 많은 아랍인 정착 지역이 철거되고 그 지역에 이스라엘인 주거지가 재건되고 있습니다. 이 때문에 이스라엘인들과 아랍인들 사이의 적대감이 고조되고 있죠. 많은 기독교계 아랍인들에게는, 다른 지역으로 이주하는 것이 최선의 해결책입니다. 이것이 레반트 지역에서 기독교계 아랍인들의 수가 감소했던 가장 큰 원인이었죠. 그리고, 안타깝지만, 다른 지역으로 이주하여 스스로 더 나은 삶을 영위하고자 하는 이들에게는 이주하는 것이 최선의 방법이며 현명한 선택이 되고 있습니다.

Actual Test 10

Reading Section   p.117

Answers

1. D [Vocabulary Question]
2. B [Negative Factual Question]
3. B [Reference Question]
4. A [Vocabulary Question]
5. C [Factual Question]
6. D [Sentence Simplification Question]
7. A [Factual Question]
8. A [Reference Question]
9. A [Rhetorical Purpose Question]
10. B [Factual Question]
11. B [Vocabulary Question]
12. A [Vocabulary Question]
13. B [Inference Question]
14. A, B, D [Prose Summary Question]

Translation

석유 유출

석유는 전세계 산업과 교통 시스템에 있어서 혈액과도 같은 존재이며, 주로 송유관과 유조선에 의해서 전세계에 운송된다. 대부분의 석유 운반은 목적지까지 안전하게 이루어 지지만, 때때로 사고가 발생하여 석유가 유출되는 경우가 생긴다. 유조선에서 석유가 유출되어 이러한 사건이 발생하면, 엄청난 환경 재해가 발생할 수 있다; 석유는 물고기와 바닷새들을 죽일 수 있으며, 해안 지역을 더럽히고, 그 지역의 수산업을 파괴한다. 석유 회사와 정부는 석유의

유출이 확산되는 것을 막으려 노력해야 하며, 가능한 빠르게 환경을 정화해야 한다. 시간이 지남에 따라, 유출된 석유를 에워싸서 정화할 수 있는 수많은 방법들이 발견되고 발명되었다. 여기에는 기계적, 화학적, 생물학적, 그리고 물리적인 방법들이 있다.

유출된 석유를 둘러싸기 위한 최초의 시도는 기계적인 방법과 관련이 있다. 작은 배에 의해 설치된, 물에 떠있는 울타리인 방책은, 유출된 석유를 둘러싸고 다른 지역으로 퍼져 나가는 것을 막기 위해서 사용된다. 방책이 유출된 석유를 특정한 구역 밖으로 퍼져나가지 못하게 한 다음에는 오염된 지역을 정화하는 다른 방법들이 사용된다. 한 가지 방법은 석유를 불태우는 것이다; 하지만, 이 방법에는 단점이 있는데, 가장 큰 단점은 이 과정을 통해서 발생하는 연기가 공기를 오염시킨다는 사실이다. 다른 방법은 스키머를 사용하여 물에서 기름을 걷어내는 것이다. 스키머에는 세 가지 종류가 있다: 위어식 스키머, 친유성 스키머, 그리고 흡입식 스키머가 그것이다. 위어식 스키머는 기름을 표면으로 떠오르게 하여 울타리를 넘게한 다음 스키머가 둘러싸고 있는 구역에 가두어 둔다는 점에서 마치 댐과 같은 역할을 하는데, 이 때 회수되는 물의 양은 최소화된다. 그 다음, 석유와 혼합된 물은 나중에 저장하거나 처리하기 위해서 펌프로 제거한다. 반면, 친유성 스키머는, 석유를 흡수하는 걸레나 띠 형태의, 석유를 빨아들이는 재료를 활용하는데, 빨아들인 석유는 나중에 이 장비에서 짜내어진다. 마지막으로, 흡입식 스키머는 표면에서 석유를 빨아들이는 진공청소기와 비슷하다. 이 모든 스키머들에는 장점과 단점이 있으며, 석유가 유출된 장소와 기상 상황, 그리고 다른 요인들에 따라서 사용할 장비의 종류가 결정된다.

유출된 석유를 정화시키는 화학적인 방법은 분산제를 사용하는 것인데, 유출된 기름으로 뒤덮인 지역에 비행기나 배를 이용하여 분산제를 살포하게 된다. 분산제에 포함된 화학 물질은 석유 분자와 결합하여, 석유를 물 분자와 분리시킨다. 그 결과, 거대한 하나의 기름 덩어리 대신, 수백만 개의 작은 석유 방울들이 물위에 떠있게 된다. 이 방법의 장점은, 이러한 방울들이 거대한 수면에 뜬 기름에 비해서 더 쉽고 빠르게 자연 분해될 수 있다는 점이다. 분산제를 사용한 것의 단점은 이 화학 물질이 환경에 피해를 줄 수 있다는 점이다. 분산제를 생산하는 기업들과 이를 사용하는 석유 회사 모두 분산제의 성분이 위험하다는 사실을 알고 있지만, 이 화학 물질보다 석유가 더 위험하기 때문에, 분산제가 둘 중에서는 덜 해롭다고 판단한다.

유출된 석유를 제거하는데 일반적으로 사용되는 생물학적 방법을 생물적 환경 정화라고 한다. 생물적 환경 정화의 목적은 석유의 자연 분해를 가속화시키는 것이다. 두 가지 주요한 방법이 – 비옥화와 씨 뿌리기가 – 사용된다. 비옥화 방법에서는, 질소와 인과 같은 양분을 물속에 첨가한다. 이는 석유를 분해할 수 있는 특정한 미생물의 성장을 촉진시킨다. 씨 뿌리기는 석유 유출이 발생한 지역에서 살지 않는 자연 분해 박테리아를 첨가하는 방법이다. 이들을 첨가함으로써, 석유는 더 빠른 속도로 분해된다. 실험에 따르면, 이러한 조건에서, 생물적 환경 정화 방법을 통해 석유의 분해 속도를 200배 이상 증가시킬 수 있다.

이러한 방법들이 실패하거나, 유출된 석유의 양이 너무 많거나, 석유 회사와 정부가 빠른 대응을 하지 못하게 되면, 기름 덩어리가 해안에 도달한다. 이렇게 되면, 석유를 제거하기 위해서 물리적인 방법을 써야 한다. 작업자들은 양동이, 삽, 그리고 호스를 들고 피해 지역을 정화한다. 모래나 바위로부터 석유를 퍼 담거나, 고압의 물 호스로 석유를 날려버린다. 석유 유출에 의해서 넓은 지역의 해안이 수개월에서 수년 동안 훼손될 수도 있다. 수천 명의 자원 봉사자들이 협력하여 일을 한다 해도, 유출된 기름을 쉽게 정화시킬 수는 없으며, 모든 지역의 석유를 제거할 수도 없다. 하지만, 시간이 흐르면, 유출된 기름의 마지막 흔적까지도 결국 사라지게 된다.

Listening Section   p.123

Answers

1. Ⓒ [Gist-Purpose Question]
2. Ⓒ [Detail Question]
3. Ⓐ [Making Inferences Question]
4. Ⓒ [Understanding Attitude Question]
5. Ⓐ [Understanding Function Question]
6. Ⓐ [Gist-Content Question]
7. Ⓓ [Gist-Purpose Question]
8. Ⓒ, Ⓓ [Detail Question]
9. Ⓐ [Making Inferences Question]
10. Ⓑ [Understanding Function Question]
11. Ⓓ [Understanding Attitude Question]

Script

| 10-02 |

W Registrar's Office Employee: Number thirty-seven, please. Would the person with number thirty-seven please come to this booth?

M Student: Good morning. I've got number thirty-seven. Here's my number.

W: Great. Oh, and good morning to you as well. So, what can I help you with today?

M: There's a mistake on my transcript that I need to have taken care of immediately.

W: A mistake? Um, I'm very sorry, but we aren't allowed to change grades for students. That is something that only professors are authorized to do. So, if you have a problem with a grade a professor gave you in a class, you need to take it up with him or her. Okay?

M: No, no. Wait. I don't need a grade changed.

W: Is that so?

M: Well, okay . . . To be honest, I'd love to have a few of my grades changed. You know what I mean?

W: Not really.

M: Er, sorry. Anyway, uh, you see, the name of one of my courses is written down incorrectly on my transcript.

W: The name? What do you mean?

M: Okay, here's a copy of my transcript . . . Take a look at the classes for the fall semester of my senior year. Uh, you know, last semester.

W: Right. So, tell me . . . What am I supposed to be looking at?

M: Ah, yes. You see, um, I took an independent study course in the History Department with Professor Marconi. It wasn't a regular class, so we had to make up the name of the course. Then, we submitted it to the Registrar's Office here.

W: Oh, I understand now. Ah . . . I can see it right here. [4]Your class was called "Concepts in Medical History." Hey, that sounds like it was a pretty interesting class.

M: Sure, but here's the thing . . . It is supposed to read "Concepts in Medieval History."

W: Oops.

M: Yeah, oops. There's quite a big difference between those two titles. Wouldn't you agree?

W: Yes, you're absolutely right about that.

M: Normally, I wouldn't really care too much about a mistake like this. But I've been giving some thought to applying to graduate school to study history. I can't do that this year, of course. It's way too late for me to apply now. But I might apply to them in a year or two, and I'll probably be focusing on medieval history. So, uh, it would be a good thing to show these schools that I took some medieval history classes when I was an undergraduate. You know what I'm saying?

W: Totally. Okay, we can change this. But you are going to have to get a note from your professor confirming that the name of the course should be changed.

M: [5]I've taken care of that already. Here you are.

W: You're on the ball, aren't you?

M: I try my best. I really want to make sure that this error gets straightened out.

W: All right. It looks like all of the paperwork is in order. I will put in a request on the computer that we change the name of your course. It is going to take about forty-eight hours to do so. We'll notify you of the results by email. And thanks for bringing this mistake to our attention.

Translation

W Registrar's Office Employee: 37번 학생. 37번 학생 이쪽으로 들어와 주시겠어요?

M Student: 안녕하세요. 제가 37번 입니다. 여기 번호가 있어요.

W: 좋습니다. 아, 저도 인사를 드릴게요. 그러면, 무엇을 도와드릴까요?

M: 제 성적 증명서에 문제가 있는데 지금 즉시 수정을 해야 해서요.

W: 문제라고요? 음, 죄송하지만, 이곳에서는 학생의 성적을 수정해 주지는 않습니다. 교수님께서 허가를 해 주셔야 하는 사항입니다. 그러니, 교수님께서 주신 학점에 문제가 있다면, 그 분을 찾아가야겠죠. 그렇죠?

M: 아니오, 아니오. 잠시만요. 학점을 변경하려는 것이 아니에요.

W: 그러면요?

M: 음, 그래요… 솔직히 말씀 드리면, 몇몇 학점을 바꾸고 싶긴 하군요. 무슨 말씀인지 아시겠지요?

W: 모르겠군요.

M: 음, 죄송합니다. 어쨌든, 어, 그러니까, 성적 증명서에 적혀있는 과목의 명칭 중 하나가 잘못 기재되어 있어요.

W: 명칭이요? 무슨 말씀이세요?

M: 네, 여기 성적 증명서를 보세요… 4학년 가을학기의 과목들을 좀 보세요. 음, 그러니까, 마지막 학기죠.

W: 네, 그러면, 말씀해주세요… 무엇을 봐야 하죠?

M: 아, 예. 그러니까, 음, 역사학과의 *Marconi* 교수님과 독립 연구 과정을 수강했는데요. 이 과목이 정규 과정이 아니어서, 과목 명칭을 우리가 정해야 했거든요. 그래서, 학생회관에 그 명칭을 제출했었어요.

W: 아, 이제 이해가 가는군요. 아… 여기에 있군요. 과목 명칭이 "의료 역사의 이해"군요. 와, 상당히 흥미로운 수업인 듯하네요.

M: 그럼요, 하지만, 그게 말이죠… "중세 시대 역사의 이해"라고 되어있어야 하거든요.

W: 저런.

M: 네, 그렇죠. 두 명칭 사이에는 확연한 차이가 있죠. 그렇지 않나요?

W: 네, 학생 말이 맞아요.

M: 보통의 경우에, 저는 이러한 종류의 실수는 별로 신경 쓰지 않는 편이지만, 제가 역사 전공 대학원에 지원할 생각이거든요. 물론, 올해에는 불가능하지만요. 이제는 지원하기에 너무 늦었죠. 하지만 1년에서 2년 내에 지원할 것이고요, 아마 중세 시대의 역사를 중점적으로 공부하게 될 것 같아요. 그래서, 음, 학부생일 때 중세 시대의 역사에 관한 수업을 들었다는 사실을 명시해 두는 것이 도움이 될 것 같아요. 무슨 말씀인지 아시겠죠?

W: 그럼요. 좋아요. 변경해 드릴게요. 하지만 교수님께 이 과목의 명칭에 대한 확인서를 받아야만 합니다.

M: 제가 이미 받아왔어요. 여기 있습니다.

W: 학생은 업무 과정을 잘 알고 있네요. 그렇죠?

M: 최선을 다 하는 것이죠. 이 문제가 올바르게 수정되길 바랄 뿐이고요.

W: 좋습니다. 모든 서류가 다 갖춰진 것 같네요. 컴퓨터에 과목 명칭 변경에 관한 요청을 할게요. 48시간 정도 걸릴 것 같군요. 결과는 이메일을 통해서 학생에게 알려줄게요. 이러한 문제에 주의를 기울일 수 있게 해줘서 고마워요.

Script

| 10-03 |

M Professor: Good morning, everyone. Today's our last class before the midterm exam, so we've got a lot of ground to cover. And, yes, today's lecture will be covered on the test, so please pay close attention. I want to start by examining the atmosphere and focusing in particular on the following: its composition, its divisions, and how the atmosphere affects life on Earth. [10]As a reminder, the atmosphere is comprised of a variety of, uh, things that, altogether, we call air.

Chemically, air consists of nitrogen, oxygen, argon, and a variety of other gases in small quantities. Overall, let's see . . . The atmosphere contains 78% nitrogen, 21% oxygen, slightly less than 1% argon, and trace amounts of the remaining gases. But air doesn't consist only of gas. It includes water vapor, which we call humidity. The amount of humidity typically varies from 0.3% to 4% by volume.

Air also contains a large number of particles called aerosols, which may be liquids or solids. Aerosols are so small that they remain suspended in the atmosphere. The most common aerosols are water droplets. Finally, there are salt particles near oceans, dust and smoke particles, ice crystals, and, on occasion, volcanic ash. These particles are one factor that's responsible for precipitation such as rain and snow. You see, water vapor attaches itself to these particles, which then form clouds. Eventually, the clouds become saturated with water vapor, so it's then released, whereupon it falls to the ground as some form of precipitation.

Structurally, we've divided the atmosphere into four main layers. They are, from the surface up, the troposphere, the stratosphere, the mesosphere, and the thermo- . . . Excuse me. The thermosphere. The troposphere extends from the surface to about nine miles up. The stratosphere goes from nine to around thirty miles up. The mesosphere extends from thirty to fifty-six miles up. And, last of all, the thermosphere extends from fifty-six to more than 430 miles up. At that point, the atmosphere is so thin that it's at the edge of space. Take a look at this chart up here on the board . . . Notice how there are, uh, layers between each zone . . . We call them pauses. There are three: the tropopause, the stratopause, and the mesopause. These three pauses are places where temperatures may stabilize and then suddenly change, either becoming warmer or colder. Also, most of the mass of the atmosphere—say around 90% of it—is found in the troposphere. By mass, I mean water vapor and particles of salt, dust, ash, and ice. Not surprisingly, the troposphere is where most of the weather that affects us takes place.

Weather itself is the result of the movement of the atmosphere. Please remember that the atmosphere is not static but is constantly moving. This movement is the result of temperature and pressure changes as well as the rotation of the Earth. We all know that hot air rises while cold air sinks. This movement is called convection and is mostly the result of the Earth being a sphere. Because of this, the sun's rays don't hit the planet at the same angle everywhere, so different parts of the planet absorb varying amounts of heat. Air, in turn, moves in an attempt to, uh, even out these differences. Also, the different temperatures result in the air pressure in the atmosphere being, er, different. Warmer air usually has low pressure while colder air has high pressure. These pressure areas, uh, chase each other as they try to balance the atmosphere. The last factor that affects atmospheric movement is the Earth's rotation. This creates belts, or zones, of air movement. There are three such belts in the Northern Hemisphere and the same number in the Southern Hemisphere. Since the Earth rotates, these belts aren't static but move, typically, from west to east.

So, how does the atmosphere, uh, help us? Aside from giving us air and water of course. Well . . . it heats the Earth and protects it from sunlight. As we know, the sun is vital to life. The atmosphere has two main roles pertaining to the sun. [11]The troposphere contains heat-absorbing gases, such as carbon dioxide, that help warm the Earth by absorbing heat and reflecting it back to the ground. However, the sun also emits ultraviolet rays. **Too much exposure to these rays can be extremely harmful—by which I mean fatal—to life on the planet.** Fortunately, we're protected from ultraviolet rays by the ozone layer in the stratosphere. It limits the amount of ultraviolet rays that get through the atmosphere. The ozone layer extends all around the planet although it varies in thickness from place to place. It's thinning in some places, which is a cause for alarm, but it is fine in other places. Fortunately, it has shown an ability to repair itself, so, no matter what alarmist material you may have heard or read, I wouldn't be too concerned about the ozone layer disappearing.

Translation

M Professor: 모두들 안녕하세요. 오늘은 중간고사 이전의 마지막 수업이기 때문에, 공부해야 할 것들이 아주 많습니다. 그리고, 예, 오늘의 강의 내용은 시험에 나오는 것들 이므로, 집중해 주시기 바랍니다. 대기에 대하여 설명하고, 특히 다음과 같은 사항들에 초점을 맞춰서 강의를 시작하도록 하겠어요: 대기의 구성, 대기의 구분, 그리고 대기가 지구상의 생명체에 미치는 영향입니다. 이미 언급한 바와 같이, 대기는 다양한, 음, 모두 다 우리가 공기라고 부르는 기체들로 구성되어 있지요. 화학적으로 공기는 질소, 산소, 아르곤, 그리고 소량의 다양한 다른 기체들로 구성되어 있습니다. 전체적으로, 어디 봅시다… 대기는 78%의 질소, 21%의 산소, 1% 미만의 아르곤, 그리고 이와 비슷한 양의 나머지 기체들로 구성되어 있습니다. 그러나 공기가 기체만으로 구성되어 있는 것은 아닙니다. 수증기가 포함되어 있는데, 우리는 이 수증기를 습기라고 부릅니다. 습기의 양은 다양한데, 일반적으로 0.3%에서 4%정도에 이릅니다.

또한 공기에는 에어로졸이라고 불리는 다양한 입자가 포함되어 있는데, 이는 액체 상태이거나 고체 상태입니다. 에어로졸은 너무 작아서 대기에 머물러 있습니다. 가장 흔한 형태의 에어로졸은 물방울입니다. 마지막으로, 염분의 입자가 해양 근처에 존재하며, 먼지와 연기의 입자, 얼음의 결정체, 그리고 가끔씩 화산재가 대기에 존재하기도 합니다. 이러한 입자들은 비나 눈과 같은 강수를 일으키는 요인입니다. 말하자면, 수증기가 이러한 입자에 달라 붙게 되면, 구름이 형성 되는 것이죠. 결국, 구름은 수증기에 의해 포화 상태에 도달하게 되고, 그리고 나면 물방울이 떨어지게 되죠. 이렇게 해서 구름은 강수의 형태로 지면에 떨어지게 되는 것입니다.

구조상으로, 우리는 대기를 네 가지 주요한 층으로 구분해 볼 수 있습니다. 이 층들은, 지면으로부터, 대류권, 성층권, 중간권, 그리고 열권으로… 죄송합니다. 열권으로 구분됩니다. 대류권의 범위는 지면으로부터 약 9마일 정도까지 입니다. 성층권은 9마일에서 약 30마일 정도, 중간권은 30마일에서 대략 56마일 정도, 마지막으로 열권은 56마일에서 430마일 이상의 범위를 차지합니다. 이 지점에서, 대기는 너무 엷어서 우주의 가장자리에 해당됩니다. 칠판에 있는 이 도표를 봐 주세요… 각각의 구역들 사이에 있는, 음, 이 층들이 어떻게 구성되어 있는지를 잘 봐 주세요… 우리는 이것을 계면이라 부릅니다. 계면에는 세 가지가 있습니다: 대류권 계면, 성층권 계면, 그리고 중간권 계면이 있습니다. 이러한 세 계면들은, 기온이 안정적이었다가 갑자기 따뜻해지거나 차갑게 변화하는 지점에 존재합니다. 또한, 대기 질량의 대부분은 - 대략 90% 정도라고 할 수 있는데 - 대류권에 존재합니다. 이 질량에는 수증기와 염분의 입자, 먼지, 재, 그리고 얼음의 결정체가 포함됩니다. 당연하게도, 대류권은 우리에게 영향을 주는 대부분의 기상 현상이 존재하는 곳입니다.

날씨는 대기의 움직임의 결과라 할 수 있습니다. 대기는 정적인 것이 아니며 계속해서 움직인다는 사실을 기억해 두세요. 이러한 움직임은 온도와 압력의 변화 뿐만 아니라 지구가 자전하는 결과이기도 합니다. 더운 공기가 상승하고 차가운 공기가 하강한다는 것은 우리 모두가 알고 있는 사실입니다. 이러한 움직임을 대류라고 하며, 이는 지구가 둥글기 때문에 일어나는 현상입니다. 지구가 둥글기 때문에, 태양열이 지구의 모든 지역에 같은 각도로 도달하지 못하고, 그 결과 각 지역마다 흡수되는 열의 정도가 다릅니다. 이 때문에, 공기는, 음, 이러한 차이와 일치하는 수준에서 움직이게 되죠. 또한, 온도의 차이에 의해서 대기의 기압도, 음, 차이가 나게 되는 것이고요. 더 따뜻한 공기는 기압이 낮고, 더 차가운 공기는 기압이 높습니다. 이렇게 기압이 존재하는 지역들은, 음, 대기의 균형을 유지하기 위해서 상호간에 이동을 하게 됩니다. 대기의 움직임에 영향을 미치는 마지막 요인은 지구의 자전입니다. 이는, 대기의 움직임에 특정 지대, 말하자면 특정한 지역을 만들어 냅니다. 이러한 특정 지대는 북반구의 세 지역에 존재하며, 남반구에도 같은 수가 존재합니다. 지구가 자전하기 때문에, 이러한 세 지대는 고정되어 있지 않고 움직이는데, 일반적으로는 서쪽으로부터 동쪽으로 움직입니다.

그렇다면, 대기는 어떻게 우리에게, 음, 도움이 될까요? 우리에게 공기와 물을 제공해준다는 사실 이외에도, 음… 대기는 지구를 따뜻하게 유지해주며 태양 광선으로부터 우리를 보호해 주기도 합니다. 우리가 알고 있는 것처럼, 태양은 생존에 필수적인 요소입니다. 대기는 태양과 관련하여 두 가지 중요한 역할을 합니다. 대류권은 열기를 포함하고 있는데 - 이산화탄소와 같은 기체들을 흡수하여, 지면으로부터 반사되는 열을 흡수하여 지구를 따뜻하게 유지해 줍니다. 하지만, 태양은 자외선을 방출합니다. 자외선에 너무 많이 노출되는 것은 상당히 해로운데, 이는 지구상의 생명체에게 치명적일 수 있습니다. 다행스럽게도, 성층권에 존재하는 오존층 덕분에 우리는 자외선으로부터 보호를 받고 있습니다. 이 층은 대기권을 뚫고 들어오는 자외선의 양을 제한합니다. 오존층은 층의 두께가 지역마다 다르기는 하지만, 전세계 모든 지역에 존재합니다. 몇몇 지역에서 이 층이 엷어지고 있는데, 이는 불안한 현상입니다만, 다른 지역에서는 상태가 나쁘지 않습니다. 다행스럽게도, 오존층은 스스로 회복될 수 있기 때문에, 여러분들이 이에 대해 경고하는 어떠한 내용을 듣거나 읽었을지 모르겠지만, 저는 오존층이 사라질 것이라고 걱정하지는 않습니다.

Compact Actual iBT Reading & Listening

4

Compact Actual iBT Reading & Listening has been designed to be used both in the classroom and by test takers working on an individual basis. Each compact test consists of one Reading passage, one Listening conversation, and one Listening lecture. All three of them are the standard length of actual TOEFL® iBT passages, conversations, and lectures. In addition, they all have the same number of questions and the same types of questions that are found on the actual test. By using this book, test takers will be more prepared for the test when they actually take it.

<Compact Actual iBT Reading & Listening Book 4> Components

- Main Book
- Answers, Listening Scripts, and Translations
- Free MP3 Downloads
- For More Student and Teacher Support Materials, Free Downloads at http://www.darakwon.co.kr